GREAT UNSOLVED
MYSTERIES
EDITED BY JOHN CANNING

GREAT UNSOLVED
MYSTERIES
EDITED BY JOHN CANNING

BOOK CLUB ASSOCIATES LONDON

CONTENTS

Editor's Note   vii

DEATHS AND DISAPPEARANCES

No. 10 Rillington Place	*Colin Wilson*	2
The Case of Lord Lucan	*Clare Smythe*	10
Crabb or 'Korablov'?	*Michael Hardwick*	21
Did Martin Bormann Escape?	*Richard Garrett*	30
Who Killed President Kennedy?	*Ronald Proyer*	37

HISTORIC AND PREHISTORIC ENIGMAS

Anastasia	*Mollie Hardwick*	50
The Princes in the Tower	*Mollie Hardwick*	57
Was Napoleon Murdered?	*Mollie Hardwick*	63
The Tragedy of Mayerling	*Mollie Hardwick*	70
Where Was Camelot?	*Rupert Furneaux*	77
The Prisoner in the Temple	*Mollie Hardwick*	83
Who Wasn't Buried at Sutton Hoo?	*Rupert Furneaux*	90
The Holy Shroud of Turin	*Mollie Hardwick*	97
Atlantis Rediscovered?	*Rupert Furneaux*	104

MYSTERIES OF THE SEA

The *Waratah* Omen	*Michael Hardwick*	114
The Bermuda Triangle	*Colin Wilson*	121
The *Mary Celeste*	*Richard Garrett*	129
What Happened on 'Little Jewel'?	*Michael Hardwick*	138

MYSTERIES OF THE AIR

UFOs	*Robert Chapman*	148
Two Stars Fall	*Richard Garrett*	156
Flight into Yesterday	*Doddy Hay*	165
Hindenburg: The Mystery Inferno	*Richard Garrett*	173

GHOSTS AND THE OCCULT

The Ghosts of Borley	*Michael Hardwick*	184
The Ghosts of Versailles	*Mollie Hardwick*	193

Strange Antics in a Tomb   *Rupert Furneaux*   200
Madame Blavatsky: Mystic or Fraud?   *Colin Wilson*   205
Reincarnation   *Colin Wilson*   212

MONSTERS

Something Queer in the Loch   *Clare Smythe*   220
The Abominable Snowman   *Colin Wilson*   227

Select Bibliography   237
Picture Acknowledgements   240
Index   241

EDITOR'S NOTE

The great Edmund Burke has written: 'A good parson once said that where mystery begins, religion ends. Cannot I say, as truly at least, of human laws, that where mystery begins justice ends.' The latter part of this judgement is manifestly true, the former assuredly false. For religion, never to be proved or disproved by reason alone, must rest on mystery. And what is true of religion is true also of ethics and aesthetics.

But let us not get too carried away by philosophy. Suffice it that much of what is colourful and good in life rests on mystery; so it is only natural that people have always been fascinated by mysteries. How dull life would be if we could not wonder and surmise. One might add to Burke's quotation by affirming that where knowledge ends mystery begins. As we near the end of the twentieth century our knowledge, despite our vanities, is still very small, and the area for surmise and conjecture proportionately large. And thank goodness for it.

So here is a selection of classic mysteries to tease and beguile. They are as widely varied in subject matter as they are in time and place; yet they all have one tantalizing feature in common: there is no answer or solution, and in most cases never will be. The reader will have to provide one for himself. It is, I suppose, just possible that Lord Lucan, Commander Crabb or Martin Bormann might yet reappear to write the last line to their stories. But the fate of the *Waratah*, the riddles of Mayerling and Anastasia, and the ambiguities and uncertainties of most of the other cases are likely to remain to torment future generations.

Some of the mysteries deal with subjective happenings. Anyone who has ever had a pre-cognitive dream, whether of a personal or impersonal nature, will no doubt have reflected that if it is possible to escape forward from the time continuum it should also be possible to recapture moments of a personal or racial past. Such an ability might explain the experiences of Moberley and Jourdain at the Petit Trianon, as well as the intimations of a previous existence, the corroboration for which is so cogently adduced in the chapter on reincarnation.

My thanks are due to the excellent team of contributors with whom it has been a pleasure to work; to Steve Dobell, the ever-helpful house editor; and to Jane Blackett for her work on picture research.

JOHN CANNING

10 Rillington Place, later re-named Rushton Place.

DEATHS AND DISAPPEARANCES

NO. 10 RILLINGTON PLACE

The climax of what has been called 'the greatest murder mystery of all time' developed on the afternoon of 24 March 1953 at a tiny, shabby house in London's Notting Hill area. A Jamaican tenant named Beresford Brown was preparing to redecorate the ground-floor kitchen, and was looking for a place where he could put up a shelf. When he tapped the wall in the corner it sounded hollow, and he realized that he was looking at a cupboard that had been covered over with wallpaper. He peeled back a strip of wallpaper from the corner and discovered a hole in the door; he switched on a torch and peeped through. And what he saw was unmistakably the back of a naked woman, who seemed to be bending forward with her head between her knees, as if being sick. It explained the offensive smell in the kitchen, not unlike that of a dead rat.

The police were there within minutes; so was the pathologist Dr Francis Camps. The cupboard door was opened, and the seated body was seen to be supported by a piece of blanket which was knotted to her brassiere. The other end of the blanket was part of the covering of a tall object leaning against the wall. A closer look revealed this was another body. And beyond it, against the back of the cupboard – which had obviously been a coal cellar – there was yet another object that looked ominously like an upright body.

The first corpse proved to be that of a rather pretty young woman, with a mark around her throat indicating that she had been strangled to death; a 'stalactite' of mould was growing out of her nose. Medical examination showed she had been dead about a month. Bubbling from her vagina was a large quantity of sperm – about 5 cc – suggesting that her killer had either had a tremendous orgasm, or had raped her more than once. The second body also proved to be of a young woman, wearing only a cardigan and vest; she too had been raped and strangled. The body had been placed in the cupboard upside down. Medical examination showed that she had been in the cupboard about two months. Body three was again of a young woman, upside down and wrapped in a blanket. And, as in the case of body two, a piece of cloth had been placed between the legs in the form of a diaper. She was wearing only a pink silk slip and bra, with two vests. She was six months pregnant, and had been in the cupboard from two to three months.

These were not the only remains found at No. 10 Rillington Place. Beneath the floor boards in the front room there was another naked body wrapped in a blanket. This proved to be a middle-aged woman, who had been dead for between three and four months. Between her legs there was

Police digging in the garden of 10 Rillington Place. The search revealed several bodies.

also a piece of silk in the position of a diaper. A search of the garden revealed that a bone propping up a fence was a human femur. Digging revealed bones belonging to two more female bodies.

There was no problem about identifying the killer. He was John Reginald Halliday Christie, who had lived in the ground-floor flat for the past fifteen years, and had had the exclusive use of the garden. Christie was described as a tall, thin, bespectacled man with a bald head. The corpse under the floorboards was that of his 54-year-old wife Ethel. Christie had left the flat four days earlier, sub-letting it to a couple named Reilly (from whom he took rent of £8). That same evening the Jamaican landlord, Charles Brown, had arrived and found the Reillys in occupation; he had ordered them to leave the following morning – since Christie had no right to sub-let the flat.

Now the hunt was on for Christie; police naturally feared he might commit more sex murders. One week later, on 31 March 1953, a police constable near Putney Bridge thought he recognized a man staring gloomily into the water and asked him if he was Christie; the man admitted it quietly, and accompanied PC Ledger to the station. He seemed relieved it was over.

The finding of the bodies brought to mind another tragedy that had occurred in the same house five years earlier. On 2 December 1949, the police had found the bodies of 20-year-old Beryl Evans and her one-year-old daughter Geraldine in the wash-house outside the back door. The husband, an illiterate labourer named Timothy Evans, had been charged with both murders and hanged. Now everyone was asking the question: was Christie the killer of Beryl and Geraldine Evans? Christie himself answered part of this question a few weeks later when he confessed to strangling Beryl Evans with a stocking; he claimed she had asked him to help her commit suicide. But Christie strongly denied murdering the baby Geraldine.

Reg Christie (as he was known) was born in Yorkshire in April 1898, the son of a carpet designer who bullied and ill-treated his family. He was a weak child who was regarded as a 'cissy' by his schoolfellows. He was often ill, and frequently in trouble with the police for minor offences – he was the unlucky type who always seemed to get caught. At the age of fifteen he became a clerk to the Halifax police, but was sacked for pilfering. And when he lost a job in his father's carpet factory for petty theft, his father threw him out of the house. He served in the First World War and, according to his own statement, was gassed. In 1920 he got a job as a clerk in a wool mill, and began courting a neighbour, Ethel Waddington, a plain, homely girl of a passive disposition; they married in 1920.

But Christie continued to be a petty criminal. In 1921 he was a postman, and people complained that letters and postal-orders failed to arrive. Investigation revealed that Christie had been stealing them, and he was sentenced to three months in jail. In 1923 he was put on probation for obtaining money by false pretences. In 1924 he was sentenced to nine months for theft. This was too much for Ethel, and she left him. He moved to London and settled down with another woman whom he met on a coach going to Margate. But Christie's dislike of work led to quarrels, and after one of these he hit her with a cricket bat, almost shattering her skull. For this he was sentenced to six months for malicious wounding. And in 1933 he received another three months for stealing the car of a priest who had befriended him. He wrote to Ethel in Sheffield, asking her to come and visit him in prison. When he came out, they again moved in together. Their new home was the small, shabby house at the end of a cul-de-sac called Rillington Place. The rent was twelve shillings and nine pence a week.

In September 1939 Christie became a war reserve policeman, and he became unpopular in the area for his bullying and officious behaviour – he loved to run in people for minor blackout infringements. During this period, Ethel often went to visit her family in Sheffield, and in 1943 Christie began to have an affair with a young woman from the Harrow Road police station. Her husband, a soldier, heard about it and went and caught them together at Rillington Place. He beat Christie up, and later divorced his wife, citing Christie as co-respondent.

It may have been this humiliation that led to Christie's first murder. Some time soon after the divorce scandal, Christie picked up a young Austrian prostitute named Ruth Fuerst – she had been stranded in England by the war – and took her back to Rillington Place. Ethel was in Sheffield. As they had sex, he strangled her with a piece of rope. The fact that he used rope suggests that the murder was premeditated; he probably decided to kill her while she undressed. But why? The answer was supplied to me by Dr Francis Camps, the pathologist on the case, when I met him in 1959. Camps told me that one of the odd things about the case that never came out in court was that he found dried sperm in the seams of Christie's shoes. For Camps, this showed clearly that Christie had masturbated as he stood over a corpse. And this, in turn, indicates that Christie had to *see* the corpse to achieve maximum stimulation. In short, he was a necrophile. In fact, he admitted later that the most overwhelming emotional experience of his life was to see the corpse of his grandfather when he was eight years old.

Christie was almost certainly lying when he said he had normal intercourse with Ruth Fuerst. In his teens, Christie was the laughing stock of the local youths because he was reputed to be impotent; after a humiliating experience with a local girl, he became known as 'Reggie No-Dick' and 'Can't do-it Christie'. With shy, passive women (like Ethel) he could achieve intercourse, although he claims that they had been married for two years before they had sex. The same is probably true of the soldier's wife with whom he had an affair. But with most women he was impotent unless they were unconscious or dead. So when Ruth Fuerst came back to his flat, he probably prepared a piece of 'strangling rope' (with a knot at either end) and placed it under the pillow, intending to kill her and make sexual use of the corpse until Ethel came back. In fact, he was interrupted. A telegram arrived shortly after the murder, announcing her return. He had to conceal the body hastily under the floor boards, and bury it in the garden at the first opportunity. Now he had killed a woman, the aching sense of inferiority – brought to a head by the beating from the angry soldier – was assuaged.

In December 1943 temptation came his way again. Now no longer a policeman, he worked for a firm called Ultra Radio, and met a plump, attractive little woman called Muriel Eady. She told him she suffered from catarrh, and Christie had an idea. He told her he had a cure for catarrh, and invited her back to Rillington Place while Ethel was away. The cure, he said, was to lean over a bowl of steaming Friar's Balsam, with a cloth over the head to keep in the steam. Christie ran a rubber pipe from the gas tap, and inserted it under the cloth. Muriel Eady passed out peacefully. Trembling with excitement, Christie moved her on to the bed, removed her clothes, and raped her. Looking at the body, he later described how he experienced a sense of exquisite peace. 'I had no regrets.' Muriel Eady also found her way into the garden.

Six years passed before he killed again, and it is possible the murder was unpremeditated. Timothy and Beryl Evans had moved into the upstairs flat, but they quarrelled a great deal; one of the quarrels was about a blonde girl who had moved in with them; the girl had to leave. In one of his confessions, Christie claimed that he strangled Mrs Evans at her own request, because she wanted to die. There may be an element of truth in this. But what Christie failed to mention is that Beryl Evans had again discovered herself to be pregnant, and wanted an abortion. Christie, who loved to swagger, had told Timothy Evans that he had once studied to be a doctor. And Evans asked Christie if he could perform an abortion.

What happened next is a matter for conjecture; but the view of Ludovic Kennedy, in his book *Ten Rillington Place*, is well argued. Christie went into the room, where Beryl Evans was waiting for him; she removed her

Above left: Mrs Beryl Evans and her daughter Geraldine, for whose murders Timothy Evans (*above*, after his arrest) was hanged. But what part did Christie play in their deaths? *Left:* John Reginald Halliday Christie, in a photograph issued by Scotland Yard.

knickers and lay down with her legs apart. Christie inserted a finger, or perhaps a spoon, then was overcome with sexual desire, and tried to climb on her. Beryl struggled; Christie strangled her, and then raped her. When Timothy Evans came home, Christie told him that his wife had died as a result of the abortion, and that he, Evans, would almost certainly be blamed.

Evans, a man of subnormal intelligence, panicked. He allowed Christie to do his thinking for him. And what Christie apparently advised was that the baby should be looked after by some people in Acton, and Evans should vanish. Evans *did* vanish – to Merthyr Vale, in Wales, and spent ten days with an aunt and uncle; then he decided to go back to London, to give himself up to the police. They came and found the bodies in the wash-house, and Evans was charged with murder.

And here we encounter the first mystery of the case. Evans then made a full confession to murdering his wife and baby by strangulation. This was, admittedly, his second confession – in the first he had stated that Beryl had died as a result of an abortion performed by Christie. But he repeated his confession to murdering his wife and child the following day. So although he withdrew this second confession a fortnight later, the police had no reason to believe his assertion that the real killer was Christie. At the trial, Christie appeared as a witness for the prosecution, and Evans was hanged on 9 March 1950.

Ethel Christie had a strong suspicion, amounting to a certainty, that her husband was somehow involved in the murders – she had noticed his extreme nervousness at the time. She confided her belief to a neighbour, and when Christie came in and caught them discussing the case, he flew into a rage. This could explain why, on 14 December 1952, he strangled her in bed. It could also have been that he experienced a compulsion to commit more sex crimes, and Ethel stood in the way. Christie told her family in Sheffield that she was unable to write because she had rheumatism in her fingers.

In mid-January 1953 Christie picked up a prostitute called Kathleen Maloney in a pub in Paddington, and invited her back to his flat. As she sat in a deck-chair in the kitchen, he placed the gas pipe under the chair; she was too drunk to notice. When she was unconscious, he raped her and put her in the cupboard.

The next victim, Rita Nelson, was six months pregnant; Christie may have lured her back with the offer of an abortion. She also ended in the cupboard – the second body.

About a month later, Christie met a girl called Hectorina Maclennan, who told him she was looking for a flat. She and her boyfriend actually spent three nights in Christie's flat, now devoid of furniture (Christie had sold it). On 5 March Hectorina made the mistake of going back to the flat alone. She grew nervous when she saw Christie toying with a gas-pipe and tried to leave; Christie killed her and raped her. When her boyfriend came to inquire about her, she was in the cupboard, and Christie claimed not to have seen her. As Christie gave him tea, the boyfriend noticed 'a very nasty smell', but had no suspicion he was sitting within feet of Hectorina's corpse.

This was Christie's last murder. Two weeks later, he left Rillington Place, and wandered around aimlessly, sleeping in cheap lodgings and spending the days in cafés until he was arrested. He confessed to all the murders of women, usually insisting that it was *they* who made the advances. He was executed on 15 July 1953.

The major mystery remains – was Timothy Evans innocent? Long after his death, he was officially absolved of all responsibility and guilt; yet that leaves some major questions unanswered. For example, why did he confess to the murders?

Ludovic Kennedy, in *Ten Rillington Place*, takes the view that Evans was innocent of both murders. He confessed, says Kennedy, out of misery and confusion. But this is almost impossible. Evans had had ten days in Wales to think things over. There is no earthly reason why he should have confessed to strangling Beryl (after a quarrel) and then Geraldine. (Kennedy argues that he was too fond of both).

In *The Two Stranglers of Rillington Place*, Rupert Furneaux takes the opposite view. He points out that Beryl and Timothy Evans often quarrelled violently, and that nothing was more likely than that Evans would kill Beryl in a rage. He argues closely and convincingly, and is, on the whole, more plausible than Kennedy. And he believes that it was Christie who murdered the baby.

But this still leaves a major mystery: why, in that case, did Evans also confess to murdering Geraldine?

The answer is surely supplied by a curious piece of evidence from another murderer, Donald Hume, who was in prison at the same time as Evans, on a charge of murdering a man named Stanley Setty and throwing pieces of his body out of an aeroplane. Evans asked Hume's advice, and when Hume asked 'Did you kill your wife?' Evans replied: 'No, Christie murdered her.' Here he could well have been lying, for by now his defence was that Christie had killed her in the course of an abortion. But when Hume asked if he killed the baby, Evans made the surprising statement that Christie had strangled Geraldine while he, Evans, watched. He said that the baby's crying had got on his nerves.

This rings true. Evans was in a frantic state, and he could well have stood by while Christie killed Geraldine. In doing so, he had become, in effect, her killer, so his confession to murdering her was not far short of the truth. Guilt probably increased his sense of being her murderer. And this, I would argue, is almost certainly the answer to the riddle. There *were* two stranglers of Rillington Place. And baby Geraldine was, in a sense, killed by both of them.

As an interesting footnote to this case, Donald Hume was acquitted of the murder of Stanley Setty. He went to Switzerland, became a bank robber, and in 1958 shot a taxi driver in the course of escaping from a bank; for this murder he was sentenced to hard labour for life.

THE CASE OF LORD LUCAN

One chilly November night in 1974, Ian Maxwell Scott telephoned his wife Susan at Grants Hill House, their home on the outskirts of Uckfield, to tell her he had decided not to come home that evening as he had planned. He had had a couple of drinks with friends, wasn't prepared to drive down to Sussex, and was staying the night with them. As so often happens, a simple decision such as this almost certainly influenced the behaviour of the central character in what was to become an overnight sensation.

With four of her children away at school and the other two fast asleep, Mrs Maxwell Scott decided to have an early night and take herself off to bed with a book. By a coincidence which she remembers to this day, the book was *The Best of Beachcomber* by John Bingham Morton. She was dozing when, at around 11.30, the doorbell rang. Her bedroom was at the back of the house so Mrs Maxwell Scott climbed out of bed, went to a bathroom which overlooked the front door, peered out of the window and called out.

Lord Lucan stepped back from the shadows of the house and called back, 'It's me, John Lucan. Can I come in?'

Richard John Bingham Lucan, 7th Earl of Lucan, had been a friend of the Maxwell Scotts for nearly twenty years. He and his wife Veronica, whom he married in 1963, had often visited Grants Hill House with their children, and the Maxwell Scotts had watched their marriage thrive, stumble and finally perish in acrimony. Lord Lucan now lived separately from

Richard John Bingham Lucan, 7th Earl of Lucan, who disappeared in November 1974.

his wife but frequently saw his children, to whom he was devoted and who – since he had failed to obtain custody of them in a bitterly fought case – were wards of court, living with their mother. Lucan and Ian Maxwell Scott were close friends and frequently in each other's company. So when she saw Lord Lucan on the doorstep, Mrs Maxwell Scott immediately feared that he had come to tell her that something had happened to her husband.

She grabbed a dressing-gown from the back of the bathroom door, ran downstairs and let Lord Lucan in. His first words, 'Is Ian here?', reassured her. (Lucan had in fact expected to find his friend at home since Maxwell Scott had turned down a dinner invitation from the Earl for that evening, saying that he intended to go home.)

But although her own fears were allayed, Mrs Maxwell Scott guessed from Lord Lucan's distracted manner and slightly dishevelled appearance that something was, indeed, wrong. She led him into the drawing-room and he confirmed her guess. 'Something awful has happened. I'll tell you about it in a minute. Can I have a drink?' There being none of his favourite vodka in the house, Mrs Maxwell Scott poured him a whisky, got herself a cup of coffee and sat down to listen to the story that would soon have the whole country speculating.

Earlier that evening, Lucan said, he had been walking past his house in Belgravia on his way to his own flat close by, to change for dinner. He still had a front-door key to the house and would often look through the windows to see if he could catch a glimpse of his children. And that night, through the window of the basement kitchen, he had seen his wife Veronica struggling with a man.

He ran up the steps to the front door, let himself in and rushed down the basement stairs, shouting something. He slipped in a pool of blood, picked himself up and ran to his wife who was hysterical and also covered in blood. The man was nowhere to be seen; he had in Lucan's phrase 'run off' somewhere.

Mrs Maxwell Scott listened in horror and near disbelief as Lord Lucan described the scene as 'ghastly' and 'nightmarish'. He paused for a moment, covering his eyes with his hand, and then continued quite calmly. There was blood everywhere, he said, and Lady Lucan was hysterical. He tried to calm her but she shouted, 'You sent him to kill me! You hired him!'

Incredulous, Mrs Maxwell Scott began to protest, but Lucan explained that his wife was an excitable and neurotic young woman who had several times accused him of having a 'contract out on her life' – an idea Lord Lucan simply put down to her watching too much television.

On the night the Lucans' nanny Sandra Rivett (*left*) was murdered, Lord Lucan arrived in a distracted state at the Sussex home of his friends the Maxwell-Scotts (*below*).

It was then, Lucan continued, that his wife had pointed frantically at a sack lying on the floor and cried that it contained the body of the children's nanny, Sandra Rivett, who had been murdered. Confused, Lucan's first thought was to calm his still hysterical wife, and he finally managed to persuade her to come upstairs with him. In her bedroom he found their eldest daughter, Frances, watching television. He sent her off to bed, telling her that her mother had had a slight accident, and persuaded his wife to lie down. Then he went to the bathroom to fetch damp towels to clean the blood from her face and to look for the tranquillizers which she habitually took. While he was doing this, Lady Lucan got up and rushed out of the house.

'I'm afraid at this point John panicked', says Mrs Maxwell Scott. 'He was positive that Veronica would try to get him into trouble.' (She had, in fact, run barefoot and blood-stained down the street to the local pub screaming 'Help me ... murder ... he's murdered the nanny!')

So Lord Lucan, too, fled from the house. He was sufficiently in command of himself, however, to think immediately about the children, now alone in the house, who might wake up and go down to that horrific basement. He went straight to the house of the mother of a school friend of Frances, who lived nearby, but there was no answer to the doorbell. Then he went to a telephone-box and rang up Bill Shand Kydd, an old friend, who was married to Lady Lucan's sister. Again there was no answer, so he telephoned his mother, the Dowager Countess, told her briefly what had happened and asked her to go to the house and either stay there with the children or take them back to her own home. (In fact, within half an hour both the police, called by the landlord of the pub, and the Dowager Countess arrived at the Lucans' house in Lower Belgrave Street, while Lady Lucan, who proved to have head wounds, was taken to hospital.)

Having failed to contact one of his close friends, Lord Lucan continued, he had then thought of Ian Maxwell Scott, whom he believed would be at home, and thus had driven down to Sussex.

By the time he reached the end of his story Lucan was, says Mrs Maxwell Scott, completely calm. But she could not persuade him that nobody would for a moment imagine that he had tried to kill his wife. Lord Lucan would not be reassured. His gambling and other debts, plus the upkeep of two establishments, had almost bankrupted him. Also it was well known that he wanted to have his children with him, and he thought that these two facts would be considered motive enough for murder. (He had, in fact, once tried unsuccessfully to 'snatch' them.) He could not bear his children to see him tried for murder. What could he do?

Perhaps, Mrs Maxwell Scott suggested, the murderer, having killed the nanny, had attacked Veronica because she had surprised him with the body. But, Lucan argued, why should anyone want to kill Sandra? After a succession of nannies who had only stayed a short while, he believed that they had at last found a 'good one'. No, he thought it must have been some maniac, or a violent burglar.

For a while they talked of other things: mutual friends, old times, Veronica and the marriage, but most of all about their children. Mrs Maxwell Scott suggested telephoning her husband to ask him to come down, but Lord Lucan said no, he would be all right now. He asked if he could use the telephone to call his mother and see if the children were OK? He did so and was reassured. (When his mother asked him if he wanted to speak to the police, who were there, he said no, he'd call them in the morning.)

Lucan then asked for some writing paper so that he could write to Bill Shand Kydd. He wrote one letter – which was mainly concerned with the welfare of his children and which explained that he was going to 'lie doggo' for a while – and then remembered something and wrote a second letter to his friend, this time concerned with his business affairs. Then he said he had better be going.

By now it was about 1 a.m. and Mrs Maxwell Scott tried without success to persuade him to stay the night. 'Ian will be back in the morning,' she said. 'There's nothing you can do tonight and you must be exhausted.' But Lucan would not be persuaded. He was even reluctant to let Mrs Maxwell Scott post his letters because he didn't want to 'involve her'. She said this was nonsense, and renewed her efforts to persuade him to stay. 'Would to God I had succeeded', she says. But Lucan was adamant.

He shrugged into his overcoat, kissed his old friend on the cheek, told her not to come out in the cold, and promised to let her know how things turned out. Then he got into his car and drove away. Neither Susan Maxwell Scott nor, as far as is known, anyone else has seen him since.

The following morning Mr Maxwell Scott arrived home at about 9 o'clock and, when his wife told him the story, was incredulous. John, he thought, must be wildly exaggerating the incident and be imagining things. However, he telephoned Lord Lucan's flat in London only to be told he was not there. The letters to Shand Kydd were duly posted and the Maxwell Scotts passed a quiet day. As often happened, they did not read an evening paper, nor watch television, and so it was not until the Saturday morning paper arrived next day that they realized that the story was all too true and that Lord Lucan had apparently disappeared.

Mr Maxwell Scott then telephoned Bill Shand Kydd, whom he knew to be staying in the country. The latter rushed up to London to find Lucan's letters at his London home and then telephoned the police and showed them the letters. The Uckfield postmark was explained and for the first time the police learned that Lord Lucan had visited Sussex that night. They were by now actively searching for the Earl, and were baffled by the Maxwell Scotts' failure to contact them and infuriated by the delay in the search for him, which was now switched to Sussex.

The police visited Grants Hill House and 'grilled' Mrs Maxwell Scott for four or five hours, asking all kinds of apparently irrelevant questions which she answered willingly and fully. Without producing a warrant, but with her full permission, they searched the house and examined the chairs for bloodstains, which they failed to find. (Mrs Maxwell Scott had seen no signs of blood on her friend: although she had noticed what appeared to be a damp patch on his trousers.) As the police were about to leave, she asked them if they did not wish to search the grounds. No, they replied, they would not bother.

The police apparently found it hard to believe that the Maxwell Scotts had known nothing about the facts – actually did not watch television all day Friday – and were suspicious of their natural reaction in contacting Bill Shand Kydd rather than the police about the letters. Both husband and wife were required to visit Uckfield police station, where they made lengthy statements – and returned to face the barrage of the Press.

On Sunday afternoon Newhaven police reported that observant neighbours had noticed that an old Ford Corsair had been left in a side street sometime between 5 and 8 a.m. on Friday 8 November. The car turned out to have been the one used by Lord Lucan and to have been borrowed from a friend, Michael Stoop, a couple of weeks earlier. It was Stoop's 'second' car, which Lucan had asked for in preference to Stoop's Mercedes, and it had been assumed by Stoop that he wanted an ordinary looking car to enable him to keep a watch on his wife without being noticed. Bloodstains of the type belonging to both Lady Lucan and the nanny were found in the car, and other clues linked it with the murder.

The following evening Michael Stoop collected some letters from his club which included one from Lord Lucan. In this letter his friend apologized to Michael Stoop for not returning his car, and told him he had left it in Newhaven. He also expressed concern for his own situation and his conviction that no judge would believe his story. He asked Stoop to keep an eye on the welfare of his children. Stoop telephoned the police about this letter but when they arrived, several hours later, they found that Stoop had thrown away the envelope with its possibly tell-tale postmark. The letter must have been written on paper which Stoop recognized as having been left in the Ford, and presumably written by Lucan while

Lord Bingham (as he then was) with his bride Veronica after their wedding in 1963. The marriage began happily but ended with an acrimonious separation, Lady Lucan winning custody of their children.

he was sitting in the car. The police searched all the waste-bins of the club, but the envelope was never found. Once again the police expressed annoyance and frustration at the destruction of evidence. They found it hard to believe that it was a natural and innocent act.

The search for the missing Earl was now being carried out in earnest. Fishermen at Newhaven reported seeing a 'distinguished looking' man walking along the quay early in the morning. But stringent checks at immigration points at Newhaven and Dieppe and aboard the only ferry to leave Newhaven that day produced nothing. Lord Lucan's passport had been left in London and there was no record that he had bought a temporary passport anywhere. He was known to have little money on him. On the other hand, it was also known that he had friends in northern France. All inquiries drew a blank.

The police also searched the beaches around Newhaven and sent frogmen down into the harbour. They searched the tunnels of the medieval castle on the hill above the town, and large areas of the local countryside. A few weeks later they sent up helicopters fitted with infra-red cameras which could detect decaying animal matter, but all that was turned up was a dead sheep or two and a dog.

There were the usual false alarms and mischievous reports – including that of a man who claimed he had seen a third person come out of the Lucans' house at the time of the murder. There were reports that the Earl had been seen in northern France and that he had stayed on three occasions in a hotel at Cherbourg. Although the proprietors of the hotel identified Lucan from photographs, they also said that the man spoke almost perfect French, while Lucan's friends told the police that his French was virtually non-existent.

The inquest was adjourned to March in the hope that meanwhile Lucan would be found, but during the intervening weeks a bankruptcy order was granted against Lord Lucan and most of his realizable assets were sold. A number of friends, who refused to believe either that Lucan was guilty or that he had killed himself, hired private investigators to try to find out where he was.

When the inquest was finally held in March 1975, the jury brought in a verdict of murder, and named Lord Lucan as the guilty party. This extraordinary departure from the usual 'person unknown' caused such a furore that Lord Lucan's family, headed by his mother, worked to get the verdict overturned. Although the verdict of the court was not changed, the law eventually was, and a coroner's jury is no longer allowed to name a person as a murderer.

Meanwhile the hunt went on. Although the police had failed to find any

While a policeman keeps guard outside Lady Lucan's Belgravia home (*left*), the search for the missing Earl centres on the cliff-top above Newhaven (*below*).

boats missing from the Newhaven harbours, they believed that Lord Lucan could have sailed to France. They also believed that his friends were involved in a big cover-up: the actions of the Maxwell Scotts and of Michael Stoop no doubt helped them to this theory. The fact was, of course, that the police were working in a milieu and among a class of people with which they were largely unfamiliar. Their conviction that 'the aristocracy' were more likely to gang up to protect one of their own than were the criminal or working classes among whom they normally operated was ludicrous, but so firmly held that even after his retirement Detective Chief Superintendent Roy Ranson, in charge of the case, wrote to the *Daily Star* in September 1982 expressing his bitterness towards what he described as the 'Lucan set'. They thought they were rather special, he claimed, 'living in their own world, quite apart from the rest of us'.

Lord Lucan's friends regard this as ridiculous. They were friends, yes, like any other group of friends, but there was nothing special about them. Nor had they ever done anything more than behave with the ordinary loyalty one would show to a friend, while giving the police every help possible. Nevertheless, the idea that he must have had help persisted while the police continued their search, which gradually extended all over the world.

'Lord Lucan' was seen in places as far apart as Las Vegas and the Seychelles. He was seen several times in South Africa (he was known to have some money in a bank account in Rhodesia) and he was pursued to Rhodes, Rio de Janeiro, Dublin and Bogota. Sometimes it was found that deliberate hoaxes had been perpetrated.

The suicide of a friend, Dominic Elwes, nearly a year after Lucan's disappearance, was said to have been connected with it. Such a continuation of the scandal, said their close friends, was ridiculous.

But to this day the mystery continues. A modern day 'bounty hunter', the same man who first found train-robber Ronald Biggs, claimed to have found Lord Lucan in South America, but failed to produce either any concrete proof or the Earl himself. For some time his friends assumed that someone was, indeed, helping him. He could never have managed to disappear so successfully on his own. But ten years have passed and his friends, once convinced he was alive somewhere, are now more pessimistic. 'Knowing John', said one of them, 'I just don't believe that he is clever enough to have stayed hidden so long without anything being heard of him. I have a horrible feeling he must be dead and I really worry about all the misery he must have suffered.'

John Lucan's friends, and many reporters and other people who have looked into the story objectively, are still totally convinced that he had no part in the murder of the nanny or the attack on his wife. It was not in his character, say his friends, while those who never knew him point out that the theory that he attacked his nanny in mistake for his wife is not only far-fetched but hardly borne out by the fact that, presumably having realized his error and his degree of commitment to the situation, he then proceeded not to murder his wife and make good his escape, but actually tried to comfort her. The theory that he hired a murderer (who could possibly have made such an error) is equally far-fetched. Lord Lucan was not in touch with the 'underworld', and even if he had been, he would hardly have put in a voluntary appearance on the scene of a crime he had instigated.

This is a story in which both the crime itself and the subsequent disappearance of a leading figure are full of extraordinary and baffling factors.

And while the mystery remains unsolved, problems continue. Lord Lucan's son, Lord Bingham, now sixteen years old, cannot officially become the Eighth Earl; tenants of the Earl's 62,000 acres in and around Castle Barr in County Mayo, Ireland, are harassing the lawyers whose job it is to collect rents for a non-existent landlord and deal with other problems: innumerable details connected with the Earl's estate remain unresolved.

And the police have not given up. 'Until a body is found,' said a senior detective, 'this case will never be closed.' And even then the mystery of who killed nanny Sandra Rivett, and why, may never be solved.

CRABB OR 'KORABLOV'?

No one who was there will forget that April evening of 1956 in the Painted Hall at the Royal Naval College, Greenwich. The long parallels of tables; the glow of the innumerable lamps at each diner's place reflected by napery, silver, glass; the gold of braid and buttons and the starched shirt fronts, set off against dark blue serge and black bow ties. All around, Wren's and Hawksmoor's columns, soaring up to where royal, allegorical, nautical and scientific figures riot colourfully to populate one of the world's finest ceilings.

But it was not towards Sir James Thornhill's creation that eyes most often turned that evening. The focal point was the top table, where among the most heavily braided and beribboned of the uniforms sat two men in civilian clothes: distinctly foreign-looking men, the elder rather sinisterly bearded, the other with the broad, round face of the merry peasant.

'B. and K.', the British Press and people had playfully dubbed N.A. Bulganin and N.S. Khrushchev, leaders of the Soviet Union now that Stalin was no longer alive. Their busy mission to many countries, of which this visit to England was part, was to deplore the enormities of Stalin's repressive and murderous reign, salute the ending of the bad old days, and assure the West that war was no longer inevitable nor to be desired.

It was not only the significance of their visit, coupled with the ceremonious glitter, which imprinted this occasion indelibly on the minds of those present. It was the later speculation about how much Mr B.'s earnest conversation with his hosts, and Mr K.'s playful quips and loud laughter, had overlain a knowledge of happenings of a very different order at an equally historic Royal Naval establishment some eighty miles away.

Perhaps one or two of the other diners were aware of it. Most of what the world at large has found out since has come through rumour, deduction and documentation which may be honest or fabricated. Unless a man by now old and decrepit enough to be deemed harmless should emerge from that almost impenetrable mass which is Russia's empire, and tell his own story, we are unlikely to learn the truth behind the disappearance of 'Buster' Crabb.

If alive now, Lionel Crabb will be time-expired, so far as the biblical span goes. In April 1956 he was forty-six. His career had been the sea, though not exclusively. After a Merchant Marine apprenticeship he had taken a number of shore jobs, in foreign parts, without much success in any of them. With the coming of war he got into the Royal Naval Volunteer Reserve, and then the Royal Naval Patrol Service. With a commission, he went to Gibraltar in 1942 as a mine- and bomb-disposal officer.

The dapper little man suddenly found himself literally in his element – not on the sea, but under it. 'Frogmen' were not part of the Royal Navy's establishment yet. The Italians had them, though, and they were causing much nuisance and damage, riding in their rubber wet-suits on torpedo-like underwater craft, sneaking beneath Allied merchantmen and warships to clamp explosive charges to their hulls.

As a countermeasure, the Royal Navy at Gibraltar had fitted out three launches with spotlights and small depth-charges for patrolling the anchorages. Two amateur divers, with improvised equipment, took to crawling about under vessels at anchor, locating and detaching these explosives.

It was this highly dangerous, uncomfortable and nerve-racking work at which Buster Crabb and a few colleagues made themselves expert, saving tens of thousands of tons of shipping from destruction. It earned him a

Commander Crabb, whose disappearance in the murky waters of Portsmouth Harbour was a source of acute embarrassment to the British Government.

George Medal and appointment to the Order of the British Empire. He was promoted to Lieutenant-Commander.

The war's end more or less deprived him of his role in life, and even his place in the service. The Admiralty gave him some diving work as a civilian; he was prominent in attempts to rescue the trapped crew of the submarine *Truculent*, sunk in a Thames estuary collison in 1950. He returned to the Navy briefly, but by early 1955 was a civilian again.

He took a job as representative of a firm supplying equipment to Espresso coffee bars. Conjecture is that he did other things, too, sometimes, involving going under water; a firm in Leatherhead had a record of selling him in October 1955 an Italian-made rubber underwater suit, of a different design from those used by the increasing numbers of Royal Naval frogmen. His invariable dry-land outfit was a tweed suit, with an eyeglass in one waistcoat pocket, a pork-pie hat, and an ebony swordstick with a head in the form of a gold crab.

It must have made him quite the most exotic of all Espresso reps. Former Naval colleagues in Portsmouth, where his business seemed to take him a lot, sensed better than to question his assertion that he had just dropped into town to visit his favourite hairdresser.

It was at Portsmouth on 18 April 1956 that the well-publicized visit to Great Britain of Messrs Bulganin and Khrushchev began. They came in show-off style in the 12,000-ton cruiser *Ordzhonikidze*, a fine warship which had raised speculation among Western intelligence agencies because of her remarkable speed and manoeuvrability, implying some revolutionary form of hull or rudder. With two attendant destroyers she anchored in Stokes Bay, at the entrance to the historic harbour.

Less ostentatiously, there had arrived at Portsmouth the previous day, by train from London, the tweed-suited little man with the pork-pie hat and the distinctive cane. He went to the modest little Sallyport Hotel, a survivor in the High Street of the badly bombed Old Town. He was joined there by a younger man, who registered as 'Matthew Smith'. They had separate rooms, but knew one another well enough to spend that evening out together.

Next day, from before breakfast until evening, Crabb was out of the hotel – a prolonged session at the hairdresser's? On 19 April he went out early again. This time he did not come back. 'Mr Smith' left later that day, paying both their bills by cash and taking his friend's baggage and swordstick with him.

Three days later, the head of Portsmouth CID came in person to the little hotel and asked to see the register. Without explanation, he tore out its April pages, and, invoking the Official Secrets Act, cautioned proprietor and staff not to discuss or answer any question about Messrs Crabb and Smith.

It was already too late, though. Crabb's employer in the Espresso business had tried to telephone him at the Sallyport, and had been told that he had gone. Surprised, he managed to get in touch with an officer friend of Crabb's, who agreed to find out what he could, which proved to be nothing. More significantly, perhaps, another friend of Buster Crabb's telephoned the Admiralty in London to ask after him. The unelaborated answer was that he was dead.

Rumour buzzed throughout Portsmouth's tight-knit Royal Naval community, and spread through the Navy at large. Those present at the splendid banquet in the Painted Hall looked speculatively at the honoured guests, and not a few Portsmouth residents stared long and hard at the Russian warships in Stokes Bay, as though trying to divine what had happened and what might still be happening out there.

Fleet Street was quickly on to the story. The Admiralty was saying nothing, neither confirming nor denying rumours ranging from the inevitable ones that Crabb had been spotted spying on the *Ordzhonikidze*'s hull, and had been shot, to the more bizarre suggestion that some automatic anti-sabotage device had killed him, perhaps by electrocution or by pinioning him until he drowned. A more intriguing theory still was that he had been captured and was at this very moment a prisoner – a British subject, held in a foreign warship in British waters – undergoing interrogation under unspeakable circumstances. A reporter who sought a statement from the Soviet Embassy in London got only the answer that one of the cruiser's lookouts had briefly seen a frogman nearby, but that to have taken any measures against him would have been out of the question in a British port.

HMS *Vernon*, the Royal Navy's underwater establishment at Portsmouth, was making no statement, but it was rumoured that several of Buster Crabb's friends there, wanting to go out and search for him, had been warned off. The official silence was understandable. The Anglo-Russian talks in London were sensitive and of potentially great importance. A spy drama, with perhaps grisly details, would not have helped them.

On 28 April Messrs B. and K. departed in their fine cruiser. Their double act had been a lively success. They had been entertained to tea by the Queen. They had agreed a joint communiqué with the Prime Minister, Sir Anthony Eden, expressing a common desire for the lessening of international tension, for disarmament, and for better Anglo-Soviet trade and cultural contacts. And Mr K. had become so incensed by speeches at a dinner given him by the Parliamentary Labour Party that he declared

that if he lived in Britain he would be a Tory. It was all very different
from those decorous proceedings in the Painted Hall. Yet a man had
disappeared; and the question many were asking was: had the Russians
taken him away with them?

The day after the Russian ships' departure, the Admiralty issued a
statement: 'He is presumed to be dead as a result of trials with certain
underwater apparatus.' Pressed in the Commons, the Prime Minister replied carefully:

It would not be in the public interest to disclose the circumstances in which
Commander Crabb is presumed to have met his death ... I think it is necessary,
in the special circumstances of this case, to make it clear that what was done was
done without the authority or the knowledge of Her Majesty's Ministers. Appropriate disciplinary steps are being taken.

That satisfied only those whose theory it was that Crabb, who was believed
to have been willing to render his services to any Allied agencies requiring
them, had been examining the cruiser in his freelance capacity, perhaps on
behalf of the US Secret Service; though who might be disciplined, in that
case, it was hard to imagine.

A further Parliamentary attempt to force the Prime Minister's hand met
his flat refusal, in the interest of the newly forged understanding with the
Soviet leaders. A formal Russian request for information could not be so
blandly evaded. According to their news agency, Tass, the Foreign Office
replied:

As has already been publicly reported, Commander Crabb carried out frogman
tests, and, as is assumed, lost his life during these tests. The frogman who, as
reported in the Soviet Note, was discovered from the Soviet ships swimming
between the Soviet destroyers, was to all appearances Commander Crabb. His
presence in the vicinity of the destroyers occurred without any permission whatever and Her Majesty's Government express their regret for the incident.

It was not enough to end Press interest. In August, a skeleton was washed
ashore near Portsmouth, but tests proved that it had been in the sea far
longer than Crabb had been missing. Then a West German newspaper
quoted a French left-wing politician, just back from Moscow, as disclosing
that Crabb was alive and being held in the Lefortovo prison there. French
Socialist sources denied that any such report had been made. From Co-
penhagen came a story that some crewmen of the *Ordzhonikidze*, paying
a courtesy call there, had told how part of the cruiser's sick bay had been
sealed off and closely guarded on the voyage home from that English visit.
No one had glimpsed the unidentified occupant.

The Crabb story returned sporadically until, in June 1957, the sea cast

Above: 'Buster' Crabb, on the left, photographed at work in 1950 during attempts to salvage the submarine *Truculent*, which sank after a collision in the Thames Estuary.
Below: The Russian cruiser *Ordzhonikidze*, with Bulganin and Kruschev aboard, nears Portsmouth. Was Crabb aboard her when she left port? If so, was he dead or alive?

up another body, this time at Chichester Harbour, twelve miles from Portsmouth. It was headless and handless, and the trunk was little more than skeleton. The lower half, though, was fairly well preserved, protected by the tight fit of a frogman's suit, of Italian make.

An inquest was held. Physical characteristics of the missing Crabb, including hammer toes and a leg scar, approximated to what the pathologists found. The coroner summed up: 'Looking at the evidence in this case, I am quite satisfied that the remains which were found in Chichester harbour on 9 June were those of Cdr Crabb ...' The body was buried at Portsmouth, though neither with Naval honours, nor with any Royal Naval representative present.

Speculation did not end at the graveside. A few days before the finding of the remains, three Soviet submarines had passed through the English Channel. It was irresistible to suggest that the body had been brought in one of them and slipped into the sea near to where it was found. There were rust marks on the legs. Perhaps it had been towed part of the way, to increase the semblance of prolonged immersion. The suit and underclothing seemed to be Crabb's; but was the body his, or the deliberately mutilated remains of another? In which case, why the elaborate deception?

The 'answer' came sensationally, three full years later. A Czech-born naturalized British journalist, J. Bernard Hutton, who specialized in Eastern European affairs and had many Iron Curtain contacts, published in 1960 a book, *Frogman Extraordinary*, which was based largely on a 30,000-word Russian dossier smuggled out to him and providing the full details of the Crabb affair.

His *Ordzhonikidze* mission had been doomed before he even donned his wet suit that April 1956 morning. A Soviet agent in Portsmouth had already recognized him, guessed why he was in town, and given the warning. He was captured easily as he swam towards the cruiser. He was kept prisoner, heavily sedated, throughout the ships' stay. When they were out of British waters, heading back to Russia, he was lifted off by helicopter and conveyed to a Soviet Naval Intelligence establishment in Moscow.

There and in the Lefortovo prison he was interrogated at great length. The dossier contained purported transcripts from which the interrogators emerge as alternately threatening and cajoling, their aim seeming to have been to get an admission that he had been engaged to spy on the cruiser for US Naval Intelligence. He denied it adamantly, refusing to sign a confession. He was not tortured, but threatened with death. It elicited nothing further from him than that he had been going to spy on the cruiser's hull out of personal curiosity.

Faced with such intransigence, the Russians were in a dilemma. They could not break his story – and as time passed, there was less and less point in trying. He would give up no Allied naval secrets. They could not let him go free, to rekindle indignation about the kidnapping of a British subject in British territory. His own Government had disowned him, and would certainly not bargain for his return. He would simply have to be 'rubbed out', his latest questioner told him – unless he would make himself useful by passing on his frogman expertise as a member of the Red Navy.

The proposal was made in friendly terms, with an offer of decent pay and treatment. The questioner produced a corpse on a stretcher. The physical resemblance to Crabb was close enough. By the time the head and hands had been cut off, and the body kept in the sea for a year or so, no one would be able to tell the difference. Then it would be planted where it could reasonably be expected to turn up, speculation about Crabb's disappearance would be at an end, and he could get on with his life and the work he so enjoyed, under new management.

'Better Red than dead' presumably reasoned the brave man, who had held out so resolutely, and who had become too recognizable to hope for any more Allied assignments, even if the Russians did let him go. He accepted. He was given a crash course in the Russian language and way of life at a 'Rehabilitation Centre', and, as 'L.L. Korablov', taken into the Red Navy, quickly becoming a frogman instructor. He was commissioned, rising by 1967 to captain, commanding a special underwater task force.

Such was Hutton's account of Crabb's disappearance, and in 1970 he published another book, *The Fake Defector*, retelling the story, adding corroboration from people who claimed to have met or seen Crabb in Russia. Its hypothesis was that attempts had been made by the Soviets to persuade him to admit to the West that he had defected voluntarily.

He has never done so, and since those days there have been far more important and sensational defections than his, in both directions. The ultimate fate of Western defectors who have chosen to make the USSR their home generally emerges. Yet Buster Crabb's has not, so the probability is that he was never taken there at all, but killed in Portsmouth Harbour, intentionally or accidentally, and his body taken away to avoid the mutual embarrassment which might have disrupted that olive-branch mission of the Russian leaders. The headless, handless remains, which turned up a year later, were either his or a substitute's; and what little scope any of it offered for a propaganda coup was worth no more than the labour involved in forging a dossier. Remember the 'Hitler Diaries'?

And yet, the world of espionage is as murky as the depths of harbour water beneath a big ship's hull. There is still time for 'L.L. Korablov' to resurface finally, and surprise us all.

DID MARTIN BORMANN ESCAPE?

Hitler presumably liked Martin Bormann, his secretary and head of the Nazi Party Chancellery. Rudolf Hess conceivably did. Frau Bormann probably did. The other Nazi leaders took a less favourable view, and his underlings detested him. Albert Speer wrote: 'Even among so many ruthless men, he stood out by his brutality and coarseness. . . . A subordinate by nature, he treated his own subordinates as if he were dealing with cows and oxen. He was a peasant.'

Bormann was short, stocky, and his face made a bad job of concealing a certain slyness: a suggestion that, in some department of his mind, he was carefully calculating the odds. Unlike his colleagues he avoided publicity, and this may have been his strength. As the only top war criminal yet to be accounted for, he has been hunted in both hemispheres. The trouble is that so few people know what he looks like.

He was born in 1900, the son of a minor post-office official. In the First World War he served in the artillery – though he never heard any shots fired in anger. Afterwards he was employed in estate management. He also joined the Freikorps – a voluntary organization with a large proportion of thugs in its ranks, which professed to maintain law and order.

In 1923 Bormann was involved in the murder of a Freikorps member who was believed (wrongly) to have been a traitor. He was sentenced to a year in jail, which may seem excessively moderate. But this was his technique: he helped to plan villainy without actually becoming involved in its execution.

Like many other Freikorps members, he eventually joined the Nazi Party. He became a minor functionary, and he might have remained one had it not been for his marriage. In 1929 he was betrothed to Gerda Buch, a rather dowdy young woman nine years younger than he was. Her father, Major Buch, was a fairly influential member of the Party, and he persuaded Hitler to be a witness at the wedding. When, in the following year, their first child was born, the boy was named Adolf – and Hitler accepted the role of godfather.

Bormann was now on his way up. Part of the Nazi doctrine was to increase the Aryan population of Germany, no matter whether the infants were born inside or outside wedlock. Gerda obliged by producing nine; her husband increased the score with assistance from his mistresses. Gerda, one has to assume, did not complain. In 1933 the ambitious Martin Bormann was appointed Chief-of-Staff to Hitler's deputy, Rudolf Hess. Once Hess had flown to Scotland on his abortive peace mission in 1941, Bormann insinuated himself even more zealously into the Führer's favour – until he became as near indispensable as anyone could be.

By the end of April 1945 the war was nearly over. Most of the leading actors had fled. But Bormann remained in the doomed Chancellery as the Russians closed in for the *coup de grâce*. On the evening of 29 April, Hitler went through a form of marriage with Eva Braun. Bormann, returning the favour of 1929, served as witness. After luncheon on the following day, the Hitlers (as they should now be called) committed suicide. The stage was set for a funeral pyre – if not of Wagnerian proportions, then at least Wagnerian in concept.

Some years ago, I spent an evening at a small hotel on the edge of Stuttgart with Erich Kemptka, a smallish, neatly dressed man who was working at the Porsche plant, and who had been Hitler's driver. Kemptka recalled that he had been instructed by Hitler's SS adjutant to procure 200 litres of petrol: that Martin Bormann had approached the Chancellery garden carrying Eva Braun's body, and that he, Kemptka, had taken her from him. The corpses were placed on the ground and drenched with petrol. It then transpired, however, that nobody had any matches. Complete disaster was averted by the arrival of Goebbels who, being a heavy smoker, had a cigarette lighter.

Erich Kemptka applied the small flame (how much more fitting a blazing torch would have been); the founder of the Third Reich – the Reich which Hitler had predicted would last for a thousand years, but which now came to its shabby end after twelve – and his bride went up in smoke.

His last duty done, the chauffeur could depart. With one or two others he made his way through the vaults and tunnels of the Chancellery until he reached the Friedrichstrasse station on the U-bahn (the Berlin underground). They came up to street level in the midst of thunderously heavy fighting, the Russians by now being well lodged in the surrounding ruins.

Presently the small, dazed group was joined by Martin Bormann. 'What's the matter here?' Bormann asked – a question so meaningless that it might have raised a laugh in other circumstances. 'Look around you', Kemptka told him. 'Listen', Bormann said, 'I need a tank quickly. I must get out of here – it's very important. I have an appointment outside Berlin.' There were, presumably, many other people with similar ideas, though it seems possible that Bormann really did have an appointment – with Admiral Dönitz, who was now head of state, and whose headquarters were 200 miles away on the Baltic.

At that moment three German tanks clattered down the street. They were all that remained of an armoured division. Bormann was about to commandeer one of them when a shell burst dangerously close. They took shelter behind the vehicle which, within seconds, was hit by a round fired from a bazooka. Kemptka was momentarily blinded. When he could see again, Bormann had vanished. (One account asserts that Kemptka saw him destroyed in a sheet of flame, but he made no mention of this and it seems unlikely.)

Nevertheless, Kemptka felt sure that Bormann was killed by the explosion. Such was his testimony at the Nuremberg war crimes trial; and his testimony, such as it was, was rejected. For want of proof that he was actually dead, Bormann was condemned to death *in absentia*.

What, then, were the alternatives? In his autobiography, Reinhard Gehlen – Hitler's Intelligence expert on Red Army matters, who sold his secrets to the Americans for six million dollars – alleged that Bormann had been a Russian agent; that he had been rescued by a Russian patrol and removed to the safety of Moscow. Gehlen even recounted the evidence of two agents who claimed that they had seen a fleeting glimpse of him on a cinema newsreel – watching a football match.

It was good, sensational stuff and doubtless it helped to sell the book. But had Gehlen forgotten that, nearly twenty years earlier, he had told quite another story to a representative of the CIA? According to this version, Bormann's fate after leaving the Chancellery was unknown. It appeared likely that he had been killed, and he was certainly *not* in Russia – nor, come to that, in East Germany.

An even wilder hypothesis was that he had been working for the British: that he had reached the Baltic and handed himself over to a headquarters unit from which he was taken to an unknown address in England. For a number of years, the report continued, he had been employed by the Foreign Office until finally he was given a pension and quietly repatriated to West Germany.

South America has always been a happy hunting ground for Bormann watchers, and there are two basic notions of how he got there. One story finds him, first of all, in the Austrian Tyrol – helping himself to hidden Nazi gold valued at five million dollars. The other suggests that he reached the Baltic, looking for a U-boat that would take him to Argentina and the hospitality of President Peron. Having discovered that all the vessels had been captured, he made his way south in the direction of Bavaria.

Whichever the case, the ODESSA organization (*Organisation der ehemaligen SS-Angehörigen*) – an escape system operated for ex-members of the SS) is held responsible for his get-away. Using forged documents, he left Europe either from Spain or (more likely) Italy. At least two reports allege that, before arriving in South America, he had undergone some rather indifferent plastic surgery – which disguised his features adequately, but left all too obvious traces of the operation.

Thereafter, Bormann sightings cropped up with a frequency comparable to those of the Loch Ness monster in Scotland. Adolf Eichmann's son went on record as having seen him in Buenos Aires. Tadek Friedmann, a dedicated Jewish Nazi-hunter, was also sure that he was in Argentina, but suggested that he was now a man of no importance. Eichmann had been abducted to Israel since he had been specifically concerned with the extermination of Jews. Bormann's crimes were less well defined – against whom and in what places were not itemized. Consequently in Israeli eyes he was not a comparable target.

CIA offices throughout South America were instructed to investigate the possibility of his presence. None produced any evidence. Nevertheless there were at least fourteen supposed sightings from other sources – in Argentina, Paraguay, Brazil, and Chile. According to one report, he was living in territory occupied by SS survivors on the border of Paraguay and Brazil. The commune – if such it can be called – owed much to the dictatorial President of Paraguay, the son of a German brewer whose methods were not very different from those of the Nazis.

By 1959 the West German Government had taken up the hunt. In that year it received information that Bormann had died in Paraguay, and was buried near the capital, Asunción. The grave was opened up: inside lay the mortal remains of a Paraguayan citizen named Hormoncilla.

Five years later Dr Fritz Bauer, who was handling the investigation, offered 25,000 dollars for any pertinent clues. That March, a man claiming to be Bormann's younger brother, Richard, reported at the police station at São Paulo, Brazil. He was, he said, tired of leading a fugitive existence. This semed to be promising until it was discovered that Bormann's younger brother was, in fact, named Albert – and Albert was living a normal life in Bavaria. The impostor turned out to be a 52-year-old former SS man, who had arrived in Brazil with false papers and was now mentally deranged.

Nor were things more satisfactory in 1967 when the police in Guatemala arrested a man answering to Bormann's description. He was an innocent itinerant carpenter named Juan Martinez.

Back in Germany, Frau Bormann seemed to be a possible source of information: her husband, surely, would have been in touch with her were he alive. When Berlin fell, she was sheltering at Hitler's Berchtesgaden residence. Since then, she had moved to the Austrian Tyrol, where she was running a school for young children and slowly dying of cancer. She had nothing to offer. The last she had heard of her husband was a telegram

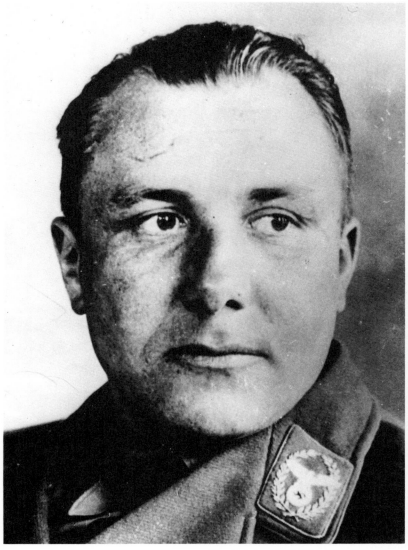

Martin Bormann in 1933, the year he was appointed Chief-of-Staff to Hitler's deputy, Rudolf Hess.

Opposite: The scene in Invaliden Strasse, Berlin, in 1965, as police search for the bodies of Martin Bormann and Hitler's surgeon, Dr. Ludwig Stumpfegger.

dispatched from the Chancellery. It read: 'Everything is lost. I will never get out of here. Take care of the children.'

A Munich bus driver thought he had seen Bormann, and clearly had not. A man was arrested in an East German town for marching down the main street dressed as a colonel in the SS. When questioned he stated that he had been promoted from corporal at a secret midnight ceremony conducted by Martin Bormann. He was judged to be in need of psychiatric care.

What, then, is the closest we can get to the truth? There is no doubt that Bormann got away from the Chancellery: and, so far as it goes, Kemptka's account appears to be true. It does not, however, seem to go far enough. Bormann was not destroyed when the tank blew up near the Friedrichstrasse station. Accompanied by Hitler's personal physician, Dr Ludwig Stumpfegger, he made his way about three miles westward to the Lehrter station, where the U-bahn emerges into the daylight. Up to this point, he must have had some hope of survival, for he had torn the badges of rank from his tunic, hoping to be mistaken for a private soldier.

But something must have gone wrong. At about 3 a.m. a party of refugees from the Chancellery – among them Artur Axmann, head of the Hitler Youth in Berlin – found the bodies of Bormann and Stumpfegger on the ground not far from the station. There was no indication of injury, and yet both men seemed to be dead. Had they taken poison? Had they been knocked out by the blast of a shell? Were they perhaps pretending to be dead? In Axmann's opinion this was unlikely: there seemed no reason for such deception. He had no time to investigate. The Russian fire was intense and he and the others had to run for cover.

During Dr Bauer's inquiry, he came across a 68-year-old retired Berlin postman named Albert Krumnow. On the night in question, he and three other Lehrter post-office employees had been ordered by a Red Army officer to bury two bodies. One resembled Stumpfegger; the other, Martin Bormann. He was vague about the actual burial place: it was, he thought, somewhere in the nearby park. The industrious Dr Bauer had the entire park dug up. There were no human remains.

In *Martin Bormann*, the former CIA official James McGovern poses the interesting possibility that Bormann had, in fact, been recognized by the Russian officer; that, indeed, the Nazi's diary was found in his pocket. On instructions from Stalin, Bormann's corpse was dug up and removed to an unmarked grave in East Germany. Dr Stumpfegger's body presumably went too.

But without proof there can be no certainty, and reports of a wandering Bormann still crop up occasionally. If he is indeed still alive, he is well into his eighties. It seems much more likely, however, that he died in Berlin on that fire-torn night in 1945.

WHO KILLED PRESIDENT KENNEDY?

After three years in the White House John Kennedy's plans to secure his re-election to the presidency were already in gear. Former Vice-President Richard Nixon, his narrowly defeated Republican rival in 1960, had decided not to run against him next time. 'No one's going to beat Jack Kennedy in 1964,' he told friends.

But not all the President's men were so sure. In many parts of the US Kennedy was unpopular. In the South, particularly, his proposals for equal rights for the blacks were viewed with hostility; and the Kennedy court saw it as the job of his Vice-President, Lyndon Johnson, a Texan, to overcome this and unite the Democratic Party. A presidential visit to Texas was arranged. The Kennedy magic and the reassuring presence of Johnson ought to pull the party factions together and secure the twenty-five electoral votes of Texas in the following year's election.

John Kennedy, at forty-three, was the youngest-ever President. With his beautiful wife Jacqueline by his side and their children John and Caroline playing on the White House lawn, and with brothers Robert and Edward ambitious for their turn at the White House, it appeared that a dynasty had been founded.

When the US-backed Bay of Pigs invasion of Cuba failed soon after Kennedy took office, he escaped much of the blame for the debacle, which was laid at the door of the previous Eisenhower administration.

In 1962, when US spy-planes detected rocket sites being prepared on Cuba, Kennedy warned Khrushchev, the Soviet leader, that he would tolerate no nuclear build-up in America's back yard, and that Russian ships bringing missiles to the island would be stopped, if necessary sunk, by the Navy.

As the two leaders stood eyeball-to-eyeball, the world waited with bated breath to see if the superpowers would begin the Third World War. Khrushchev backed off, and the world breathed again. What a giant was Kennedy, many thought, a match for any man on earth.

His security was a great problem for his protectors. In his first year of office he had been the subject of 870 threatening letters, and it was a daunting fact that since 1840 every President elected at twenty-year intervals had died or been killed in office: Harrison, elected 1840, Lincoln 1860 (assassinated), Garfield 1880 (assassinated), McKinley 1900 (assassinated), Harding 1920, Roosevelt 1940. Kennedy had been elected in 1960. 'That's one jinx I'll break,' he laughingly told friends.

Whenever he travelled, his personal bodyguard of thirty-five special agents was increased, and there was a White House police force of 170 uniformed men who guarded the residence. Incoming parcels were checked with X-ray equipment, and all food and liquids were inspected on delivery. Gifts of chocolate and candy were destroyed untasted, and when the President dined out, even at the homes of friends, Secret Servicemen watched the meal being prepared in the kitchen.

A group of agents travelled ahead of him to check security and study the layout of every building he entered. Agents mixed with the crowds on his route. When he travelled by rail, the bridges along the way were guarded, a pilot train preceded his to test the track, and his carriage had a steel floor and bullet-proof windows.

His aircraft was guarded twenty-four hours a day, his pilots taking their meals two hours apart in case their food should be poisoned. The presidential guards had to look inconspicuous and so men of exceptional height were ruled out. All were crack shots and judo experts, usually aged between twenty-four and thirty, strong, athletic, well spoken and mostly university graduates. As soon as the presidential election result was known, these men immediately guarded him day and night. If he played golf they caddied, if he swam they rowed a boat close by.

A group of agents investigated the thousands of suspect persons, cranks and fanatical organizations, and every threatening letter was checked out. When the President visited the vicinity of such people, they might be restricted to their homes until he moved on. It is a criminal offence to threaten to harm the President. On 21 November 1963, when John Kennedy flew to Texas, there were dossiers on 50,000 such threateners.

The tour was to include San Antonio, Houston, Fort Worth, Dallas, and Austin. The state was a breeding ground for lunatic fringe organizations, and guns could be bought as easily as fishing rods, so an enormous security operation was mounted to protect the President.

On Friday 22 November, Kennedy rose early at his Fort Worth hotel. The trip was going well and he was in good mood. San Antonio and Houston had seen large, cheering crowds out to greet him. Behind the barriers several thousand people gathered that misty morning for a glimpse of the President. There was a burst of applause as he stepped outside, and he walked over to the parking lot to greet them, making them laugh with his easy, attractive manner, thrilling them. It was his way to pretend that the crowd was really waiting to see Jacqueline, and he apologized: 'I'm sorry. Mrs Kennedy takes longer to get ready than I do – but then she looks so much better than me. No one ever wonders what outfit *I'm* going to wear!'

On the flight from Fort Worth to Dallas Kennedy went over the speech he was to deliver at the civic lunch. Its theme was: 'Only an America which practises what it preaches about equal rights and social justice will be respected.' And he would close with the words of Psalm 127 – 'Except the Lord keep the city, the watchman waketh but in vain.'

Dallas was a violent place, formerly the seat of the Ku Klux Klan, and still a stronghold of the extremist John Birch Society, anti-everything except the WASPS, White Anglo-Saxon Protestants. Adlai Stevenson, the former presidential candidate, had been set upon by extremists that autumn, and Lyndon and Lady Bird Johnson had been manhandled by a jeering mob while campaigning for Kennedy in 1960.

The pastor of the largest of Dallas's many churches had preached against Kennedy and the Roman Catholics from his pulpit, condemning any form of integration with blacks. The day before Kennedy's visit handbills were being distributed in the streets with pictures of the President, side face and full face like criminal mug-shots, with the caption 'Wanted for Treason'.

Shortly after 11.30, in fine, sunny weather, the plane landed at Dallas and the Kennedys were driven into the city in the blue Lincoln convertible, its bubble top removed to enable the President to stand and acknowledge the cheers. Jacqueline in pink woollen suit and pill-box hat carried a bouquet of red roses. Texas Governor John Connally and his wife Nellie sat in front of the Kennedys. In the following car was a party of Secret Service agents.

At a gentle fifteen miles an hour the motorcade proceeded. The crowds were ten-deep and warm in their applause. As it neared the triple underpass approaching the intersection of Elm, Main and Commerce Streets in the business area, with a mile to travel to the lunch venue, Nellie Connally turned to the President and said above the cheers: 'No one can tell you now that Dallas people don't love you.'

'No, they sure can't,' John Kennedy replied. And those were his last words. There came a sharp crack of rifle fire and he pitched over to his left, across his wife, his poor wounded head falling into her lap. 'My God, they've killed Jack!' she screamed.

Governor Connally slumped forward, wounded in the chest, as another shot rang out. The driver didn't react immediately, and for several seconds the Lincoln slowed down. Agent Clint Hill jumped from the following

The assassination of John F. Kennedy, in a Dallas motorcade, on 22 November 1963. *Top:* Kennedy slumps forward after being hit. *Above:* Mrs John Connally bends over her wounded husband, while a Secret Service agent stands over Mrs Kennedy.

Opposite: The depository building where Lee Harvey Oswald worked, and from where at least one shot was fired at the President. The arrow shows the window behind which Oswald's rifle was discovered.

car, sprinted forward and leapt onto the Lincoln's rear bumper. He saw Kennedy's head torn open, blood everywhere. The limousine pulled out of the motorcade, and roared off to the Parkland Memorial Hospital, three miles away, Jacqueline cradling her husband in her arms.

Surgeons fought for his life, in vain. There was a wound below the Adam's apple, and the bullet had split the back of his skull high up on the right of his head. Shortly before 1 o'clock they abandoned their task. A sheet was drawn up over his body. Jacqueline knelt beside him, in prayer. John Fitzgerald Kennedy, aged forty-six, the thirty-fifth President of the United States, was dead: the eighth President to die in office, the fourth by an assassin's bullet. He had failed to beat what he himself had called a jinx.

But who killed him? An Italian-made rifle with telescopic sight was found in a room of the Texas School Book Depository building near a window overlooking the route of the motorcade. Checks revealed that it belonged to a young man who had worked there for the past month. His name was Lee Harvey Oswald. And he was missing from the building.

Shortly after the assassination Patrolman J.D. Tippit challenged a young man hurrying along East Tenth Street. The man pulled out a revolver and shot the policeman dead. A citizen notified police headquarters on Tippit's car radio.

An agitated young man was seen to run into the nearby Texas Cinema. The manager called the police. As the main feature, *War is Hell*, was about to go on, the house lights went up and policemen crowded in. 'This is it!' the suspect cried, drawing a gun. It misfired, and police officers fell upon him. He was identified as Lee Harvey Oswald, and charged with two murders, that of Patrolman Tippit, and of President Kennedy.

Oswald was never brought to trial. Two days after the assassination, as he was being taken from the City Hall cells, handcuffed to a detective, a man named Jack Ruby pushed his way through the crowd of onlookers, pulled a revolver and shot Oswald in view of millions on television. He died in a hospital room a few yards from where Kennedy had died forty-eight hours earlier.

Oswald, twenty-four, born in New Orleans, had been a strange, lonely, social misfit, described at school as withdrawn, belligerent and hostile, without friends. A psychiatrist had reported that he was a potentially dangerous character, with a hatred of authority. Oswald became a Marxist, joined the US Marines, qualified as a sharpshooter and learned Russian. Discharged from the Corps to take care of his sick mother, he left her after three days.

Oswald went to Russia, saying that leaving America was like getting out

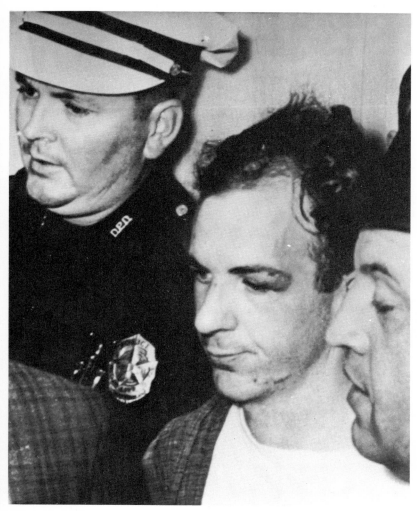

Lee Harvey Oswald, in police custody, before himself being killed by Jack Ruby. 'I am just a patsy,' he had repeatedly told police.

The dramatic moment at Dallas city jail as Jack Ruby steps forward to fire a bullet into Oswald's stomach.

Opposite: Jack Ruby, a Dallas nightclub owner and a minor Mafia figure, at Dallas city jail after shooting Oswald.

of prison, and he applied for Soviet citizenship. The Russians weren't keen to grant this. He worked in a factory, married a Russian girl and they had a baby daughter. He joined a rifle club. Angered when he found that his Marine discharge had been on the grounds that he was an undesirable, he wrote a bitter letter to John Connally, thinking mistakenly that he was still Navy Secretary. The honeymoon with Russia lasted all of two and a half years, after which he pleaded with the US Government to allow him home. Generously they paid the family's fare.

Oswald found it hard to hold down a job, and his wife was pregnant once more. In the spring of 1963 he bought the Italian rifle, and gave his support to the Fair Play for Cuba Committee, carrying 'Viva Castro' banners. He read books on the assassination of Governor Huey Long, and the life of Mao Tse-tung.

The pathetic Oswald's private life was in disarray. Shortly before the birth of her second baby, his wife moved into the home of a woman friend. The woman got Oswald a job at the Texas School Book Depository, and on the night of 21 November allowed him to sleep with his wife. Next day Oswald took his rifle, wrapped in brown paper, to work.

Why Jack Ruby killed Lee Oswald is not clear, for he gave various reasons during his three years in prison, including his wish to spare Mrs Kennedy giving evidence in court. His death from cancer was in the same hospital where Kennedy and Oswald had died, and where Marina Oswald's second girl was born. Ruby's background was glossed over by the Warren Commission, but it transpired that he was a minor Mafia figure, a pay-off man who 'took care' of numerous corrupt Dallas officials.

The task of the President's guards was to anticipate trouble, not wait for it to happen, so it was extraordinary that Oswald, a known oddball, was not, at the very least, kept under surveillance that fateful day.

Had there really been an elaborate plot to kill the President? The Warren Commission investigation published twenty-six volumes of evidence, including 3,154 exhibits and 25,000 FBI interviews. They came to the conclusion that Lee Harvey Oswald, acting alone, and with no accomplices, had been the sole assassin. Robert Kennedy accepted the finding, and publicly stated that if he were to become President and had the power to do so, he would *not* reopen the inquiry.

But many poured scorn on the Warren report, and in the late 1970s a committee of Congressmen spent more than two years delving into previously unexamined aspects of the assassination. They found many vital leads had been ignored or overlooked by Warren, and although they came up with no definite solution they concluded that Kennedy *had* been the victim of a conspiracy. Lyndon Johnson, Kennedy's successor, always suspected a Communist plot, and saw the hand of Khrushchev or Castro behind the killing. Others held that a group of rich and powerful southern businessmen, angered at the liberal President for 'stirring up the blacks', had put out a contract on him.

Neither the FBI nor the CIA were displeased at the 'lone nut' theory. Both had files on Oswald and his left-wing activities, and would have faced censure for gross incompetence if the Red Plot theory had been proved.

The number of shots fired has never been positively established. Undoubtedly *a* shot was fired from the book depository, but the evidence is overwhelming that more gunfire came from the grassy knoll one hundred yards from that building. The fence there would have provided good cover for a gunman, and behind the fence a carpark would have enabled a getaway car to wait, unnoticed. A young soldier, Gordon Arnold, home on leave, went behind this fence seeking a good point from which to watch the motorcade, but was ordered away by a man with a badge claiming to be Secret Service. The inquiry found that there had been no such officers on the grassy knoll. Arnold gave evidence that he felt 'a shot whizz only inches over my left shoulder' from behind him.

Abraham Zapruder, the amateur cameraman who took the famous movie film of the assassination from the grassy knoll, was one of a dozen people standing there who also told of bullets fired from *behind* them. The Connallys were sitting in front of the Kennedys, facing forward, and the Governor always maintained that he was struck about a second after the President was hit. The bullet which wounded him entered through his chest, travelled through his body, and finished up, almost undamaged, in his thigh. So there is little doubt that there was more than one assassin firing from more than one vantage point.

Was the President's murder carried out by order of big crime bosses? A man named Jim Braden, held by the police for acting suspiciously after the shooting, was released when Oswald was charged with the crime. But it was learned later that his real name was Eugene Brading, that he had a criminal record, and that he was associated with Carlos Marcello, then one of the richest and most ruthless figures in America's criminal underworld. The night before the Kennedy slaying Brading had stayed at the Cabana Hotel. Jack Ruby had also called there that evening.

Another of Marcello's men was David Ferrie, an ex-pilot with extremist right-wing sympathies and a hatred of Kennedy. When it was learned that he might have flown a gunman out of Dallas in a private plane, orders were given for Ferrie's arrest. Before he could be picked up he was found dead, apparently from natural causes, although he had left two notes indicating suicide.

Within an hour of Ferrie's death his associate, Eladio del Valle, also wanted for questioning by the police about the Kennedy killing, was found murdered in a car in Miami. He had links with Florida crime boss Santos Trafficante, a friend of Carlos Marcello.

The Warren Commission decided that Oswald killed Patrolman Tippit, and several witnesses had identified him as the policeman's murderer. But by that time Oswald's face was known all over the world through television and newspaper pictures. And some witnesses of the street killing testified that the gunman had looked nothing like Oswald.

Was Oswald really a pawn, placed on the board as a Marxist red herring by wealthy criminals whose operations were being attacked by the Kennedy brothers? If so, they would have assured Oswald that he would have protection. During his brief period in custody he had repeatedly said: 'I'm just a patsy.'

The theory could be consistent with the subsequent killing of Oswald himself, for he would have had to be silenced before he could appear in open court.

A number of other violent deaths occurred during the investigations, including those of three newspaper reporters who had interviewed Jack Ruby. One died of gunshot wounds, one from a karate chop, the third from a drugs overdose.

Were Cubans responsible for the President's death? After his triumph in the missile crisis, Kennedy had adopted a more relaxed attitude to the Castro regime, wanting operations against them to cease. American-based anti-Communist Cubans were furious, and could have found willing allies in the Mafia whose lucrative crime empire of gambling and prostitution in Cuba had been ended by Castro's revolution.

For more than two decades there have been investigations, allegations, accusations, innuendo. But no satisfactory conclusion. The death of John Fitzgerald Kennedy remains an unsolved mystery.

HISTORIC AND
PREHISTORIC ENIGMAS

ANASTASIA

For every royal person who has disappeared, presumed murdered, in mysterious circumstances, there has been someone – often more than one person – who has claimed his or her identity. Yet never have so many claimants come forward as those who have asserted themselves to be members of the Imperial Family of Russia, supposedly murdered by their Bolshevik guards in July 1918, after the revolution and the outbreak of civil war.

The Romanovs, Tsar Nicholas II and his family, were happy and united in private life, and very much more English than Russian in their looks and ways. Nicholas was the nephew of King Edward VII's Queen, Alexandra, and so closely resembled his cousin King George V that they might have been taken for twins. The Tsarina Alexandra was the grand-daughter of Queen Victoria, her mother being Princess Alice of Hesse. They had five children: Olga, Tatiana, Marie, Anastasia, and the Tsarevich, Alexis, a boy of fourteen who suffered from the hereditary disease haemophilia. The eldest daughter, Olga, was twenty-three, the youngest, Anastasia, seventeen.

In April 1918 they had been taken by the Bolsheviks to the mining town of Ekaterinburg in the Ural Mountains, where a villa owned by a merchant, Ipatiev, had been converted into a prison. Previously their imprisonment had been hardly more than house arrest; but now they were subjected to harsh, insulting treatment by drunken guards who delighted in humiliating them. In early July these were replaced by the Cheka, secret police. It was known that loyalist forces under Admiral Kolchak were rapidly closing in on Ekaterinburg, and this development was the execution warrant of the Imperial family.

On the night of the sixteenth the prisoners were wakened by Jacob Yurovsky, head of the Cheka squad, who told them to get dressed and come downstairs, since their rescuers were approaching and it was necessary to move them. They went with him to a semi-basement room, together with the family's doctor, the Tsar's valet, their cook and parlourmaid. And there, in a hail of revolver bullets, they all died.

Working quickly by the light of lanterns, the Cheka squad wrapped the corpses in sheets and loaded them on to a waiting truck. Fourteen miles from Ekaterinburg, at a disused mine-working called 'the 'Four Brothers', the bodies were dismembered and burned in a bonfire fuelled with gasoline; any bones remaining were dissolved with sulphuric acid, and the ashes and debris thrown down the mine-shaft.

The real Anastasia, in a family group taken in about 1910. *Left to right:* Marie, Tatiana, Anastasia, Olga and Alexis. *Below:* The blood-stained basement room in the Villa Ipatiev at Ekaterinburg, where the Tsar and his family were massacred on 16 July 1918.

Such were the findings of Nicholas Sokolov, a legal investigator on behalf of the White Government in Siberia, in January 1919. The information he obtained from depositions was less impressive than the mute evidence supplied by the contents of the mine – hundreds of fragments and objects. Among them were two belt-buckles, an emerald cross, a sapphire and diamond cross, a pearl ear-ring from a pair the Tsarina always wore, three icons, six sets of women's corsets, and the small hacked body of Tatiana's spaniel, Jemmy. These grisly discoveries, and the blood-stained condition of the basement room, were enough to make it certain that all the Imperial family and their domestics had been murdered.

Yet before very long many self-proclaimed Romanovs had come forward, each declaring that he or she had escaped the mass slaughter; among them were a Tsar or two, several Tsarevichs, an Olga, a Tatiana and a Marie – and one whose identity has caused more debate than any other, Anastasia.

There have been no fewer than fifteen women claiming to be this youngest daughter of the Tsar. All except one have been proved to be impostors. The remaining claimant, best known as Anna Anderson, has been at the centre of a controversy which has raged for over half a century.

Her story began in Berlin, on the evening of 27 February 1920, when a young woman tried to drown herself in the Landwehr canal. She was rescued by a police sergeant and rushed to hospital. She seemed to be about twenty, had no papers nor identification of any kind, and refused to answer questions about herself or her motives for attempting suicide. Transferred to the Dalldorf asylum with 'mental illness of a depressive character', she was given the name of 'Fräulein Unbekannt', Miss Unknown. Her body was covered with scars, and she seemed terrified of any sort of identification, even of photography. But an X-ray showed that the bones of her upper jaw had been damaged by a blow of some kind. She spoke German, with a foreign accent.

As she improved in health, the nurses were impressed by her intelligence, courtesy and graciousness, the qualities of 'an aristocratic lady'. Someone was struck by her likeness to the Imperial family, but when she was shown a photograph of them, she became distressed. In Autumn 1921 she declared that she was Her Imperial Highness the Grand Duchess Anastasia Nicolaievna.

Clara Peuthert, a patient in the same ward, claimed to recognize Fräulein Unbekannt as a Romanov, and, when released, she informed Russian *émigrés* in Berlin of her discovery. One of them, Baron von Kleist, was convinced, and in May 1922 he took Fräulein Unbekannt into his own care. In the fourth-floor flat at Nettelbeckstrasse 9 she became the focal point of attention, surrounded by a constant stream of curious visitors, coaxed, fawned on, stared at, badgered with questions. Some of the *émigrés* said they recognized her immediately as Anastasia, others claimed there was not the slightest resemblance.

On 29 June 1922, Baron von Kleist and his wife gave an evening party. The occasion proved too much for their guest; she suffered a nervous collapse, and became so ill that she was given morphine. Under its influence the spell of silence was broken. Disjointedly, over a period of months, she told her story, fragmentary, wild at times, though it was later adapted by Baron von Kleist into a coherent narrative.

With the rest of her family, she had followed the Red soldiers down to the basement at the Villa Ipatiev on that July night. She remembered that shots had rung out, her father had died first, the body of her sister Tatiana had fallen across her, protecting her own. Then she had felt a violent blow on the head, and had fainted. The next thing she remembered was lying in a farm waggon, badly wounded in the head and body, travelling for weeks, perhaps months. She had been rescued by a family called Tchaikovski, who spoke in Russian and Polish. Alexander Tchaikovski must have been one of the Red guards at Ekaterinburg, for he told her that he had found one of the bodies – herself – still alive, and had smuggled her out to their farm.

They had taken her to Bucharest, she said: and this part of her story was much later corroborated by a Lieut-Col Hassenstein, who had been communications officer at a bridge which some peasants were waiting to cross with a turnip cart; he had been told that the cart contained the Tsar's youngest daughter, Anastasia.

In Bucharest, where they lived for a year, the Tchaikovskis had lived off the sale of the jewellery which Anastasia, like her sisters, had worn sewn into her clothes – diamonds, a long pearl necklace, and other gems. In 1927, after Anastasia's story had been publicized, a witness came forward to confirm that he had been in a jeweller's shop when a very valuable pearl necklace from Russia was brought in; his description of the would-be seller matched that of Alexander Tchaikovski.

In 1919 Anastasia had borne Tchaikovski a son, then married him. Soon afterwards he was killed, shot by Bolsheviks. The baby was taken away from her, and she embarked on a journey to Germany, a country she had known as a child, hiding from police and soldiers. Her companion, Sergei Tchaikovski, disappeared in Berlin. Alone, she was gripped by despair, and jumped into the dark waters of a canal.

That was all she would say. The continual badgering she received irritated and depressed her. She refused to speak in Russian, a language she

apparently identified with the horrors of the Villa Ipatiev. She was unhappy with the Kleists, and after August 1922 she was passed from one
émigré household to another. In January 1924 she was offered hospitality by
Detective-Inspector Grünberg at his country house at Funkenmühle.
Anxious to have her identified, he persuaded Princess Irene of Prussia,
sister of the Tsarina, to see her, using a false name. If Anna (as the girl
was now generally called) were to recognize her visitor as the Princess, it
would be a point in her favour.

But the meeting was a failure. Princess Irene was not satisfied with
Anna's resemblance to her niece, and Anna gave way to an hysterical
outburst; later she said that she had been hurt and offended that her
mother's sister should have pretended to be a stranger, in order to trick
her.

The scene was to be repeated many times in the coming years. Anna's
obstinate pride, her refusal to answer questions, her erratic behaviour,
were to cost her the support of many would-be sympathizers. Her detrac-
tors saw her strange conduct as proof of the falseness of her claim. Her
refusal to speak Russian told strongly against her, for the Grand Duchess
Anastasia had been an excellent linguist, who spoke good English (the
domestic language of the Imperial family) and had a good grasp of French
and German.

The Dowager Empress Marie Fedorovna, mother of the Tsar, firmly
refused to believe that her son and his family had died at Ekaterinburg.
In her opinion they were still alive, all together, in hiding, and the woman
in Berlin claiming to be Anastasia was an impostor. Her daughter, the
Grand Duchess Olga, shared her views. The Prussian Crown Princess
Cecilie visited Anna, but found it almost impossible to communicate with
her. Anna's flashes of memory – a waltz tune that made her break down
in tears, a song the Tsarina used to sing in English – could not counter-
balance her seemingly obstinate refusal to co-operate with those who gen-
uinely wanted to identify her. The Grand Duke Ernst Ludwig of Hesse
was approached and shown plaster casts and photographs taken of identifying marks which Anna shared with the Grand Duchess Anastasia – scars,
and a deformed toe-joint. But he was unimpressed.

Pierre Gilliard, who had been the Tsarevich's tutor and had shared the
family's imprisonment, went to see Anna with his wife, who had been
Anastasia's nurse. The visit was inconclusive, but there were better results
from a meeting between the Grand Duchess Olga and her supposed niece.
But, regretfully, the Grand Duchess could not bring herself finally to
acknowledge Anna, though she conceded that there were many remarkable
things about her case.

The sole survivor of the massacre? The mystery woman who claimed to be Anastasia, photographed in her hospital bed in Berlin in 1920, after trying to drown herself in the Landwehr Canal.

The rest of Anna's life was a confusion of assertions and denials, conflicting evidence, and bickerings about the so-called 'Romanov fortune', which, if it were ever discovered, would have to be shared among the Tsar's relatives. In February 1928 Anna sailed for America, where she stayed for a time with the Princess Xenia of Russia, second cousin of Anastasia. She now called herself Mrs Anna Anderson. But the Princess's attitude towards her guest changed – again, money seems to have been connected with the break. In 1938 a legal battle which was to become the world's longest law-suit began when Anna applied for a cancellation of the Berlin Court's ruling that the entire Imperial family were dead, and that the Tsar's property in Germany should pass to his secondary heirs.

After the Second World War Anna, living in an army hut in the Black Forest, became world news, by way of books and films. In 1968 she married in America a professor of history, John Manahan. In 1970 the hearings, dismissals and appeals of the legal battle ended in a rejection of Anna's plea for recognition by the West German Supreme Court, just fifty years to the day after she was pulled unconscious from a Berlin canal. She died in 1984, aged eighty-three.

Possibly the strangest thing about the mystery of Anna's identity, a strange enough story in itself, is that there is no actual, concrete evidence that the Imperial family was ever slaughtered *en masse* at the Villa Ipatiev. Probability, yes, for of all the 'sightings' of alleged escaped Romanovs no indisputable proof ever emerged that they were who they said they were. But reliable witnesses were never found.

Only one man, a Bolshevik who had been taken prisoner, made a declaration, drawn up by the Siberian White Army and signed under torture, to the effect that he had seen the bodies of the Tsar and his family lying in pools of blood on the floor of the basement room. Shortly afterwards he died of typhus – or probably more torture. No recognizable human remains were found in the 'Four Brothers' mine: a box whose grisly contents were said to be part of what was found there went the rounds of relatives and inquirers, was never satisfactorily investigated, and finally vanished without trace, as did two of the three copies of the testimony elicited by Sokolov in 1919. The third, when it turned up, threw curious doubts on the entire investigation, suggesting that it might have been politically motivated without much regard for fact. The White Russians needed the assurance that the Romanovs had been butchered to blacken the reputation of the Bolsheviks.

Sokolov never, it seems, bothered to investigate the contemporary rumours that the Grand Duchess Anastasia had escaped the slaughter. In 1938 Franz Svoboda, who had been an Austrian prisoner-of-war in 1918, made a sworn statement that when the bodies were being loaded up after the massacre one of them – a girl – was still moving. He and a companion rescued her and took her to a nearby house. The rumours of her escape, and of other possible escapes, were so widespread that the Cheka posted notices all over Ekaterinburg claiming that certain persons in the firing squad acted insubordinately and abducted female members of the family, taking with them certain valuables. These 'valuables' were the jewellery sewn by the Empress and her daughters into the lining of their clothes. The Cheka were alarmed enough to institute searches of houses and trains. With so much smoke, there may very well have been fire.

It is unlikely, now that so many trails are cold, that the mystery of Anna Anderson will ever be resolved. Anastasia herself had certainly expected to die. After the family's disappearance in 1918 there was found at the Villa Ipatiev a pathetic fragment of a letter from Anastasia to a friend, written in English. She had been reading a poem by Browning, about a girl called Evelyn Hope. 'Sixteen years old when she died!' Anastasia had ended her letter: 'Don't forget me.'

THE PRINCES IN THE TOWER

In July 1674 workmen employed in demolishing a stone staircase in the Tower of London made a gruesome discovery. Beneath the bottom stair, buried ten feet deep, they found an old wooden chest. Inside were the skeletons of two children; one lay on its back, the other, face downwards, on top of it. The bones were sent to the King's surgeon, who pronounced them to be those of two boys aged about eight and thirteen.

It seemed that a mystery had been solved: the disappearance of the young uncrowned King Edward v and his brother, Richard Duke of York, in 1483. It was popularly supposed, and had been for almost two centuries, that they had been murdered by their uncle, Richard Duke of Gloucester, so that he might claim unchallenged the throne which, it was said, he had committed many crimes to gain.

For sixteen years, 1455–71, the civil conflict later known as the Wars of the Roses had raged between the Houses of Lancaster and York for the right of succession to the throne of England. The issue had arisen as long before as 1424, with the death of one of the hereditary claimants, Edmund Mortimer, Earl of March. He died childless, leaving as his heir Richard Duke of York, a prince of the Plantagenet line.

In the early years of the fifteenth century the reigning kings, Henry IV and his son Henry V, were able to fight off any challenge from the Yorkist claimants. (Shakespeare's *King Henry IV* is a dramatic history of Yorkist risings, and their defeat by the Lancastrian Henry and his son, the future Henry V.) But the early death of young King Henry V in 1422 left his throne in peril. His son, Henry VI, was only eight months old, and, as he grew up, he proved to be feeble-minded. His long minority, the unpopularity of his wife, Margaret of Anjou, and the loss of Normandy ended in an outbreak of civil war in 1455.

The Duke of York had a strong ally in Richard Neville, Earl of Warwick, the powerful 'Kingmaker', and together they defeated Henry VI's army at the first battle of St Albans. But fortunes were reversed in 1460 at the battle of Wakefield, when York was killed – beheaded, it was said, on the battlefield. Queen Margaret thought herself triumphant now that her chief enemy was gone, but a year later, after some savage retaliatory slaughter on both sides, the second battle of St Albans gave the victory to the dead York's son, Edward. Extremely handsome, virile, and royal in aspect, he provided a complete contrast to the feeble Henry VI, now a prisoner, and amid popular acclaim he was crowned Edward IV.

Two further battles, at Barnet and Tewkesbury, raised Lancastrian hopes again, but at Tewkesbury Margaret was taken prisoner and her only son, Prince Edward, killed. Within a few weeks the captive Henry was murdered in the Tower of London, by the Duke of Gloucester some said. The Monk of Croyland, whose *Chronicles* are a valuable source of information about the period, recorded that 'he who perpetrated this has justly earned the title of tyrant'; but he named no names, and may have been referring to Edward IV, who would certainly have been the instigator of the deed.

Edward had come to the throne at the age of twenty-three, still a bachelor. In the middle of delicate diplomatic negotiations for his marriage to a French princess he announced to a shocked Council that he was already married, to the Lady Elizabeth Grey. She was the widow of a Lancastrian knight, and by birth a Woodville, connected through her mother to the Plantagenet line. She was four years older than Edward, and the mother of two sons. Violently unpopular as the marriage was, it could not be undone. She bore her husband nine children – three sons and six daughters, all, like their parents, beautiful and healthy.

But in April 1483 King Edward died suddenly, at the age of forty-two. He left his kingdom in the care of his brother, Gloucester, who was to govern it as Protector until the young King Edward, at that time only twelve and a half, came of age. This was a perfectly normal arrangement, and might have worked perfectly well but for one factor: ambition.

Ever since her coronation Queen Elizabeth had been busily securing positions of power and wealth for members of her family. Through her influence her sisters had married into ancient families, and among her brothers were the Bishop of Salisbury and the commander of the Fleet. Her father had been given an earldom and promoted to the office of Lord Treasurer. Still beautiful, proud and ambitious, Elizabeth no doubt saw herself as the virtual ruler of England in control of the child King.

There was no love lost between the Woodvilles and Richard of Gloucester. He had, as a boy, fought valiantly in the Wars of the Roses and had always loyally supported his brother King Edward. The time would come when it would be whispered that Richard had been responsible for the murders of his brother George, Duke of Clarence, and of the deposed Lancastrian king, Henry VI, carried out on Edward's orders. Richard was an austere, grave, single-minded young man who took kingship extremely seriously; the prospect of a kingdom ruled by the upstart Woodvilles must have seemed abhorrent to him. Yet how could it be avoided? Only by taking control himself, as King, and two lives were between him and the English throne – the lives of his two small nephews.

Young Edward was brought from Ludlow Castle to London, for his coronation; but before he reached the capital two kinsmen of his had been arrested and beheaded without trial, on flimsy charges. The Queen, hearing of this, sought sanctuary in Westminster Abbey with her younger children. There she heard that the two men who had been executed were her brother Anthony and one of her sons by her first marriage; then that Richard's one-time friend and ally, Lord Hastings, had also lost his head, and that Richard was accusing her of witchcraft.

Reluctantly, she allowed her little son Richard, Duke of York, to be taken from her and lodged in the royal apartments of the Tower, with his brother the young King. And the coronation was put off, from May to June, from June to November. In June a shocking story spread throughout London: a bishop had declared to Richard, the Lord Protector, that the children of King Edward and Elizabeth Woodville were illegitimate, because Edward had been precontracted to marry another lady. On 26 June, before a great concourse, the Lord Protector modestly agreed to become King Richard III.

The small boys in the Tower were seen less and less. In July they were to be observed shooting and playing in the gardens, and later at the windows of the inner apartments; then they were seen no longer, and rumours began to circulate that they were dead, by Richard's order.

Long after Richard himself was dead, killed at the battle of Bosworth, various stories were put about. Sir Thomas More, writing thirty years later, had it that one Sir James Tyrell had been hired to murder the Princes, employing two brutish men, Forest and Dighton, to smother the boys in bed and to bury them 'at the stair foot, meetly deep in the ground under a great heap of stones', the remains afterwards being removed by a priest to a more respectable place of burial.

But More's account (echoed by Shakespeare in his play *King Richard III*) is full of errors and inconsistencies, though it damaged Richard's character permanently. He became 'Crouchback', a deformed monster of unprecedented savagery, the wicked uncle who 'waded through blood to a throne'. Only in recent years has opinion swung round to produce a body of strong supporters convinced of Richard's innocence, beginning in 1906 with Sir Clements Markham's biography, attempting to fix the murder of the boys on Henry VII. There are reasonable grounds for the consideration, at least, of this theory. Henry, when he became King, never accused the dead Richard of the murder. His behaviour in the matter of James Tyrell's alleged confession was casual in the extreme. He took no steps to find the bodies of the Princes and give them a proper tomb. He was, in his own way, every bit as calculating and unscrupulous as Richard, as he demonstrated when he tricked the poor half-witted young Earl of Warwick, dead Richard's nephew, into a faked conspiracy for which he was executed.

Another candidate has been put forward as the possible murderer of the Princes. Henry Stafford, Duke of Buckingham, was of the noblest blood in the land after the reigning Plantagenets, descended from Edward III's fifth son, Thomas of Woodstock. If the line of Edward IV were removed, his claim to the throne would be very strong. So he had a motive, and also he had opportunity. He held the office of Constable of England, which would have made it easy for him to reach the Princes. He did not set out with Richard on the summer progress of 1483, but lingered in London for a few days before joining the King at Gloucester, after which he rode into Wales and began plotting against Richard. If he succeeded in deposing Richard, the lives of the two boys still lay between him and the throne; to get rid of them quickly would cast a deadly stain on Richard's reputation, and win over the Woodvilles to Buckingham's cause, without implicating himself.

It was Buckingham who, before Richard accepted the crown, spread rumours not only that the Princes were bastards, but that Edward IV himself was not the son of his alleged father. It was all anti-Yorkist propaganda. This did not go unnoticed at the time, and contemporary chroniclers had their suspicions of Buckingham's guilt. A scrap of narrative in the Ashmolean MSS asserts that Richard murdered his nephews 'at the

Edward and Richard, the sons of Edward IV, being parted from their mother by their uncle, Richard, Duke of Gloucester. (After N. Gosse)

Richard III. Did he order their deaths in the Tower?

prompting of the Duke of Buckingham, as it is said'. A French chronicler, Molinet (on the whole unreliable), said that 'on the day that Edward's sons were assassinated, there came to the Tower of London the Duke of Buckingham, who was believed, mistakenly, to have murdered the children in order to forward his pretensions to the crown', and Philippe de Commynes, the French statesman and historian, declared flatly that though Richard was responsible for the Princes' death it was Buckingham '*qui avoit faict mourir les deux enffans*' – who had actually killed the two children.

A definite pronouncement on the age of the bones exhumed in 1674 would settle the question to some extent. If they could be dated as being between 450 and 500 years old, that would be proof that they were the bones of the Princes, who must have died in mid-1483. If they were newer, post-1485, Henry might well have been the culprit.

In 1933 permission was given by the Dean and Chapter of Westminster for the urn to be opened, in order that the bones might be examined by experts. Their findings were not entirely satisfactory. Some of the bones were missing, and those that remained were mixed up with the bones of animals, possibly put there by those who had stolen the missing ones. (It is known that in 1728 some of the bones were sent by an antiquary to the Ashmolean Museum, Oxford, where they disappeared.) From what remained of the skeletons it was estimated that the taller one had been four feet ten inches, the lesser one four feet six and a half inches. From the dental evidence, the children seem to have been about twelve and ten respectively. The elder one, presumably Edward, had a disease of the jaw which must have caused pain and depression – this would explain one account of Edward as being dejected and nervous. A stain on one of the skulls might indicate death by smothering, or might have been a bloodstain.

But in children so young, even their sex could not be positively stated. They might have been girls. Because no tests existed in 1933 which would determine date, it could be assumed that the two children died at any period in history up to 1674. It has even been suggested that they were the remains of two children sacrificed when the White Tower was built in the eleventh century.

The pertinent question is: if these were not the Princes, who were they? For all the Tower's violent history, the murder and secret burial of two children would surely have given rise to some comment which would have come down to us. The bones were found where More said they were, assuming that a re-interment by a priest did not take place. There can be no substantial doubt that the boys died in 1483; early apologists for

Richard, and some later ones, have ignored the fact that there were widespread contemporary rumours that they were dead, both in England and abroad. A young man who turned up in Henry's reign claiming to be the Duke of York, rescued from the Tower, was discredited. Two documents which might seem to suggest that both boys were alive as late as 1485 can be assumed to have other explanations. One, of March 1485, refers to an order for clothing for 'the lord Bastard'. This probably refers to Richard's illegitimate son, John, who was appointed Captain of Calais in that month. The other concerns ordinances for the regulation of the King's Household in the North, in July 1484, and lays down the breakfast arrangements for 'my lord of Lincoln and my lord Morley' and 'the children'. One of these obviously important children was certainly the young Earl of Warwick, the others very probably the younger daughters of King Edward and Queen Elizabeth, since the eldest daughter certainly joined the household in 1485.

In view of the great advances in science which have taken place in the half-century since 1933, it would surely be justifiable for a re-examination of the bones to take place. The unfortunate children are past hurt; Richard's reputation can hardly be more damaged, and if new evidence pointed to Henry VII as the murderer, that cold-blooded Tudor's memory would not be too seriously stained. After all, the Princes were barely related to him, and he can only have been thankful for their deaths, whoever murdered them, since that murder ensured him the Crown.

WAS NAPOLEON MURDERED?

A little before six on the evening of 5 May 1821, Napoleon Bonaparte died at Longwood House, St Helena. He was fifty-one years old, and had been in exile for six years after his armies had been totally defeated at Waterloo. From being the terror of Europe, Emperor of the French, would-be master of the world, he had deteriorated into a listless, sickly invalid, suffering from varied symptoms, steadily growing weaker. St Helena was not a healthy island, and the conditions of his captivity were not conducive to cheerfulness or vigour. He had submitted himself to great privations during his campaigns, his eating habits had always been irregular, and he had recurrently suffered from what appears to have been an acute haemorrhoidal condition. Even more important, his spirits were low, his son kept from him, his wife so indifferent to his fate that she had neither visited nor communicated with him in exile.

His health had been variable, with occasional days of malaise, and no more alarming symptoms than sharp pains in the side or chronically cold feet. For a whole year, from 1818 to 1819, he had had no personal physician. Then a Dr Antommarchi had arrived from Corsica; he was not particularly sympathetic to his patient, but the island's Governor, Sir Hudson Lowe, was anxious to have a doctor of almost any sort in attendance on Napoleon, to testify that his sickly condition was not due to liver trouble caused by the bad climate. That would have thrown discredit on him personally, and on England, for condemning the prisoner to exile in such a poor climate. Besides, Napoleon had often expressed a fear that the English would somehow try to poison him. It would never do for rumours of that kind to get about.

In October 1820 Napoleon and some of his small entourage paid a visit to Sir William Doveton, a leading citizen of St Helena, now retired and living a peaceful life at Sandy Bay, some distance from Longwood. He had never before met Napoleon, and his impression was that the ex-Emperor was pale, but otherwise seemed perfectly well – 'as fat and round as a China pig', was his expression. In fact, Napoleon's shape had changed noticeably since his fortunes had begun to decline sharply after the disastrous retreat from Moscow. Once lean and hollow-cheeked, he had become increasingly stout; a drawing made of him in 1820 shows an immense stomach and an obvious unhealthy gain in weight.

In January 1821 he was at a low ebb, telling people 'it won't be long now'. His companion the Count de Montholon thought that he was suffering from a *maladie de langueur*, a wasting disease. This description, usually a euphemism for cancer, would be mentioned in the communiqué to the French Government as the cause of death. Montholon expressed himself unhappy with the ministrations of Antommarchi, and suggested to Hudson Lowe that he should be replaced by a French doctor. The suggestion was not taken up.

From that time onwards Napoleon's symptoms multiplied: a dry cough, constant thirst, weak pulse, nausea, internal discomfort with a 'burning feeling', icy chill and shivering. He refused to take medicines, as he had always done, but in March was persuaded to try an emetic, repeated doses of which were administered without his knowledge. His thoughts went to the death of his father, at thirty-five, from cancer of the pylorus (the exit from the stomach to the small intestine). He asked an English physician, Dr Arnott, who had arrived, whether the disease could be hereditary, and was told that nothing seemed to be wrong with his digestive organs beyond inflammation.

The orange drink, orgeat, which was the only one he cared for, seemed to satisfy him no longer. He was afraid someone was putting something into it, and consented to drink a little wine. In mid-April, now seriously ill, he made his Will, and on 28 April told Dr Antommarchi that after his death he wished an autopsy to be performed on his body – but no English doctor was to be involved, other than Dr Arnott if his help was absolutely necessary.

He begged Antommarchi to promise to have his heart preserved in spirits of wine and taken to his wife. (This was not done; by medical orders it was buried with him.) He also suggested that his stomach be examined very carefully, overlooking nothing, reported upon and sent to his son; another wish that was not fulfilled. Two days before his death he was given calomel for the first time. Nothing was of any use now. After several days of suffering he died.

Seven doctors performed the autopsy, six of them English. Their decision on it was not unanimous, except that an ulcer existed in the stomach, near the pylorus, which Antommarchi described as cancerous, and the other doctors as being of the nature of a hard tumour 'leading to cancer'.

Three days later Napoleon was buried in Slane's Valley, about two miles from Longwood, in a grave unmarked because Hudson Lowe refused permission for it to be inscribed 'Napoleon', with the dates of birth and death; he insisted on 'Napoleon Bonaparte' or nothing. Nineteen years later the body was removed and taken to France, to be re-interred in the crypt of l'Église Royale, in the Hôtel des Invalides in Paris. The body had not been embalmed, as materials were not available. It was enclosed in four coffins. When the last one was opened, those watching were astonished to see the corpse in a perfect state of preservation, completely recognizable and undecayed.

So, any secret which Napoleon's remains held was finally buried in that much-visited tomb, under an immense weight of porphyry which it would take an atomic explosion to dislodge.

In 1955 a Swedish dentist, Sten Forshufvud, was reading the memoirs of Napoleon's chief valet, Louis Marchand. He had been wholly devoted to his master and had been at his side continually throughout his final illness. Forshufvud was a man of wide medical interests, who had done research on poisons. He was also a strong Bonapartist, in line with a family tradition, surrounding himself with portraits of Napoleon and books dealing with his life and times. He was reading Marchand's memoirs in the hope of finding in them the true reason for Napoleon's death – for he did not believe, as some others had not believed, that it was from cancer.

As he read, he began to wonder whether the cause of death could have been poison, and poison by arsenic? Some of the symptoms struck him as significant. The doctors who performed the autopsy might well not have discovered anything suspicious because the sick man had been dosed with tartar emetic and calomel, which would have destroyed any arsenical traces. One thing in particular struck Forshufvud – Napoleon's great increase in bulk and weight, quite the reverse of what might be expected in a cancer victim, but typical of someone poisoned with arsenic. Other symptoms fitted: a feeling of intense heat, burning pain, thirst, weak pulse: altogether, taking into account the details left by Dr Antommarchi, Forshufvud deduced twenty-two out of the thirty recognized symptoms of arsenical poisoning. Even if any of the doctors had entertained suspicions (and the last thing English doctors would have wanted to do would have been to suggest that poison had been administered), no tests existed then which might have been used, such as those now used – Reinsch's, Fleitmann's, Marsh's and Gutzeit's.

That was his theory. To prove it would be no easy matter. The body was now beyond his reach, or anybody else's. There was only one chance – that he might be able to get hold of a portion of Napoleon's hair. Hair is a well-known retainer of arsenic, as it is the means through which the body attempts to rid itself of the poison. Not merely a small lock of hair would be needed, or a few strands, but a substantial amount – about as much as would be contained in a pigtail. The odds seemed impossible, until, glancing through a chemical journal, Forshufvud read that a new test had been discovered by which only a single strand of hair was necessary. The scientist concerned was a Dr Hamilton Smith of the University of Glasgow.

Forshufvud's quest began. His first move was to make contact with Prince Napoleon Louis Jerome Victor Bonaparte, who might well have a lock of Napoleon's hair. He travelled to Paris; an appointment was made by telephone, but not kept. A Commandant Henri Lachouque was more forthcoming – he was a leading Bonapartist, and, to Forshufvud's delight, he had a lock of the hair, shaved off the day after death. Forshufvud was given a strand, and on returning home sent it to Dr Hamilton Smith for analysis. The test was positive, showing that the owner of the hair had been exposed to relatively large amounts of arsenic.

Forshufvud visited Dr Hamilton Smith in Glasgow, and learned from him that a newly invented test could analyse hair in sections, showing at what rate arsenic had entered the system during the growth of the hair – whether in large doses, or gradually. More hair was needed, the first specimen having been destroyed during the test. Forshufvud obtained some from another source. Tests on it showed that Napoleon had received largish, but not fatal, doses of poison at times roughly approximating to the times of his illnesses.

Napoleon Bonaparte,
depicted in 1820 in a
brooding pose on St Helena.
His health had deteriorated
and his shape had changed –
'as fat and round as a China
pig' was how one resident of
the island described it.
Below: Napoleon on his
deathbed.

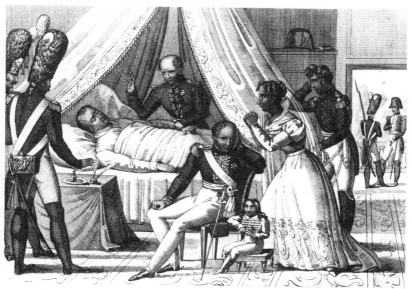

Forshufvud now had all the laboratory results he needed, and the statement from a descendant of Betsy Balcombe, Napoleon's child friend on St Helena, that a tradition ran in her family that he had been poisoned. No more evidence was necessary; he had only to work out a theory of how the poison was administered.

He eliminated some suspects. Dr Antommarchi did not arrive in Napoleon's household until 1819, and the time-tracing test had shown poison administered in 1818. Other companions of Napoleon could be eliminated, the English very easily, for they would not have risked an international scandal. In the end only one suspect was left – Montholon. He had no particular cause to be devoted to Napoleon, and his attachment to the household in St Helena was rather inexplicable since he could have been a good deal more comfortable at home in France.

There was only one explanation, Forshufvud thought. Montholon had been sent out to kill Napoleon. The method was not hard to guess; Montholon was the wine-steward, in sole charge of supplies. Nobody else would drink the wine (and those who had been offered it as a gift had been sick). And when his fatal campaign was nearing its end, Montholon sided with the doctors who wanted to give the patient calomel, which would effectively remove traces of the poison.

Who instigated the murder, and why? Forshufvud had an answer ready. The Count d'Artois, known as Monsieur, was the younger brother of the newly restored Bourbon king, Louis XVIII, and, of course, of Louis XVI, murdered under the Terror. Not surprisingly he hated everything connected with the French Revolution, and most of all he hated Napoleon Bonaparte, who had, so to speak, jumped on the back of the Revolution and ridden himself into a position of enormous power. Exiled in Scotland, d'Artois launched plot after plot against Napoleon; all, including an assassination attempt, failed.

D'Artois would become the next King of France, on the death of his brother. Fanatically anxious to restore something like the old régime, he ran a spy network which had uncovered a truly alarming number of plots to bring back the Revolution and Napoleon with it. The man was still alive; he had escaped from exile once, and while he was still sturdy and fit he could do it again. Therefore he must be destroyed, slowly, in unsuspicious circumstances. And therefore Montholon was entrusted with a mission to kill.

These were Forshufvud's conclusions, and he was perfectly happy with them, convinced that he had fulfilled Napoleon's last wishes and unmasked his murderers. His curious life-work had not been in vain.

But how correct were his theories? On the face of it they are most ingenious, and he undoubtedly proved that there was arsenic in Napoleon's body. But arsenic can enter a body in various ways, with or without fatal results. Copper arsenic, known as Scheele's green, was at one time much used as a pigment for colouring various materials, including fabric and wallpaper. And in 1982 Dr David Jones did intensive research which produced the fact that Napoleon's wallpaper at St Helena had contained arsenic. His findings were broadcast in a BBC feature programme, *The Saga of Napoleon's Wallpaper*.

So a source of the poison, unconnected with Montholon or any other possible murderer, actually existed. Whether Napoleon could have absorbed enough of it from the colouring matter used in the wallpaper is a doubtful point. Forshufvud thought he had eliminated such a possibility, since it would have involved others in the household becoming ill. Could Napoleon have been in the habit of leaning against it, touching it frequently, tracing patterns with his finger? It is impossible now to discover.

It must be remembered that medical science in the early nineteenth century was still at a very immature stage. Whatever the doctors found at the autopsy, they evidently did not really understand it; but a modern view is that the tumour in the dead man's stomach was just what they thought it was – a cancerous growth, not something that might have been caused by arsenic. Napoleon's father had died of the same thing. He himself was not a particularly healthy subject. For many years he had bolted his food so quickly that he had sometimes vomited at the table; not a habit which can have done his digestion much good. He seems to have had a lifelong tendency to complaints of the bowel and excretory organs. The violent exercise he had taken in the past had suddenly ceased; his body, from 1815 onwards, must have been suffering withdrawal symptoms. The growing stoutness which Forshufvud attributed to arsenical poisoning had not set in with exile – it is obvious in portraits of 1813 and earlier.

Napoleon was not a healthy man when he landed on St Helena, but not a sick one either. There was no particular reason why he should die, but equally no particular reason why he should live, having no longer anything to live for. There have been rumours of poison round almost every unexplained death in history; they were inevitable in Napoleon's case. If indeed he was murdered, how futile that murder was, happening when it did, and not before the mass slaughters for which he had been responsible.

THE TRAGEDY OF MAYERLING

Below the small church of the Capuchin friars in the Neumarkt, Vienna, is a dark, chilly crypt. Within it lie the remains of members of the House of Habsburg, from ancient times up to the twentieth century. The oldest are enclosed in caskets on shelves, later ones within stone sarcophagi richly engraved with emblems of royalty and death, skulls among garlands of roses and heraldic devices. The vault is dominated by the enormous tomb of the Empress Maria Theresia, mother of kings and queens, above which the sculptured forms of the Empress and her husband rise from the sleep of death to greet each other, so lifelike that one expects them to step down from their high platform and make their way back to their great palace, the Hofburg, only a little distant, in the heart of Vienna.

Not far from this awesome monument are three coffins, unburied, like the other Habsburgs around them; they are those of the Emperor Franz Josef of Austria, who died in 1916, his wife the Empress Elisabeth, assassinated by an Italian anarchist in 1898, and their only son, the Crown Prince Rudolf, whose mysterious death by his own hand in 1889 shocked Europe, and has been debated ever since.

Rudolf, born in 1858, should have grown up into the archetypal Prince Charming. His father was a powerful monarch, his mother the most beautiful woman of her time. But things began to go wrong for him very early. The Empress, born a Wittelsbach, had grown up wild and free, sometimes roaming the countryside with her father in gypsy disguise. The restrictions of Court life irked her, and interference by her mother-in-law came between her and her husband. When Rudolf was only two she went away to Madeira on the first of many escape-journeys which would separate her more and more from her growing son. He was an intelligent boy, but like her highly strung, a condition not improved by being put in the care of thoroughly unsuitable people at an early, impressionable age. It was a tradition that royal children should be brought up by authoritative strangers, but Count Gondrecourt, his first guardian, was a tough soldier noted for his narrow piety, who believed in 'hardening' the young prince by such devices as the firing of pistols in the child's bedroom, without warning, in the dead of night. After three years he was replaced by a milder character, but too late for the damage to Rudolf's nerves to be cancelled out.

A superior education by the best brains in Vienna turned Rudolf into a young man of highly cultivated intelligence, politically aware, liberal-minded, frustrated by the knowledge that he would never be able to exercise power while his father lived; and Franz Josef was very healthy and had been reigning since he was eighteen. Rudolf's appointment at twenty-nine to the post of Inspector-General of the Infantry resulted in a military disaster which humiliated him deeply, though a year earlier there had been a family tragedy which had affected him even more – the mysterious death by drowning of his mother's cousin King Ludwig of Bavaria. Rudolf represented his father at the funeral, and saw with alarm the effect it had on his mother.

King Ludwig had been incurably insane, as had his brother. There was a history of mental illness further back in the Wittelsbach family, and Elisabeth and Franz Josef were first cousins, and related in other ways. It was at this time that Rudolf may have suspected the germ of madness in himself, and begun to brood on death, especially death linked with sexual love.

A loveless marriage to the young Princess Stephanie of Belgium drove him into dissipation; he contracted a venereal disease. Among the young women he associated with was a high-class prostitute, Mitzi Kaspar. She was surprised when one day he suggested to her that they should go into a public garden and shoot themselves. She laughed, but made sure that the police were informed. To others he spoke of his own death, and prophesied that he would never inherit his father's throne.

It was his cousin, Countess Marie Larisch, who introduced him to Mary Vetsera. She was the daughter of a baroness, rich, lovely, seventeen years old, and already infatuated with the Crown Prince from a distance. Their meetings, chaperoned (but not too closely) by the Countess Larisch, became more and more frequent. On Mary's first visit to Rudolf's apartments in the Hofburg she saw lying on his desk a revolver and a human skull. She laughed, taking Rudolf's morbidity for a kind of game; she was amused by a ring given by him to her inscribed 'United in love until death'. As their flirtation turned into an *affaire*, rumours began to spread through the Court, through Vienna.

It was January 1889 when matters came to a head. An angry interview took place between the Emperor and his son. The cause was not known publicly, but what was known was that Rudolf had been involved, if only marginally, in Hungarian intrigues which might include a plot to incite the Magyars to rise against the Emperor; and Rudolf often supplied material for articles to a liberal editor, Moritz Szeps. But more likely to anger Franz Josef was a complaint by Rudolf's wife, Princess Stephanie, about his conduct with Mary Vetsera. In all likelihood the Emperor commanded him, during that interview, to renounce her.

At about the same time there was a stormy scene between Mary and her mother over a cigarette-case the Countess had discovered, inscribed

Crown Prince Rudolf of Austria.

Rudolf's lover Mary Vetsera. The ring he gave her was inscribed: 'United in love until death'.

The body of Rudolf lying in state. Mary's body was smuggled out of Mayerling and secretly buried at a nearby monastery.

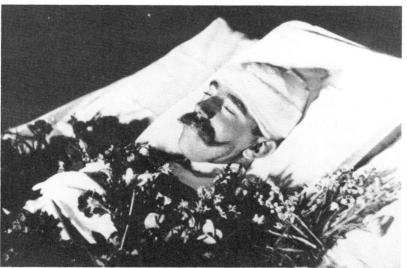

'Rudolf', and a tale which was going round the Court about another cigarette-case which had been given by Mary to Rudolf. The drama was coming to a head: the lovers must be parted.

On 27 January, at an evening reception at the German Embassy, Mary was glowing with happiness and almost supernaturally beautiful. She asked Count Hoyos, a great friend of Rudolf's, whether he ever went shooting with the Crown Prince. He was, indeed, going to join a shooting-party on 29 January, at Mayerling, a Habsburg hunting-lodge in the Vienna woods. Then, the next day, Mary Vetsera ran away, leaving a note for her mother saying that she was going to jump in the Danube. But nobody, in the ensuing panic, bothered to look for a body in the river. Her mother and Countess Larisch had a very good idea where she had gone.

She was, indeed, at Mayerling with Rudolf. Count Hoyos and Prince Philipp of Coburg were there, too, but had no knowledge that Rudolf had anybody else with him. Prince Philipp returned to Vienna for a dinner party; Hoyos and Rudolf dined alone on the evening of the twenty-ninth, after which Hoyos went to his lodging in an annexe. Later that evening Rudolf's coachman, Bratfisch, entertained Rudolf and Mary by singing and whistling, a performance they seemed to enjoy greatly.

Next morning, at 6.30, Rudolf emerged from his bedroom in a dressing-gown and told his valet that he wanted another hour's sleep, but must be wakened at 7.30. Failing to get an answer at that time, the valet called Hoyos. Together with Prince Philipp, who had returned from Vienna, they smashed down the bedroom door. In the dark, shuttered room they could see enough: Mary's body lying on the bed, Rudolf half-sitting by it. Both had been shot through the head, and the revolver was still in Rudolf's hand. Evidence showed that he had been drinking brandy all through the night. Mary had been dead some hours.

It was Hoyos's unenviable task to take the dreadful news back to Vienna. The Empress was at the Hofburg, for once; it was she who had to tell the Emperor. Then Mary's mother arrived, seeking news of her daughter, only to hear that both Mary and Rudolf were dead – of poison, as it was generally thought at the time.

The first official news given to the Austrian people was that the heir to the throne had died of a heart attack, an unlikely story. Mary's death was not mentioned, nor the fact that she had been with him at Mayerling. While doctors were examining Rudolf's body, hers was concealed, and later smuggled out of Mayerling and buried, with hasty secrecy, at Heiligenkreuz, a Cistercian monastery not far away. Her death certificate stated that she had committed suicide, which everyone now knew to be untrue. But it was out of the question to admit publicly that the Crown Prince was

The courtyard of the Mayerling hunting-lodge as it was in Rudolf's lifetime.

a murderer. Only the Abbot of Heiligenkreuz was told the truth, since he refused to give Christian burial to a suicide.

Both Rudolf and Mary left letters, written during that fateful night. Rudolf left none for his father. Mary's, to family and friends, were curiously worded, with ambiguous phrases which might be taken to mean that she did not expect to die. If these were misleading, and she had fully accepted Rudolf's proposal of a death-pact, she cannot have comprehended what she was doing. An excitable, passionate girl, little more than a child, she had been dazzled out of all sense and reason by Rudolf's persuasiveness, and had been quite unable to see that he was dangerously abnormal. Wagner's opera *Tristan and Isolde* had been performed in Vienna as recently as 1885; the theme of death in love, or love in death, was a popular one. Under his fatal influence, she sacrificed her beauty, wealth, prospects of a brilliant marriage; all her family's hopes for her were buried in an obscure, secret grave.

Whatever she died for, it was not love. Rudolf was doubtless fond of her, as he had been of many women, but she was not worth dying for, in herself. It seems as though he had reached the point when he felt he had no choice but to die. Perhaps he sensed that he was going out of his mind, and could not face the prospect.

There were other possibilities, mentioned by Countess Larisch in her memoirs, *My Past*, published in 1913. According to her, Rudolf was heavily involved with Hungarian intrigues, possibly even planning to become King of Hungary, which was part of the Austro-Hungarian Empire but had a strong separatist faction. One of these separatists was Count Stephen Karolyi, with whom he was frequently in communication. There is little evidence that he had actual plans which would have implied disloyalty to his father; but at least one shred of it may be found in a will made by Rudolf in 1887. In it he requested his executor to open his study desk in the presence of his wife. The executor was to use his own judgment about which papers were to be destroyed and which kept. But Rudolf wrote again to his executor, apparently before leaving for Mayerling: in it he directed that 'my desk in the Turkish room here in Vienna' should be opened by the executor 'immediately and alone', and any papers found in it destroyed.

He may well have been drunk when he wrote this (and certainly was drunk throughout the night at Mayerling). The letter was written in Magyar, and there was a reference in it to 'our dear beloved homeland'. The executor, Ladislas von Szoegenyi-Marich, was himself a Magyar. He destroyed much, but not everything. Enough remained to ensure that Countess Larisch was forbidden the Court, but no political papers – if there were any – were allowed to survive.

If any clues remained, they might have come to light at the opening of the Imperial archives, when the First World War was ended and Franz Josef was dead. But no file on Rudolf was among them. There was a story that the Emperor had given them to Count Taafe, his Prime Minister, and that Taafe had taken them to his home in Bohemia, where they had been accidentally destroyed by fire. The Taafe family did, in fact, hold relevant documents; long after the events, an old lady came forward to testify that she had seen them, and that among other things they revealed was the fact that Mary had been pregnant. Another story says that when the sensitive subject of Rudolf's burial was under discussion, the Emperor sent Pope Leo XIII an immensely long explanatory telegram. But the Vatican is not in the habit of releasing such information without very good reason.

Whatever the truth behind the events that took place at Mayerling on the night of 29 January, the cover-up story for them was one of the most elaborate ever mounted. Disclosure of them could have unsettled the Emperor's throne, discredited the Habsburgs and invited attempts at revolution or invasion. The Prince of Wales conveyed a version of the facts to his mother, Queen Victoria, in tactful terms. There had to be an admission that Rudolf was mentally disturbed, in order to obtain Christian burial for him; but hereditary madness was not mentioned, if only out of deference to his mother.

Mayerling still stands, but it is no longer a hunting-lodge. In accordance with Franz Josef's wishes, a memorial chapel was built and the place was taken over by Carmelite nuns, so that the crimes committed there might be expiated in prayer. Rudolf's only child, the Archduchess Elisabeth, lived until 1963. Descendants of the House of Habsburg are still alive, but as a ruling power it is as dead as the killer and the victim of the Mayerling tragedy.

WHERE WAS CAMELOT?

Out of the blue, and for no apparent reason, twelfth-century England and France suddenly became flooded with legends about a mythical King Arthur, the founder of a knightly order. His knights quest for the Holy Grail. Arthur marries his lady-love and builds his palace at Camelot. Betrayed and mortally wounded in battle, he is buried at Glastonbury. This legendary Arthur was the creation of the age of chivalry, designed to express its ideals of bravery, virtue and courtly love.

The real Arthur appears to have been a British general who fought the Saxon invaders about AD 500. He won great battles, culminating in his victory at Badon. His great feat was to delay the conquest, thus giving the uncouth Saxons time to become more civilized and enabling his Celtic countrymen to retire to their Welsh and Cornish fastnesses and survive as a racial entity. Arthur himself was probably a Romanized Briton, possibly of mixed ancestry, educated, sophisticated and versed in Roman military techniques.

Britain had been a Roman province for 400 years, defended by the legions. They were withdrawn from the frontiers after the sack of Rome by the Goths in AD 410. The Dark Ages had begun. Britain fell under the rule of a number of petty kings. They were too weak to resist the waves of Saxons, Angles and Jutes who poured across the North Sea. By 465 they had overrun Kent and established themselves east of the line from the river Humber in the north to the town of Southampton on the English Channel. They encroached westwards, raiding and pillaging. The Celtic kings, it is thought, placed Arthur in command of their combined forces. He may have raised a body of mailed horsemen, some of them possibly the sons or grandsons of legionaries who had married and settled in Britain.

The earliest reference to Arthur is by the chronicler Nennius who died in 811. Referring to the Saxon conquest, he said: 'Then Arthur fought against them in those days with the kings of the Britons.' Nennius lists Arthur's battles, the twelfth being at Mount Badon, 'where fell nine hundred and sixty men in one day'. None of the battle-sites has been definitely located. Badon has been identified as being fought at Badbury Rings in Dorset, at Badbury Camp in Berkshire, and at Badbury by Liddington Castle in Wiltshire, and is variously dated in 499 and 518.

Nevertheless, tentative identification of the battle-sites suggests that Arthur ranged Britain, and may have campaigned in Scotland, employing his mobility to throw back the Saxons. His soldiers may have been mounted on black horses, a cross between the native fell ponies and the larger black Frisians left behind by the Romans. This possibility led in 1971 to the suggestion that the inn sign 'The Black Horse', widespread in certain areas, recalls the scenes of Arthur's great victories,* his black horsemen having become so enshrined in legend that their memory was perpetuated by pub signs. Mr Wildman presents his case with persuasive logic. None the less, it may be one of the dottier theories of history.

* S. G. Wildman, *The Black Horsemen: English Inns and King Arthur*, Garnstone Press, 1971.

There is nothing to link Arthur definitely with a place named Camelot. The name is thought to have been invented by the twelfth-century poets to provide Arthur with a palace fit for a king. Or did they derive it from local tradition as chronicler John Leland claimed he did in 1542? Visiting the county of Somerset he was told that 'Camalat' was the name borne by the hill by the village of South Cadbury and that Arthur 'much resided there'. Corroboration for this local identification appeared to be supplied by the ancient fortifications girding the hill's summit, 1,200 yards (1,100 metres) in circumference, and recorded in the Domesday Book under the name 'Camelle' or 'Camel'. The local people called the hill 'Arthur's Palace', as the antiquarian John Camden learned in the sixteenth century. Arthur was still associated with the site in 1723 when William Stukeley visited 'Camelet Castle'.

Encouraged by these ancient traditions several local antiquarians dug on the hill, unearthing pottery and coins. Several items were donated to the Somerset County Museum at Taunton. Then a chance discovery revived interest in the 1950s. Pieces of pottery from the site were recognized by Dr Ralegh Radford as belonging to the fifth and sixth centuries, Arthur's period. Radford was a recognized authority on Dark Age Britain. His report in the *Proceedings of the Somerset Archaeological Society* caught the attention of other archaeologists.

Could the local folklore embody an ancient memory of the time when Arthur had made 'Camelot' his stronghold? Such a possibility was not as remote as it may seem. Tradition lingers long in rural England. For example, at Bosham in Sussex the story was passed from generation to generation that King Canute's teenage daughter had been accidentally drowned in the harbour. This verbal tradition was startlingly confirmed in the early 1900s by the discovery, during repairs to the church, of a coffin containing the bones of a young girl. These ancient clues, and Dr Radford's discoveries, led to the formation in 1965 of the Camelot Research Committee. Sir Mortimer Wheeler became its president, and his one-time pupil, Leslie Alcock, was appointed its archaeological director.

Alcock and his many helpers faced a huge task, the excavation of the hill's plateau, 18 acres (7 hectares) in extent. South Cadbury Hill rises 250 feet (76 metres) above the surrounding countryside, commanding a wide view from its ancient earthen ramparts. Trial digs showed that it had been occupied as a hill fort, one of the many which dot southern England, since Neolithic times. In their early reconnaissance the archaeologists were guided by the crop marks, the green patches disclosed by aerial photography. These indicated the places where pits and trenches had been dug. Smaller excavations in three zones disclosed ancient storage pits and the post-holes which had provided the frames of houses. Some of these were 15 inches (38 centimetres) in diameter, indicating large buildings.

These discoveries suggested that a major operation would be worthwhile, though that would require considerable money and a band of devoted workers. The committee's appeal raised £15,000 and offers of help came from the students of University College, Cardiff, interested parties in so far as they were descended from Arthur's Celtic retainers. Enthusiasm for the search for Arthur's Camelot reached national proportions. The BBC sent its cameramen to record the work, and the site was visited by so many eager tourists that the committee found it necessary to appoint guides and issue leaflets explaining its work.

At the start of the 1967 season, the archaeologists were offered by a Mr Mark Howell the use of an instrument he had devised to locate metal objects and rock fractures under the surface. This 'banjo', as it became called from its shape, comprised a boom with a radio transmitter at one end and a receiver at the other. Tests showed that it was sensitive to metal and required no expert qualifications to operate. It enabled the archaeologists to set up a grid system of recordings, which greatly assisted their work. The Oxford Laboratory for Archaeology also provided a formidable range of electronic instruments including the well-proven proton magnetometer which is highly sensitive to geophysical anomalies. The early test digs and the readings obtained by these instruments encouraged the archaeologists to excavate at two places, at the ramparts on the southern side of the hill and at the plateau's highest point, where the post-holes indicated traces of large buildings.

Exploration at the south-western gateway in the ancient ramparts disclosed successive chronological layers. On the top layer was the wall-face of a massive mortared stone rampart and gateway. Coins, pottery and the building style identified this as the rampart, 12–20 feet (3.6–6 metres) thick, built by the Saxons during the reign of King Ethelred the Unready, who had used the hill as a mint. The structure was dated about AD 800–900. The lower, more ancient layer disclosed a pit containing the bones of thirty men, women and children jumbled together. Nearby were found hoards of sling shots, Roman coins and the hinge of a Roman cuirass. Lower still ran an ancient cobbled roadway, worn by feet and rutted by cart tracks. Weapons and burnt pottery dated the massacre in the first century AD, in the decade of the Roman conquest when the general Vespasian had captured more than twenty British hill forts. The ancient Britons had defended Cadbury, dying in its defence. The Romans, to prevent refortification, had destroyed the ancient Celtic ramparts, the earthen bank and ditch which dated from Neolithic times.

Top: Cadbury Hill from the air. Was this the site of King Arthur's Camelot?
Above: Part of the fortifications at Cadbury Hill, destroyed in about A.D. 50 and rebuilt in about 550.

These discoveries showed that the hill's ramparts had been destroyed in about AD 50 and had been rebuilt by the Saxons after their conquest of the region in about 550. Between these layers – the pre-Roman and the early Saxon – the archaeologists found a chaotic mass of earth and piled stones, separated by a thick layer of soil from the pre-Roman, and by a thinner layer from the Saxon period of occupation. This 'stony bank', as it became termed, comprised four courses of stone, one above another, on which had been piled an earthen rampart topped by a timber breastwork. This fortification had been built in the Celtic manner, but no Celts had lived on the hill for 400 years. Someone had refortified Cadbury Hill between 450 and 550, in the period of the Saxon westward advance.

Evidence derived from other parts of the hill suggested that Cadbury Hill had been rebuilt as the fortress of a great military leader, and had been a wealthy and important settlement.

Excavations of post-holes revealed the outline of a rectangular building 65 feet long and 34 feet wide (19 by 10 metres). It had occupied the dominant position at the top of the hill. Could it have been the chieftain's feasting hall and home? Sherds of pottery dated the building to the Arthurian period. With nothing more than its foundations to work upon, the archaeologists reconstructed the building as a wattle and daub structure held together by a timbered framework with a thatched roof. There had been doors in each long wall. An open centre hearth was likely, but the evidence had been ploughed away by modern farmers. The foundations fitted the size range of contemporary halls, for example at Castle Dore in Cornwall and Yeavering in Northumberland.

The excavations at the gate and on the hill exhausted the information gathered about the AD 500 period, though by the end of 1970 the archaeologists had investigated only one-fifth of the plateau's surface. They had found nothing to prove conclusively that Cadbury Hill had been Arthur's Camelot. But the circumstantial evidence seemed convincing. Arthur would have needed a fortified base. Why not Cadbury Hill? It was an ancient hill fort, in a commanding position, close to the Fosse Way leading north and the Hard Way coming from the east. Nearby runs the river Cam, possibly the site of Camlann, the battle where Arthur received his mortal wound from his British opponent Medrant. Twelve miles (19 kilometres) to the north-west rises Glastonbury Tor, and beside it the abbey which is Arthur's traditional resting-place.

Arthur's reputed relics and those of his wife were discovered in 1190 enclosed in a hollow tree trunk in a grave of great depth. The bones were exhumed and transferred to a tomb within the church. The tomb was opened in 1278 in the presence of Edward I. The contemporary account, the *Annals of Waverley*, states that the bones of King Arthur were of great size, in keeping with his traditional height and girth. They were dispersed when the tomb was destroyed during the Reformation.

People at Cadbury believe that Arthur sleeps in a huge cavern within the hill. Somewhere on the plateau is a stone slab giving access to the cave. The Reverend James Bennett, a keen antiquarian, stated in 1890 that on opening up a hut there he found a flagstone, the manhole leading to the cave. Unfortunately he did not record the hut's position.

But Arthur does not always sleep. Twice a year, on Midsummer Eve and Christmas Eve, you can hear the hoof beats of the horses as the King and his men ride down from Camelot to drink at the spring which bears his name.

THE PRISONER IN THE TEMPLE

On a July day in 1793 a small boy was taken away from his mother, aunt and sister, and put into solitary confinement in the care of a cobbler and his wife. So far as is known, he did not come out alive. But there were those who said he did, and many who claimed his identity for themselves.

Louis Charles had been born to Marie Antoinette, Queen of France, in 1785, only four years before revolution swept away the French monarchy and its old régime. He was only the Dauphin, heir to the throne, because his elder brother had died at the age of seven, the victim of rickets, a disease caused by vitamin D deficiency; his baby sister, Sophie, died aged eleven months.

In October 1789 the rabble stormed the Palace of Versailles, and dragged the royal family back to Paris. They were imprisoned in the Palace of the Tuileries, which had been for many years uninhabited and neglected; to the child Louis Charles it was a strange, unpleasant place. 'Everything is dirty here, Mama,' he said. The King's captors were still polite enough to ask how he would like the place redecorated. 'Each may lodge as he can. I am well enough,' he answered coldly.

For three years the royal family lived under fairly civilized conditions. But in summer 1792 a significant thing was done: a tricolour ribbon was stretched across the Tuileries gardens, a demarcation line between what was royal and what was national. The revolutionaries sardonically named it Coblenz, after a town which had become one of the refuges of fleeing *émigrés.* Admission was only by ticket, and ticket-holders were suspiciously scrutinized.

Within it, the King, fearing what might come to himself and his family, plotted continuously. He had made one daring bid to escape, in June 1791, when the prisoners had left the Tuileries under the cover of night, Louis Charles dressed as a little girl. The party was on the way to Metz, a royalist stronghold. But at the village of Varennes-en-Argonne the King was recognized, and they were brought back among humiliations that turned Marie Antoinette's fair hair white in a night.

Now there was little pretence of politeness. On 10 August 1792 a revolutionary mob stormed the Tuileries and massacred the King's Swiss Guard. He was forced to wear the red cap of the revolution, and to drink a toast to Liberty, Equality and Fraternity, and the Queen heard herself called *L'Autrichienne* – the Austrian bitch. From the Tuileries the family was taken, amid shouts of '*Vive la nation!*', to the Temple, in the Faubourg St Germain, and formally imprisoned.

They bore it with patience and good sense. The King gave lessons to his small son; they played draughts together, and strolled in the garden. After four months the King was taken away to a tower in another part of the Temple. He was still allowed to join his family for meals, but early in December was warned that he must prepare himself for public trial.

They must all have known what that meant. On Christmas Day 1792 he made his will, in which he forgave his enemies. There was a tender last reunion, on 20 January 1793, at which the King impressed on the Dauphin that no revenge must be attempted for what was going to be done to him. He was calm and resigned, the Queen furiously indignant. To his guards she cried '*Vous êtes tous des scélérats*' – 'You are all villains'. Next morning he went to the guillotine, the first monarch to be judicially murdered since Charles I in 1649.

The little family in their Temple prison suffered increasingly from their harsh guards. On 3 July the Dauphin was taken away to a room below, on the second floor. His personal jailers were a cobbler, Antoine Simon, and his wife, under instructions to brainwash the child and turn him into a revolutionary. They taught him to drink and swear and to sing the *Carmagnole*, a 'saucy, rollicking, diabolic *chanson*' which was a favourite with the crowds as a rabble-rouser.

The Simons do not appear to have been actively cruel, but were coarse enough to debase an impressionable child. His shirt, according to reports, was not changed for six months on end. The most loathsome act in the whole history of the revolution was the enforced signing by the Dauphin of a document making obscene charges against his mother, which were used in court against her at the token trial which preceded her execution in October 1793. The indignities of her captivity had been such that death must have been almost welcome to the Queen.

Marie Thérèse last saw her brother on 1 August, the day their mother was taken away. In January 1794 the Simons resigned their post of foster-parents to the Dauphin. His living conditions rapidly deteriorated, for he was now imprisoned in one room, with an iron grille for a door, so that he could be constantly watched. Those who came to visit him found him completely unresponsive; he neither spoke nor showed any sign of emotion. They observed signs of rickets – swellings of the joints, and progressive deformity of the legs. No sympathy for the nine-year-old child was expressed, only remarks on his laziness and obstinate refusal to take exercise.

But somebody must have reported his condition, for a new warder was appointed and provision made for medical care, though there is no record that this was given. In March 1795 the iron grille was taken away, and an ordinary door put in its place, a fair sign that the prisoner was no longer regarded as likely to escape.

It was in May 1795 that a doctor was at last called in to examine the child. Dr Desault was head surgeon of the Hôtel Dieu, the oldest hospital in Paris. The story goes that he became mysteriously ill on the day he made the examination, after having said that he was not entirely happy about the patient's identity. Shortly afterwards he died – also mysteriously. Another doctor was summoned, and was so alarmed by the state of the child that he called in a colleague. He, equally perturbed, demanded that his patient be removed to a better room, with more light and proper ventilation. But in mid-afternoon on 8 June the child died.

A post-mortem by four doctors resulted in a unanimous verdict that death had been caused by scrofula, a tubercular condition affecting the lymphatic glands and bones; ironically, it was known in England as the King's Evil, curable only by the royal touch. On the same evening, the corpse was coffined and buried in a common grave, in the cemetery of Ste Marguerite, without a memorial. Thus, so far as the Temple jailers were concerned, came the end of the boy 'known as the late Louis Capet's son'.

But others thought that it was not the end. Rumours soon spread that he had not died at all, but had some time in 1794 been taken out of the Temple crammed into a clothes-basket, and another child substituted for him – most probably a deaf and dumb one, which would explain why the emissaries of the Convention had found him completely unresponsive. Royalist hopes were built on such rumours; after the turn of the century a series of 'Dauphins' began to appear, some forty of them in all.

Top: Louis XVI imprisoned with his family in the Temple. Painting by Ward.
Above: The Dauphin, who was retained in prison following his parents' execution.
The uncertain fate of the Dauphin sustained Royalist hopes.

The Temple prison.

Among them, Jean Marie Hervagault was attractive and persuasive, but undoubtedly a tailor's son who had seen a good deal of the inside of prisons. Nobody rallied to him, and he died in 1812. One Mathurin Bruneau adopted the title of Charles de Navarre, and set himself up in rivalry to the newly restored Bourbons in 1818. Nobody believed in him, either, but Louis XVIII, brother of the dead King, was interested enough to have the cemetery of Ste Marguerite dug up, without finding any trace of a coffin which might have been his nephew's. After his death, in the reign of his brother Charles X, another pretender arose in the person of a man whose real name was Hébert, but who called himself Baron de Richelieu and Duke of Normandy. The Bourbons knew themselves to be unpopular, and were not prepared to take risks with people who might damage them. Hébert was tried and given a twelve-year sentence; but he never served it, escaping to England until the excitement had died down.

Of the other pretenders, who rather remarkably included a half-caste Indian, the strongest was Karl Wilhelm Naundorff, whose legend persists to this day. He was born in the same year as the Dauphin, 1785, or so he said – no birth certificate or proof of baptism was ever found. In 1810, while living at Spandau, near Berlin, he married a shopkeeper's daughter; they produced nine children. In 1824 he was arrested for arson and passing false coinage. After his release from prison, in 1827, he moved to Saxony and began to press his claims to be Louis XVII (the Dauphin had technically become King on the execution of his father).

His story was that he had been hidden on the fourth floor of the Temple, and a wooden figure substituted for him in the prison room. Then the figure was exchanged for a deaf mute, who in turn was removed and a scrofulous child put in his place. It was not this child, who died of the disease, but Charles Louis who left the prison in the coffin, from which he was removed by 'friends' – organized by the dictator Barras, to please his mistress Josephine Beauharnais – before it reached the cemetery. He was then taken to the Vendée province, where there was much Royalist sympathy, then to Italy, and from Italy to England, being imprisoned in both countries but freed at the request of the Empress Josephine. His next imprisonment (in a dungeon this time) was in Germany, near Frankfurt. He escaped and became a soldier under the Duke of Brunswick, before settling down in Berlin as a watchmaker.

With this story he approached his alleged sister, now the Duchesse d'Angoulême, and got supporters to reinforce his pleas. She had inquiries made, but they only produced the information that Naundorff did indeed look very like the Bourbons. The Duchesse, however, refused to meet him; her brother was dead, she was certain.

At last he became convinced that he had no hope of gaining recognition through her, and decided to go to law. Boldly, he issued a summons to the Duc and Duchesse, and Charles x, to present themselves before the civil court and answer his claims. He was promptly arrested, his mass of papers seized, and expelled from France. Like so many refugees, he fled to London and settled his numerous family in Camberwell Green.

Was he unlucky, accident-prone, or the victim of deliberate malice? In Paris he had been stabbed by an unknown assailant; in London he was shot in the arm, and twice his premises went up in flames. He was always poor and in debt, and no nearer establishing his identity as Louis xvII.

In 1839 he published a book setting out some highly unorthodox religious views, and two years later another which very much displeased the Pope, while attracting unwanted support for Naundorff from a number of religious cranks.

Naundorff seemed fated to succeed at nothing. For years he worked on the manufacture of explosives which no government would buy, until in 1845 there were murmurs of interest from Holland. He went there, but became ill, and died on 10 August. He was buried under the name of Charles Louis de Bourbon, Duc de Normandie, born at Versailles on 27 March 1785.

His descendants fought for his claims. Now Dutch nationals, they were allowed to call themselves Bourbon. Their long struggle for recognition lasted throughout the nineteenth century, and only ended in 1954, in failure.

Those who have tried to justify Naundorff have pointed out his physical resemblance to the Bourbons. He had, they said, certain bodily marks, including a scar on the lips, which the Dauphin had had. He knew things about the family in the Temple, and particularly about the frustrated flight to Metz, which convinced many people. His vocation for watchmaking, and skill in invention, were traits shared with Louis xvI. Two jailers who were still alive in 1834 swore that they had personally seen the Dauphin die. But Madame Simon, old and ill, insisted that she had recognized Naundorff as her one-time charge when he visited her in hospital.

There was every reason why the miserable, sick child who was the real Dauphin should have died in prison. He had an inherited disease and had received appalling treatment. Yet there is a story that in 1845 the Duchesse d'Angoulême received by post a drawing inscribed 'Louis xvII on his deathbed', and was deeply moved by it. Did she see something that made her regret her refusal to meet Naundorff, so many years before?

WHO WASN'T BURIED AT SUTTON HOO?

The mounds on her estate at Sutton Hoo, Suffolk, aroused Mrs Edith May Pretty's curiosity. The old story of the ploughman who had turned up a golden brooch in 1800 hinted at buried treasure. A previous owner of the estate had set his gamekeeper digging into one of the mounds. Finding only a rabbit warren he had given up. The mounds, eleven in number, rose on the escarpment above, 450 yards (410 metres) from the eastern bank of the river Deben, a tidal estuary 9 miles (14 kilometres) from the North Sea. Mrs Pretty, a justice of the peace, contacted Ipswich Museum. Its curator, Guy Maynard, sent the museum's field surveyor, Basil Brown, to inspect the mounds. He recognized them as ancient tumuli, possibly containing burials.

Assisted by two of Mrs Pretty's gardeners, Brown started work in 1938. The first three mounds yielded comparatively uninteresting results. One contained a cremation burial and had been looted. Enough objects, including the remains of an ornamental shield and the tip of a sword, were found to identify the site as an Anglo-Saxon grave. In the second mound Brown detected the outlines of a small rowing boat, which may have been 18 to 20 feet (5.5 to 6 metres) long. Two small clench nails were similar to those which had been found within a mound 9 miles (14 kilometres) away at Snape in 1862. That mound had yielded the outline of a smaller boat. The third mound contained pieces of bowls and pottery of Anglo-Saxon type. All three mounds had been entered and ransacked.

While these early discoveries confirmed that the mounds contained Anglo-Saxon burials, there was no hint that another would yield what Sir Thomas Kendrick, the then director of the British Museum, would call 'the most remarkable archaeological discovery ever made in England'.

Work was resumed in May 1939. Doubtful as to which mound to excavate next, Brown turned to Mrs Pretty. 'What about this one?' she asked, pointing to the largest mound, the one closest to the river, which was obscured by a clump of trees. The mound was 9 feet high, 100 feet long and 75 feet wide (2.7 by 30 by 23 metres). Starting from the eastern end, Brown began to dig a trench 6 feet (1.8 metres) wide, through the mound. The gardeners' spades soon turned up clumps of corroded clench nails, evidence pointing to another ship burial. Leaving the nails in position, Brown carefully cleaned the earth around them, disclosing the outline of the forward part of a ship, a vessel clearly of considerable length. A layer of displaced earth, and the find of a tiger-ware jug and remains of a fire, showed that the mound had been previously entered. Fortunately the sixteenth-century robbers had penetrated only to ground level and missed the ship. They had cooked a meal before departing.

By 11 June Brown had cleared sufficient earth to disclose the ship's frame, or rather its outline in the sandy soil. Its timbers had decayed, leaving the clench nails which had fastened the planks to the frames. Had the central portion of the ship been used as a burial chamber? That was a fair inference because the burial of a chieftain or king within his ship had been a pagan custom adopted by both Anglo-Saxons and Norsemen. The size of the mound and the length of the ship suggested a unique discovery. Brown called a halt and informed the British Museum and the Inspectorate of Ancient Monuments. C. W. Phillips, a fellow of Selwyn College, Cambridge, and secretary of the Prehistoric Society, an experienced excavator, was sent to supervise the work. He was soon joined by a team of specialists.

The archaeologists faced a task of unprecedented difficulty. No one in England had previously attempted to excavate a ship, especially one whose timbers had disintegrated. The Viking ships discovered at Oseberg and Gokstad in Norway and at Ladby in Denmark had been recovered intact. Brown had found a much older vessel, one dating from the early years of the Anglo-Saxon conquest, a discovery unparalleled in British archaeology.

The vessel had left a perfect impression of its hull in the sand. It had been 89 feet long and 14 feet wide (27 by 4 metres), and had been clinker built, with overlapping planks of oak. It had been rowed by thirty-eight oarsmen. The helmsman had steered by means of a broad-bladed oar affixed to the starboard quarter. Its construction showed advances in technique from the row-galley which had been unearthed at Nydam Moss in Denmark in 1863. The Nydam ship had been built about AD 400 and had been 73 feet 9 inches (22.5 metres) long. It is housed at Kiel Museum. Another somewhat smaller vessel had been found near Utrecht in Holland. Both the vessels had lacked proper keels, whereas the Sutton Hoo ship had had a primitive horizontal plank, enabling it to be sailed with a following wind. Its greatest depth had been 4 feet 6 inches (1.3 metres), and it had drawn 2 feet (0.6 metres) of water. It had been a great open row-boat, longer than the later Gokstad ship (79 feet, 24 metres), the Oseberg ship (68 feet, 21 metres) and the Ladby ship (68 feet, 21 metres). These Scandinavian ships had been built with proper keels, allowing for propulsion by sail as well as by oar.

How had the Sutton Hoo vessel been carried for a third of a mile (0.5 kilometre) overland from the river, and up the 100-foot (30 metres) escarpment? It is assumed that it was hauled or pushed on rollers, and placed above the trench cut in the soil. It was then held by ropes and lowered as the rollers were removed. The mound had been built above the ship after the burial chamber had been made amidships. The labour must have been enormous.

No vestige of this wooden burial chamber remained. It had been crushed by the weight of the soil. Phillips estimated that it had been $17\frac{1}{2}$ feet (5.3 metres) long and had looked a 'bit like Noah's Ark'. Within that area probably lay the chieftain's grave goods. The difficulty was to remove the earth without allowing the sides of the excavations to cave in. The archaeologists felt they had little time, for war was imminent. They worked slowly, using paint brushes and needles to turn each speck of earth. The first piece of treasure to come to light was a golden pyramid which may have hung from a sword belt. It was in perfect condition and nothing like it had been found in England before.

'Each day of that exciting week', wrote O. G. S. Crawford, the editor of *Antiquity* and one of the specialists drawn to the excavation, 'yielded some rich find often of a type hitherto unknown.' He anticipated the hidden things to come and was not disappointed. There were objects the archaeologists did not expect to find. Many of the treasures were corroded or too delicate to touch. They were wrapped and removed for cleaning and restoration at the British Museum laboratory. Several years elapsed before they could be assessed and described.

Two early discoveries suggested a royal burial. An iron spike, 6 feet 4 inches (1.9 metres) long, and capped by a bronze stag, turned out to be a standard, a symbol of sovereignty usually carried before the king in ceremonial processions. The whetstone was another such symbol. This great four-sided stone weighed 6 lb $4\frac{1}{2}$ oz (2.85 kilos). A sombre human face had been carved on each side of the stone. It was beautifully shaped and almost in mint condition. Nothing comparable to it is known. Bruce Mitford, former keeper of the British and medieval antiquities at the British Museum, called it 'this fantastic piece'.

The burial yielded the remains of a large circular shield, fragments of a helmet, an iron-bound bucket, two heavy bronze bowls, a six-stringed musical instrument, silver bowls and platters, drinking horns, a great silver dish, an iron lamp, golden harness, epaulets, a huge golden buckle, leatherwork, a sword 3 feet (0.9 metre) long, encased in its scabbard, a purse containing thirty-seven golden coins, and two spoons marked with the names of 'Saulos' and 'Paulos'. There was also considerable jewellery which Bruce Mitford called 'the most gorgeous of the finds'. One great gold buckle weighed $14\frac{5}{8}$ ounces (414 grams).

Everything had been supplied for the needs of the individual in his after-life. The richness of the grave goods indicated his place in society. The emblems of royalty suggested a royal person, almost certainly a king.

Above: The excavation
of the Anglo-Saxon ship
at Sutton Hoo. It
revealed all the hallmarks
of a chieftain's burial –
except for a body. *Left:*
The huge golden buckle,
part of the treasure
buried with the ship.

But there was no skeleton at Sutton Hoo, and a complete absence of the personal ornaments usually found in a pagan grave. The contents of the mound conformed to the description of a ship-burial given by the Anglo-Saxon poet, Beowulf, who is believed to have lived early in the eighth century, possibly within a hundred years of the burial at Sutton Hoo. Describing the burial of a mythical Danish king, Beowulf wrote:

> Then Scyld departed at the destined hour,
> that powerful man sought the Lord's protection.
> His own close companions carried him
> down to the sea, as he, Lord of the Danes,
> had asked while he could still speak.
> That well-loved man had ruled his land for many years.
> There in the harbour stood the ring-prowed ship,
> the prince's vessel, shrouded in ice and eager to sail;
> and then they laid their dear lord,
> and giver of rings, deep within the ship
> by the mast in majesty; many treasures
> and adornments from far and wide were gathered there.
> I have never heard of a ship equipped
> more handsomely with weapons and war-gear,
> swords and corselets; on his breast
> lay countless treasures that were to travel far
> with him into the waves' domain.
> They gave him great ornaments, gifts
> no less magnificent than those men had given him
> long before, when they sent him alone,
> child as he was, across the stretch of the seas.
> Then high above his head they placed
> a golden banner and let the waves bear him
> bequeathed him to the sea; their hearts were grieving,
> their minds mourning. Mighty men
> beneath the heavens, rulers in the hall,
> cannot say who received that cargo.

The mound at Sutton Hoo had yielded the richest treasure ever found on British soil. To whom did it belong? If the objects had been buried with no intention of being reclaimed, they reverted to the owner of the land, Mrs Pretty. Her right of possession was confirmed by a coroner's inquest. If the nation wanted the treasure it would have to buy it, at some fantastic cost. Mrs Pretty solved the problem by generously presenting the entire treasure to the nation. The British Museum took possession, concealing the wonderful finds in a bomb-proof shelter for the duration of the war.

The argument, first mooted in 1939 and not yet finally settled, recommenced after the war. Who had the king been, and why had he not been buried in his ship, according to pagan practice? One thing only seemed certain. He had been a member of the royal house of East Anglia, the first kingdom established by the Anglo-Saxons who had invaded England following the withdrawal of the Roman legions. They came from northern Europe and Scandinavia, bringing with them their ancient customs and traditions.

The possibility that the body had been cremated and the ashes had disintegrated is discounted on the ground that there is no known example of a body cremation without the burning of both grave goods and ship. Otherwise the burial had been in accordance with heathen tradition, the inhumation of a chieftain surrounded by his goods of outstanding richness. The absence of the body posed both a puzzle and a possible pointer to the man's identity.

The thirty-seven gold coins provide the strongest clue. They had been minted all over western Europe, in France, Belgium, the Rhineland and Switzerland, but no two coins had been derived from a single mint. Several bore the names of identifiable kings. They were found together in the purse. How long had they been hoarded? The collection suggested a royal treasure, comprising, possibly, gifts from other kings.

All the coins belonged to the Merovingian period in Europe when more than 2,000 mints were in operation. Knowledge of this coinage is still imprecise. Several numismatic experts have given their opinions. Early on their consensus indicated that the coins had come together between AD 650 and 660. But in 1960 the French authority on Merovingian coinage, M. Lafaurie, placed the assembly of the Sutton Hoo hoard at about 625. His opinion has been supported by Dr J.P.C. Kent, keeper of the British Museum's Department of Coins and Medals. His provisional verdict is 'not later than 630 for any coin; and 625 as the likely date for the assembly'. Another leading authority, Mr Philip Grierson, adheres to the old chronology (*Antiquity*, 1952).

Thus the coins provide only a rough and controversial guide to the date of the burial. To identify the king whose ship and goods, but not his body, were buried at Sutton Hoo, we need to consult the Venerable Bede, who wrote his *Ecclesiastical History* in about AD 700. Bede describes the conversion of East Anglia to Christianity, beginning with the baptism of Redwald who ruled as 'Bretwald', or supreme king. He died in 624 or 625. According to Bede, Redwald had been 'admitted to the sacrament of the Christian faith in Kent, but in vain; for, on his return home, he was seduced by his wife and certain perverse teachers and turned back from the sincerity of his faith.' Redwald erected in the same temple both an altar to Christ and a similar one to the devil.

Redwald may have hoped to gain from both possible worlds, or he may have remained a pagan at heart. There is another possibility. Did he die a Christian and receive burial in consecrated ground? Did his pagan subjects accord him a traditional funeral, a cenotaph lacking only his body? The presence in the grave of the two spoons bearing the names of Saul and Paul is interesting. They may have been Redwald's christening spoons.

This apparently convenient identification of Redwald does not satisfy everyone. One of the coins is claimed to have been minted by the Gothic King Dagobert I, who died in AD 638, some thirteen years after Redwald's death. According to this estimate, the hoard of coins could not have been assembled in Redwald's lifetime.

Redwald was succeeded by Sigeberht and Ecgric (or Aelthelric) who acted as joint rulers. Sigeberht was exiled to France in 630, where he was converted to Christianity. He entered a monastery, leaving Ecgric to rule alone until 640, when he joined him to fight the Mercian King Penda. Both were killed soon after. Ecgric was succeeded by King Anna, a devout Christian. He died in 654 and was given a Christian burial at Blythburgh.

Sandra Glass ('The Sutton Hoo Ship Burial', *Antiquity*, 1962) has suggested that Anna erected the Sutton Hoo memorial for the heroic Ecgric, supplying his cenotaph with the symbol of royalty. She points out that a burial of such magnitude, using so much of the royal treasury, could only have been carried out by a king for a king. Did the Christian Anna allow the pagan warriors who had survived the battle with the Mercians to erect a memorial to their hero? C.W. Phillips, however, conceives the possibility that Anna was the king for whom the memorial was erected, possibly for political reasons, by his pagan subjects. He too was slain by Penda. According to yet another theory, the memorial was erected to Anna's brother and successor, the Christian Aethelhere. His body was lost in flood waters following the battle of Winwaed. That would account for the absence of a body at Sutton Hoo.

Despite these intriguing suggestions, the general choice identifies Redwald as the Anglo-Saxon king who was honoured. He was an early king of the dynasty which built its palaces at Rendlesham, 4 miles (6 kilometres) up the river Deben from Sutton Hoo. A crown weighing 60 ounces (1.86 kilos) was dug up there in 1960. That it was melted down suggests that it was made of gold or silver. The kings established their cemetery at Sutton Hoo. No clump of trees then obscured the heath from the river from where the mounds could have been clearly seen, silhouetted against the skyline, 'high and broad and visible from afar to all seafarers', as Beowulf described his own future grave.

THE HOLY SHROUD OF TURIN

Behind iron grilles, above two altars in the Cathedral of St John the Baptist, Turin, lies a piece of linen cloth wrapped in crimson silk, and contained in an iron chest enclosed within a wooden box, secured by three separate locks. It is one of the most debated objects in the world, and has been so for over six centuries. It is the Shroud, sometimes called the Holy Shroud, of Turin. If what many believe is true, it bears the image of Jesus Christ, imprinted on it as he lay in the rock-tomb after his crucifixion.

It has been seen only rarely during the past two hundred years, every exhibition of it needing permission from the Pope, the Cardinal of Turin, and its late owner, the ex-king of Italy, King Umberto of Savoy. But in 1973, after repeated efforts by an American pastor, Father Peter Rinaldi, an enormous concession was made: the Shroud was shown on Italian television, networked all over Europe. On 22 November, in the great hall of the former royal palace of Turin, the Shroud was displayed under the strong light from television lamps, before the eyes of excited spectators.

What they saw was a length of linen, obviously ancient but in good condition, herringbone-woven, 14 feet 3 inches by 3 feet 7 inches. Two lifesize images appeared on it, faintly in sepia, one the front aspect, one the back; the shape of a man, naked, in the still attitude of one laid out in death. The image is negative – the light areas appearing dark, the dark appearing light, as in a photographic negative.

Intensive modern studies have made it possible to reconstruct the appearance and physical details of the subject. He was a bearded, long-haired man, aged probably between thirty and thirty-five, some 5 feet 11 inches tall, weighing about 12½ stones. His body, slim and well built, has suffered terrible maltreatment. All over his skin, from face to legs, are the marks of a savage scourging, probably inflicted by two tormentors: there are between ninety and a hundred wounds which could have been made by metal-tipped thongs. Across the shoulders the skin is badly bruised and broken, as if by some heavy, rough-surfaced object. There is a deep wound in the side, which has produced a flow of blood and serum. The knees are cut and bruised, the left kneecap badly so, as if by a heavy fall. The visible wrist (the hands are crossed) and both feet reveal wounds made by spikes being driven through them. The face is bruised and swollen, as though the lash had struck there too, and the scalp is marked by deep punctures made by sharp objects.

All the signs indicate the body of a man scourged, made to wear a cap of spikes forced down on his head, oppressed by a heavy weight laid on his shoulders, and finally crucified by nails driven through the wrists and ankle-bones. There are no signs of decomposition. The abdomen area is swollen, as it would have been by the asphyxia which usually caused the death of the crucified.

All four Gospels describe these injuries as having been inflicted on Jesus. In the account by St Mark, after Pontius Pilate's yielding to the multitude's shouts for his death:

> ... the soldiers led him away within the court, which is the Praetorium; and they call together the whole band. And they clothe him with purple, and plaiting a crown of thorns, they put it on him; and they began to salute him, Hail, King of the Jews! And they smote his head with a reed, and did spit upon him, and when they mocked him, they took off from him the purple, and put on him his garments. And they led him out to crucify him. And they compel one passing by, Simon of Cyrene ... to go with them, that he might bear his cross.

The scourge-marks exactly correspond with those that would have been made by the Roman *flagrum*, a sort of cat-o'-three-tails whose thongs were tipped with metal or bone. Roman law allowed only forty lashes for its own criminals, but imposed no limit for the flogging of Jews. The beating received by the man of the Shroud might well have hastened his death. The 'crown of thorns', which was a cap covering the scalp, not a wreath, was not a common feature of the punishment of criminals, but in this case was a mockery of one who had proclaimed himself King. It was usual for crucifixion victims to carry the horizontal crossbeam of their gallows on their own shoulders; the fact that Simon of Cyrene was called in suggests that Jesus fell under its weight after, as St John tells, 'he went out, bearing the cross for himself'. John goes on to say that the Jews, because it was the eve of the Sabbath, asked of Pilate that the legs of the three crucified men, Jesus and the two robbers, should be broken so that they would die quickly and could be taken down from their crosses:

> The soldiers therefore came, and brake the legs of the first, and of the other ... but when they came to Jesus, and saw that he was dead already, they brake not his legs: howbeit one of the soldiers with a spear pierced his side ...

The leg-breaking was usual, causing the crucified person to slump, unable to support his weight and to breathe. But the man of the Shroud had not had his broken.

The Holy Shroud of Turin. Is this the image of Jesus Christ, imprinted on the linen as he lay in the tomb?

All these details and more, including the strong likeness of the face to the earliest known portraits of Christ, were obvious to those who first saw it at the beginning of its long, strange history, only some of which is known to us.

Soon after the crucifixion a mysterious 'portrait', with magical curative powers, was taken to Edessa in eastern Turkey, where it wrought various miracles of healing; later it was concealed safely in a niche over the city's west gate. In AD 525 it was discovered, identified as the miracle-working cloth, and transferred to a shrine built by Emperor Justinian. From this time onwards a new likeness of Christ began to appear in art; in the early days of Christianity the Christian church adhered to the Jewish ban on physical portraits, but now one artist after another began to paint likenesses strongly resembling the face of the Shroud, even to peculiarities which are caused by the texture of the cloth and the marks made when it was folded, at one time, to reveal only the face.

Now known as the Mandylion, the Shroud came in 944 to Constantinople, and in 1011 a copy was sent to Rome where it was known as the Veronica (true likeness) and began to be associated with the legend of St Veronica, who was said to have wiped Christ's face with her handkerchief and to have received a permanent image of him.

In 1203 the relic was being exhibited every Friday, to be worshipped. Then it disappeared, during the sack of Constantinople by the Crusaders, possibly remaining in the hands of the Knights Templar, and in particular Geoffrey de Charny; the Templars are traditionally supposed to have had a mysterious connection with Christ. Then, after the death of a later Geoffrey de Charny, it turned up in 1357, now the full-length Shroud, not the Mandylion portrait, in the new collegiate church of Lirey, in southern France, where it was exhibited to large crowds of pilgrims, and medals of it were struck. Two years later the Bishop of Troyes denounced it as a fraud perpetrated by an artist, an accusation which the Pope indignantly denied.

In 1449 a Margaret de Charny was exhibiting the Shroud in Liège, Belgium, and elsewhere. In 1460, after her death, it came into the hands of Duchess Bianca of Savoy, and found a home in the chapel of Chambéry castle. In 1532 a fire broke out there, but the cloth suffered only minor damage, and was repaired by nuns. There are records of its exhibition throughout the sixteenth and seventeenth centuries until, still in the hands of the House of Savoy, it came to Turin, and was shown there six times during the nineteenth century, being exposed to photography from 1898 onwards. At the 1973 showing to television and the Press various tests were taken.

Microscopic examination of the fibres showed that among the linen

threads there are minute traces of cotton. This proved conclusively that
the Shroud had been woven in the Middle East, since cotton is not grown
in Europe. In 1977 a group of scientists set themselves up as the Shroud
of Turin Research Project. Among their important discoveries was the fact
that the image on the Shroud was formed by a three-dimensional object; they
accordingly made a three-dimensional replica of the figure, and from a study
of this found that a piece of cloth had surrounded the head, passing under the
chin. This must have been a chin-band, the strip of linen used to keep the
mouth of the corpse closed, in accordance with Jewish burial customs.

Something else was revealed: the eyes had been covered by two small
objects – coins. Measurements showed them to be of the exact dimensions
of leptons, coins minted in the time of Pontius Pilate. Laboratory tests
showed no trace of blood on the cloth, nor any vestige of paint or dye,
thus putting paid to the theory that the Shroud was a fourteenth-century
forgery. The Bishop of Troyes had in 1359 condemned it as such, but
many faked shrouds, among other allegedly holy relics, were circulating at
that time, and the Bishop was seriously annoyed with the de Charny family
for going over his head to the Pope to ask permission for the Shroud to be
shown. He produced no evidence, and the charge was not investigated.
(There were, of course, no scientific tests at the time to settle the question
either way.)

Several facts about the man on the cross had now been revealed which
suggested an identification with a first-century crucifixion and burial. His
appearance is typically Jewish or Semitic, even to the long lock of hair
which falls over one shoulder – 'the most strikingly Jewish feature on the
Shroud' one expert called it. This fashion of wearing the hair, in a sort of
unbound pigtail, is typical of Jewish men of the period. The position of
the nail-wounds in the hands corresponds exactly with the findings on the
only known victim of crucifixion to have been exhumed – the skeleton of
one Jehohanan, found near the Damascus Gate of the Old City of Jeru-
salem. The nails had been driven not through his palms, but through the
wrists' end of the radius, as seen in the Shroud but not in conventional
paintings of the crucifixion. Nails through the palms would simply have
torn the flesh and allowed the arms to fall from the cross-bar.

The body of the Shroud victim had not, obviously, been washed, since
all the bloodstains were visible. The Jews always washed their dead before
burying them, but only if the body had not been moved, and never on the
Sabbath. St Luke tells us:

A man named Joseph ... of Arimathaea ... went to Pilate, and asked for the
body of Jesus. And he took it down, and wrapped it in a linen cloth, and laid him

in a tomb that was hewn in stone, where never man had yet lain. And it was the day of the Preparation, and the Sabbath drew on. And the women ... followed after, and beheld the tomb, and how his body was laid. And they returned, and prepared spices and ointments.

St John adds to this:

And there came also Nicodemus ... bringing a mixture of myrrh and aloes, about a hundred pound weight. So they took the body of Jesus, and bound it in linen cloths with the spices, as the custom of the Jews is to bury.

When, the day after the Sabbath, Mary Magdalen returned to the tomb, and found the stone rolled away from the mouth of it, she ran in panic to Simon Peter and John, who went back with her and entered the tomb:

And he beheld the linen cloths lying, and the napkin, that was upon his head, not lying with the linen cloths, but rolled up in a place by itself.

And seeing this, the two disciples 'believed'. Jesus had risen from the dead, as he had promised.

Many tests have now been made, with all the resources of science, yet no one can say conclusively how a dead body could possibly imprint its image upon the cloth in which it was shrouded. One theory is that it may have been produced by a 'vapourgraph', a chemical reaction between ammonia (proceeding from sweat) on the body, and aloes and olive oil on the linen. But much more widely believed is the theory that the image was imprinted by some process of scorching. The scorch-marks made by the fire of 1532 are not dissimilar to the colour-tones of the body 'portrait'. The theory is grimly supported by photographic images produced by the explosion of the first atomic bomb at Hiroshima – men and objects 'photographed' by radiation.

Could an extraordinarily powerful combination of light and heat have 'photographed' the body? Brilliant light is associated with the miraculous appearances of Jesus, as in the Transfiguration:

And after six days Jesus taketh with him Peter, and James, and John his brother, and bringeth them up into a high mountain apart: and he was transfigured before them: and his face did shine as the sun, and his garments became white as the light.

When the Mandylion portrait worked its first 'miracle', in Edessa, taken by the disciple Thaddeus to the paralysed King Abgar, the King saw an unbearably bright light streaming from the portrait Thaddeus carried and at once got up from his bed, cured of his disease.

It is a rational scientific guess, not fanciful speculation, that the image

Opposite: Pope John-Paul II examines the Shroud. Only he can give permission for the carbon-14 test to be carried out – which would instantly determine the date of the Shroud.

on the Shroud was created by some kind of thermo-nuclear flash. There seem to be no valid arguments against it, nor has any better theory so far been advanced. One test remains to be made that would instantly determine the date of the Shroud – the carbon-14 test. This would require a very small sample of the linen to be destroyed in the process. At the moment of writing, the decision to make the test rests entirely with the Pope, ex-King Umberto having died in 1983. If and when it is undertaken, a great mystery will be partly solved. If the image on the Shroud was not made by hands, how was it made? If the Shroud did not enfold the body of Jesus Christ, why has it been preserved as a most precious thing for almost two thousand years?

ATLANTIS REDISCOVERED?

Submerged in a single day and a night? A mighty continent sunk beneath the sea! Its population wiped out in an instant! What a stimulus to imagination; even to sheer lunacy. No wonder the famous legend of Atlantis has created a mystery which countless people have sought to solve.

The Greek philosopher Plato, who told the story, said that Atlantis lay outside the Mediterranean, beyond the Pillars of Hercules, as the gateway to the Atlantic was called in 345 BC, about the time he wrote. But modern geological research has shown that no great continent could have existed and become submerged in mid-Atlantic within human memory. So was Plato romancing? Or did he, as he emphatically stated, record history, confused and only half-remembered as it may have been? He gave as the source of his information his ancestor, Solon, who in 570 BC had visited Egypt where priests had instructed him in ancient history. After Plato's death the editor of his works, Crantor, sent inquiries to Egypt, to which the priests replied that the records of the lost continent were still extant 'on pillars'.

Using Solon's notes, Plato had composed two dialogues. In his shorter *Timaeus*, he described the island, or islands, of Atlantis as being as large as Libya (meaning North Africa, west of Egypt) and Asia Minor combined. Its king had founded a wonderful empire, extending into the western Mediterranean. Then came frightful earthquakes and inundations. Atlantis sank beneath the sea. That had happened 9,000 years before Solon's time.

Plato supplied greater detail in his *Critias*. The metropolis of the empire had been built on a small, round island, its coastline steep and precipitous. The royal palace, built on a second and much larger island, was a 'marvel to behold for size and beauty'. It was furnished with hot and cold baths. The temple, sacred to Poseidon, was resplendent with silver and gold. Every four or five years the kings gathered to administer the laws, and to hunt and sacrifice bulls. In course of time they became greedy and domineering, whereupon Zeus planned their destruction. Before this occurred an Athenian army which had gone out to fight the Atlanteans had been destroyed by a natural calamity. The Atlanteans had been contemplating war against Athens and Egypt.

Atlantis was a highly organized state, a land of conscious amenity, leisure, fine architecture, resplendent art, abundant public services, a Bronze Age society, literate, warlike, contemplating the conquest of Egypt and Athens. No such state existed 9,000 years before Solon's time. Either his priestly informants or Solon himself had confused the date, making the disaster occur millennia rather than centuries before 590 BC: 900 years is a far more realistic estimate. That would date the destruction of Atlantis to about 1500 BC. Although not yet a Greek city, Athens then existed, and Egypt was at the height of her power.

Where, then, was Atlantis? That it was not far from Greece and Athens is indicated by the apparent facts that the Atlanteans had contemplated their conquest, and that an Athenian army had set out to foil their designs. Nevertheless, Atlantis has been located in many places – in Mexico, Central Asia, the Sahara, Spain, Greenland, Newfoundland and even in Britain.

Geoffrey Ashe in *Camelot and the Vision of Albion* has presented the case for Britain, the land of the 'Hyperboreans' to the Greeks in Plato's time. It contained, according to the fifth-century-BC writer Hecataeus of Abdera, a unique shrine, the magnificent precinct of Apollo – possibly Stonehenge – and was inhabited by the 'fairest and noblest race of men that ever lived'. Britain was an Atlantic island, one of the several from which it was possible to pass to the opposite continent encircling the ocean, as Plato had described Atlantis. His topographical details seemed to fit the northern sea route to America via Iceland, Greenland and Newfoundland. Mr Ashe does not suggest that Britain became submerged, but rather that following considerable contact with the Aegean at about the time the building of Stonehenge was in progress, Britain became lost to view, swallowed up in the northern mists and forgotten. Plato, he thinks, adopted the romantic story of Britain's lost glory to portray his ideal state. However Ashe admits that the Cretan theories are more prevalent.

And possibly more persuasive. Can Minoan Crete be recognized as the seat of the Atlantean empire, the volcano Thera the cause of its decline? That possibility was first suggested in 1907 by the British scholar K.T. Frost. Sir Arthur Evans's excavations at Knossos in the 1920s, and the decipherment of the Linear B script by Michael Ventris and J. Chadwick in 1960, showed that the Minoan civilization of Crete collapsed suddenly at the height of its power and for no apparent reason in about 1500 BC. Significantly the volcanic Thera, 65 miles (104 kilometres) to the north of Crete, erupted catastrophically at that time.

In 1939 Professor Spyridon Marinatos, the chief of the Greek Archaeological Service, began his research to link the eruption of Thera and the end of Atlantis. Other scientists have contributed to the discussion, notably the American geologists Dr Ninkovitch and B.C. Heenen, who have dredged up cores of sediment containing volcanic ash from the sea-bed of the eastern Mediterranean, and Professor A.G. Galanopoulos, director of the Seismological Institute of the University of Athens. Their contributions have been summarized by Professor J.V. Luce, a specialist in Plato and classical studies.

The theory assumes that Crete was swamped by the tidal wave set up by Thera's catastrophic eruption, and the fertility of its soil ruined by heavy deposits of ash and pumice. The story of the disaster was carried by refugees to Egypt where, 900 years later, it was repeated in garbled form to Solon. He translated the Egyptian name of Keftui for Crete as Atlantis, derived from the description of that mountainous island as the 'land of the pillar', held up in the sky by the giant Titan, Atlas. Unaware that the story related to Crete, Plato located Atlantis outside the Mediterranean in the ocean also named after Atlas, in the belief that no Mediterranean power had been strong enough to have posed a threat to both Athens and Egypt.

To prove this theory, three questions require answers. What was the intensity of Thera's eruption? What evidence is there that Crete suffered from a volcanic disaster? What parallels exist between the civilizations of Minoan Crete and Plato's Atlantis?

Before the catastrophic eruption in the fifteenth century BC which wrecked it, Thera, or Santorin as it is now called, was one island, 10 miles (16 kilometres) in diameter, with a volcanic cone 5,250 feet (1,600 metres) in height. Its eruption may have been the greatest and most destructive of historical times, surpassing even Krakatoa's famous outburst in 1883. Whereas the island of Krakatoa, in the Sunda strait between Sumatra and Java, lost 8 square miles (21 square kilometres) – as is shown by the size of its caldera – Thera must have lost four times as much material, for its caldera comprises 32 square miles (83 square kilometres). A caldera is the

A landscape on Thera (present day Santorini), the volcanic island sixty-five miles north of Crete. The caldera on the right shows clearly the sequence of eruptions on its cliff-face. Could these eruptions, dated around 1500 B.C. and cataclysmic in force, have brought an end to Atlantis?

The relief head of a bull from the palace of Knossos. The hunting of bulls is one of many parallels which suggest Knossos may also have been the royal palace of Atlantis.

'cauldron' formed by the collapse of the magma chamber when it has become exhausted by eruption. The collapse forms a huge cavity into which the sea pours and is ejected with explosive violence.

In Krakatoa's case, the wave set up by the explosion swept across the strait, rising to the height of 120 feet (36 metres), submerging towns and villages and drowning many of the 36,000 victims of the disaster. It roared on around the world, raising the level of the English Channel by 2 inches (5 centimetres). The ejected pumice, the characteristic product of explosive magma, smothered Sumatra and Java and built floating islands in the sea. The ash formed a dust cloud which plunged the straits into darkness for three days and swept around the earth, lingering in the atmosphere for two years and causing climatic changes. Krakatoa's 'big bang' was heard 3,000 miles (4,800 kilometres) away across the Indian Ocean. Another Javanese volcano, Tambora, in 1815 deposited pumice and ash which destroyed the fertility of the land, causing the deaths of 80,000 people by starvation and disease.

Thera's collapse may have been even more prodigious, and so its effects far greater and more widespread. Excavations on Thera suggest that the island suffered disaster in two stages. First it was submerged beneath enormous quantities of pumice and volcanic ash. The volcano's debris destroyed the inhabitants' houses, which conformed to Minoan architecture and contained similar pots and frescoes. The removal of 65 feet (20 metres) of pumice has disclosed a Bronze Age Pompeii, a civilization similarly frozen in time, but without the bodies. No skeletons or personal treasures have been found at the lowest levels. Their absence suggests that the people of Thera, warned by the volcano's activity, had time to flee. They probably sought shelter in Crete, of which Thera was an outpost or colony.

Thera reached its peak some time between 1500 and 1470 BC, the period indicated by the pottery and the carbon-dating of timber recovered from the ruined buildings. The ancient volcano, its magma exhausted, blew its top. It exploded in violent paroxysm, plunging the eastern Mediterranean into darkness, its 'big bang' being heard probably from one end of that sea to the other. It set up a seismic wave, a giant *tsunami* as such waves are now called. Rising to prodigious height, perhaps hundreds of feet, it raced across the intervening sea, striking and inundating the coast of Crete.

Archaeological investigation has shown that every harbour, and every town and palace in eastern Crete, was suddenly destroyed and never rebuilt. Only Knossos, the capital, escaped, owing to its location some 3 miles (5 kilometres) inland where it was sheltered by a range of low hills.

Pumice and ash engulfed the fields, destroying their fertility. At Amnisos, the port of Knossos on the north coast, Professor Marinatos found evidence of the tidal wave. Buildings had been reduced to their foundations, sea-borne pumice had been forced into their crevices. The walls of the so-called Villa of Frescoes had collapsed inwards, sucked in by huge masses of receding water. The other harbours and towns so far excavated yield the same evidence of sudden destruction by water and falls of ash. The limestone gorge beside the naval base of Kato Zakro has retained its ancient name of the Valley of the Dead.

Before 1500 BC, Minoan Crete had dominated the eastern Mediterranean. So powerful was her navy that no land defences had been built. No state was capable of challenging her sea supremacy. Then, almost overnight, Crete collapsed. Shorn of her naval protection, her fertile soil rendered suddenly unproductive, she fell easy victim to the Mycenaean invaders from Greece. The once powerful Minoans succumbed to a natural calamity. No other conclusion seems possible.

Professor Luce has culled evidence from ancient myths and legends to show how widespread was the disaster caused by Thera. Greek poems mention the sudden depopulation of Crete. Herodotus stated that Crete had disappeared some time before the Trojan War, that is before 1400 BC. The legend of Deucalion's flood, dated in the Parian Marble at about 1529 BC, suggests that the mainland of Greece was also inundated, as were many Aegean islands. Plutarch records that on the island of Lycia Poseidon sent 'a wave which reared up and flooded the land'. Rhodes suffered a severe flood which caused heavy loss of life. Centuries later the Samothracians were still sacrificing on altars which had been set up in a circle round the island to mark the floodline of a great inundation from the sea. Even the famous Argonauts were caught in the aftermath of the disaster. Sailing past Crete, Jason and his crew were engulfed in awful darkness and bombarded by fragments of stone.

Egyptian texts supply no concrete information, probably because of the Egyptians' distaste for solid history. The Ipuwer Papyrus, however, indicates that trade with Crete was cut off suddenly about the time of Thera's eruption. This Egyptian silence seems strange, for Thera's eruptive violence should have been felt even at the distance of 650 miles (1,000 kilometres). Volcanic dust has been found in cores raised from the sea-bed close to Egypt. Several investigators have attributed the ten plagues of Egypt, the Israelites' crossing of the Sea of Passage, and the pillar of fire by night and the pillar of cloud by day, to Thera's eruption. But a date around 1470 BC seems far too early for the Exodus.

The vital question remains to be answered. Was Atlantis Crete? The parallels are remarkable. Both island civilizations disappeared suddenly as the result of a natural calamity.

Atlantis, according to Plato, was ruled by a monarchical and class system. Its women held high status, its people were literate, leisured, skilled in engineering, enjoying the comforts of hot and cold baths, regularly hunting bulls which ranged over a temple precinct. The islands were protected by precipitous cliffs, one island small and round, the other large and rectangular in shape.

Before Thera erupted, its island was small and round, possibly the legendary metropolis. Crete is long and thin, mountainous, with a large northern plain in which was set Knossos, the royal palace. King Minos ruled over a hundred towns. Every five years, as in Atlantis, their governors assembled to administer the laws and hunt the bulls which roamed the temple precinct. Legend tells that the Athenian Theseus came to Knossos to free his people from the tribute levied by Crete. He was forced to fight the legendary Minotaur, half-man, half-bull, and frescoes depict him dragging the slain bull from the labyrinth.

Sir Arthur Evans's excavation at Knossos disclosed a sophisticated culture, the most highly developed civilization of the ancient world, splendid in architecture, rich in artistry, elegant, leisured, yet centrally organized under a monarchy, with a code of laws giving equal status to women and dividing the classes. Springs provided hot water for baths, cold water for lavatories set in the palace walls. An extensive irrigation system ensured the soil's fertility. The Minoans' pottery, jars, weapons and frescoes are exhibited in the Herakleion museum.

Of the parallels between Crete and Atlantis, K.T. Frost had this to say in 1913, long before the two civilizations were compared. 'The whole description of Atlantis which is given in the *Timaeus* and *Critias* has features so thoroughly Minoan that even Plato could not have invented so many unsuspected facts.' Plato's account of the island which ruled over a great and wonderful empire precisely described the 'political status of Knossos'.

'The great harbour, for example, with its shipping and its merchants coming from all parts; the elaborate bathrooms, the stadium and the solemn sacrifice of bulls are all thoroughly, though not exclusively, Minoan: but when we read how the bull is hunted "in the temple of Poseidon without weapons but with staves and nooses", we have an unmistakable description of the bull ring at Knossos, the very thing which struck foreigners most and which gave rise to the legend of the Minotaur. Plato's words exactly describe the scenes on the famous Vapheio cups which certainly represent catching wild bulls for the Minoan bull fight; this, as

The bull-pit at Knossos. The Minoan bull-fight, like the one described by Plato, was remarkable in that no weapons were used.

we know from the palace itself, differed from all others which the world has seen in exactly the point which Plato emphasizes – namely that no weapons were used.'*

Young Frost did not live to see his theory vindicated. He was killed in the First World War. Plato, it seems, has also been vindicated, though he had no idea that he was accurately describing the civilization of Minoan Crete.

*K.T. Frost, 'The *Critias* and Minoan Crete', *Journal of Hellenic Studies* 33, 1913, pp. 189–206.

MYSTERIES OF THE SEA

THE *WARATAH* OMEN

The male passenger twisted restlessly in the narrow confines of his bunk, gripped by the growing menace of a dream. He had had the dream before, and his subconscious mind fought against it, because it anticipated the ending, which would jerk him wide awake, sweating and clutching at the sheets.

A few moments of wakefulness would be enough to relieve his mind. There would be no untoward sound or sensation to give his fear substance; the motion of the big steamship would not have changed. He was on his way home, to his wife, with no domestic or business worries to come flooding back into his waking mind and explain his agitation. Yet he knew, from several successive nights' experience, that when he fell asleep again his dream would recur; and although he was a seasoned voyager, in a modern, almost new ship, he would be scared for his life once more.

What he saw every time was himself standing at the ship's rail, staring out across a quiet sea. Suddenly, the surface would part, as there arose through it the anachronistic and out-of-place form of a medieval knight in armour. The armour would be stained with blood, unwashed-off by the sea, and the cloth which the figure held in one hand would be bloody too. The other hand would hold his drawn sword, brandished high.

It was not the threat of the sword or revulsion at the blood which petrified the dreamer – who was a down-to-earth businessman, by no means in the habit of retiring to bed having partaken of rich food and drink. What brought his dream to a climax, before the figure slid back under the sea, was its silent mouthing in his direction. One word only it repeated: '*Waratah! Waratah!*' – the syllables were quite distinct to him. Then it vanished, and the dreamer awoke. After lying petrified for a few minutes, he calmed down and told himself that enough was enough, and that when the ship put in at Durban soon, he would leave it and look for another to take him the rest of his way.

For the vessel in which he was at present sailing, and suffering that disquieting dream, was named *Waratah*.

The unhappy passenger was Claude G. Sawyer. This was his twelfth long voyage, a passage this time between Melbourne, Australia, and London, by way of South Africa.

The passenger and cargo steamer *Waratah*, 9,339 tons, was less than a year old: it was now July 1909, and she had been launched on the Clyde the previous October. Her maiden voyage had been to Australia with a full complement of the type of passengers she been designed to carry –

emigrants. It was a prosperous trade in those days, taking disenchanted British and Irish from the old world to the new land whose vast emptiness promised such contrast after the squalid overcrowding of ancient slums. Most of them travelled in dormitories in the holds, spacious and comfortable compared with what they had left behind. The smaller number who could afford to pay for luxury got it, in the form of very well-appointed cabins and public rooms, including a music lounge complete with minstrels' gallery and the subtlety of the new concept of concealed lighting.

Mr Sawyer was one of this privileged minority, travelling expenses-paid, his passage booked right through to London at no cost to him – yet when *Waratah* called at Durban, her first landfall on the African coast, he could scarcely wait to go ashore, taking his baggage with him.

Fellow-passengers who watched him descend the gangway shrugged or smiled. He was a crank, they agreed. Some of them had heard his story of the spectral knight from his own lips; others had had it passed on to them. If he had been seen to be a boozing type, they would have put it down to incipient DTs. He was not, though, so he must be a bit of a nut. When *Waratah*'s master, Captain Josiah Ilbery, had heard what this cabin passenger had been saying, he declared that it must stop. As a commodore of the Blue Anchor Line, with forty years' sea service in steam and sail, he did not personally condescend to soothe Mr Sawyer's uneasiness, but deputed an officer to go and warn him that spreading alarm and despondency was not a good thing, so, with the captain's compliments, would he kindly leave off. Mr Sawyer did more than that – he *got* off, at the first opportunity.

Once ashore, he sent his wife a telegram to explain why he had chosen to delay his homecoming by waiting for another ship. He said nothing of bloodstained knights arising from the sea – she, too, might have feared that he had taken to drink, or suffered a brainstorm. All the reason he gave was that he thought the *Waratah* was a top-heavy ship. As an engineer, Mr Sawyer perhaps had some knowledge of such things, centres of gravity and so forth. He may only have been referring to what he had heard others say, though, for want of any other reason to give his wife short of scaring her with his apparition. Certainly, the suggestion that *Waratah* was top-heavy had been made. When she rolled, it had been observed, she rolled spectacularly, a deep roll so prolonged as to be almost a comfortable experience, provided one was hanging on securely to something fixed.

Sportier passengers on opposite sides of the steeply tilting decks when such a roll occurred exchanged greetings with their opposites. 'How are you up there?' 'Lovely view. Your turn next.' It was as if the ship reached a point of balance from which she was reluctant to rise, but would have preferred to stay keeled over like a racing yacht. When she did at last right herself, though, it was with a less pleasant sensation. She came up with a jerk, which sent objects and unwary passengers flying, injuring some.

The professionals aboard her, the officers and seamen, were divided over her behaviour. 'Dead on the roll' was the graphically descriptive expression which came readily to the lips of older hands. For a number of them, the maiden voyage had been enough. They left her in Australia and looked for berths in other ships. For every one of them, though, there was another less apprehensive, who believed that any slight aberrations about the stability of a new ship, with characteristics of her own, would soon be settled by learning just how best to stow her and trim her ballast.

The Board of Trade had passed her. She bore the top rating of Lloyd's of London, and had been separately examined by the emigration authorities, who certified her totally acceptable to carry large numbers of emigrants on the long and often dangerous route between England and Australia by way of the Cape of Good Hope.

The carrying of emigrants was, of course, a largely one-way trade; yet with Australia already a thoroughly established colony, with its bigger cities quite populous, a good return business had developed. Ships which went out there full could reckon on coming back with at least half their accommodation taken and enough cargo to make the voyage pay. When *Waratah* had slipped her moorings for this second homeward journey, she had on board her over 200 passengers and crew and a 6,500-ton cargo. She left Adelaide, the last of her Australian ports of call, on 7 July, and reached Durban on the 25th, which was when Mr Sawyer disembarked. She sailed again the following evening, about to round the Cape of Good Hope on the way to Cape Town, 600 miles and three days' steaming away.

Increasing numbers of new ships had been equipped with radio by 1909, but not *Waratah*. Once she left a port, she was on her own, except for encounters at sea with other vessels, at which they 'spoke' to one another for weather information and greeting. The only one to encounter the *Waratah* on that often-hazardous stretch in the Cape region was the tramp steamer *Clan MacIntyre* making for East London, not far off. *Clan MacIntyre* had left Durban before the big ship, but her speed was nothing to the other's capability of 13 knots, and she was overhauled abeam of the Bashee River at about 6 a.m. on the 27th. They spoke by lamp, a brief exchange, before the big ship sped on and by 9.30 was out of sight.

It took the tramp steamer longer than anticipated to make East London though. The wind, which had been gentle north-easterly, suddenly died, to be replaced by a violent sou'wester. It was a typical phenomenon of the 'Cape of Storms', and it buffeted and tossed the small craft ceaselessly until that evening.

The newly launched liner *Waratah*, which disappeared without trace off the South African coast in July 1909, after a strange warning.

At about 9.30 p.m., further down the coast near East London, a Union Castle liner, *Guelph*, sailing eastward, sighted a large passenger ship about five miles away, going in the opposite direction. They too spoke by lamp, but the faint signal from the west-bound ship was too indistinct to be read, except for the last three letters of her name: '...*tah*'.

Waratah did not arrive at Cape Town on her due date, 29 July. No one was unduly concerned, though. The storm which the *Clan MacIntyre* and other shipping in the vicinity had just been through had been one of the worst in most people's memory. The tramp steamer had been blown backwards at times. Even a big twin-screw liner would make heavy going of such conditions. However, if Captain Culverwell of the *Guelph* had known that the liner he had spoken with unsuccessfully had been the *Waratah*, and had been aware that she had passed the *Clan MacIntyre* some fifteen hours earlier, yet had accomplished only seventy miles since, he might have suspected that something else was amiss. But there had been no signal for help, and the sighting had not even been thought worth noting in *Guelph*'s log.

Other vessels entering Cape Town had nothing to report of the *Waratah*. The insurance agents began to feel troubled. They told local shipping reporters that while several days overdue would be unremarkable for most shipping in such conditions, it seemed 'an unusual event' for a liner as well found and owned as *Waratah* to be so late.

Perhaps even the materialists of the insurance world would have been more concerned if they had known that Mr Claude Sawyer, who by now had resumed his homeward passage in a Union Castle ship, had had another and even more dramatic dream while staying in a Durban hotel. As he had told the Union Castle Line's local manager next morning, he had clearly seen the *Waratah* with her bows engulfed in big waves. One of them 'pressed her down. She rolled over on her starboard side and disappeared'. The night he had dreamed that had been 28 July – the date on which, unknown to him, *Waratah* vanished.

Two tugs were sent to search, but found nothing. Concern began to mount in both Cape Town and London. On Admiralty orders, the cruisers *Pandora* and *Forte* were ordered to sea, while all other shipping was alerted to look out for the liner, no doubt disabled and drifting, unable to tell her plight. Uneasy realization grew that an unpreventable drift could have carried her beyond where she would be likely to encounter any other shipping, far south-eastward towards the Antarctic region. A third cruiser, HMS *Hermes*, joined the search, over a considerably extended area.

The reason why hope endured that *Waratah* was intact and had suffered no disaster was that no scrap of wreckage, nor any of her plenteous lifeboats and rafts, had appeared. More terrible weather hampered the search, driving the smaller vessels back to port and so seriously straining *Hermes*'s hull that the cruiser had to be dry-docked.

There was not long to wait, though, before reports of debris and bodies came, from two sources. An apprentice in the steamship *Tottenham* claimed to have spotted a little girl in a red dressing-gown, dead in the sea about 350 miles from Durban. His second mate corroborated this, adding that the child had worn black stockings under bare knees, and that she would be ten or twelve years old. The *Tottenham*'s master had put his ship about and had stopped to examine the 'body' from over the side. The red-gowned child was nothing more than a roll of printing paper in a red wrapping. Other 'bodies' proved to be blubber, a not uncommon sight in waters where whalers often dumped useless portions.

More 'bodies' in that same vicinity were reported by the steamer *Insizwa*. Again, no tangible evidence was produced, for no boat had been lowered. A Cape Town newspaper reporter asked the master why: because his ship was already listing slightly in the heavy sea, due to shifted cargo, and anyway, he had female passengers whom he did not wish to distress.

The reporter took the statement to the Colonial Secretary, seeking official comment. The captain's evidence was accepted, and the report went into print, while a tug was sent to search the area thoroughly and bring any bodies back. By the time it returned, having found nothing but more blubber, the master of the *Insizwa* had decided that he might have been mistaken, possibly at the prompting of the ship's owners, who did not want their captain and crew kept from their duties by having to wait to attend any inquiry.

No wreckage or bodies ever turned up, merely some palpably faked messages in bottles. The missing ship was known to be provisioned for a year, but the thought of her drifting helplessly towards frozen wastes, with more than 200 souls aboard, was a piteous one. Services of intercession were held. Clairvoyants were asked to try to 'see' her. Claims and counterclaims about her top-heavy construction, her sailing characteristics, and the state of her cargo appeared in the newpapers of Australia, South Africa and Great Britain, as former crew members and passengers gave their opinions. Mr Sawyer's dreams were much cited, together with disclosures from officers whose more knowledgeable foresight had decided them to leave the ship before that last voyage, warning others that they could be sailing into danger.

The weight of expert opinion rejected the notion of a large liner floating silently with the tides while those aboard eked out their supplies, and died, one by one, as hunger, cold and despair intensified. The strongest belief was that *Waratah* had gone down in that violent storm, failing to recover from one of those steep rolls, turning turtle, and plunging to the depths. Everyone would have been indoors in such weather, everything would have been secured, so no bodies would have floated free.

The Board of Trade inquiry was not held until December 1910, almost a year and a half after the disappearance. In all that time, not a scrap of concrete evidence had appeared. The inquiry spent weeks listening to everyone with anything to say, even including a confessed stowaway on *Waratah*'s maiden voyage who admitted having been frightened by the way she rolled. There was talk of bad design, bad workmanship, bad loading, bad weather, all countered by insistences that there had been nothing wrong with *Waratah* at all: she had been a fine ship, a pleasure to sail in.

No one's evidence was more quietly impressive than Mr Claude G. Sawyer's. His story of his dreams was exactly as it always had been, moving the court to congratulate him for coming forward at the risk of exposing himself to widespread mockery for sticking to so fanciful-sounding a yarn.

The findings, not announced until 22 February 1911, could only be, in short, that *Waratah* had capsized suddenly in an exceptional gale and been lost with all aboard her.

It all happened more than seventy years ago, possibly not very far from the South African coast, in waters where Second World War U-boat packs prowled and sent many another ship to the bottom. Perhaps it was one of these later victims which a South African Air Force pilot reported seeing lying on its side in clear water in 1952. A further search revealed nothing, but refuelled the *Waratah* story yet again.

It continues to recur, with theories of 'killer' waves rearing many times the height of even the largest ships; of 'holes' which open in the sea and literally swallow a vessel at a gulp. Newer and newer techniques will perhaps some day lead to the finding of the *Waratah*, and indeed the cause of the disaster. What is the betting that it will be as Mr Sawyer saw it in his dream, with a colossal wave having crashed over her bows and 'pressed her down'? By the time that is ascertainable, we shall perhaps also have advanced enough to accept that a bloodied medieval knight could rise from an ocean to give a dreaming man a warning that would save his life.

THE BERMUDA TRIANGLE

5 December 1945 was a warm, clear day in Fort Lauderdale, Florida, and when five Avenger torpedo-bombers roared into the sky on a routine patrol that afternoon there was no conceivable reason to anticipate trouble. All had been carefully checked and refuelled; all carried radios and the latest navigation equipment, developed and tested during the Second World War. By 2.15 p.m. the planes had disappeared into the sky east of Florida; they were due back in two hours. But an hour and a half later the control tower heard a worried voice saying: 'This is an emergency. We seem to be off course. We cannot see land ... repeat ... we cannot see land.'

'What is your position?' asked the tower.

'We're not sure of our position. We can't be sure where we are. We seem to be lost.'

It was baffling and incomprehensible. It was about as likely that a squadron of planes could get lost off the coast of Florida as that a nanny pushing a pram should get lost in Hyde Park on a Sunday afternoon.

'Head due west,' said the control tower.

'We don't know which way *is* west. Everything is wrong, strange. We can't be sure of any direction. Even the ocean doesn't look as it should.'

The tower was mystified. Even if a magnetic storm had affected the compasses, surely the pilots only had to fly towards the sun in order to cross the Florida coastline?

At 4 o'clock the flight-leader decided to hand over to someone else. At 4.25, the new leader told the tower: 'We're not certain where we are.'

Unless the planes could find their way back over land during the next four hours, they would run out of fuel, and be forced to land in the sea. A rescue mission was launched. A few hours after this last message, a giant Martin Mariner flying-boat, with a crew of thirteen, took off towards the last reported position of the flight. Neither the Martin Mariner nor the five Avengers ever returned. They vanished completely, as other planes and ships have vanished in the area that has become known as 'the Devil's Triangle' and 'the Bermuda Triangle'.

But *what* finally happened to them is no mystery. The weather became worse during the course of the afternoon; ships reported 'high winds and tremendous seas'. Flight 19 and its would-be rescuer must have run out of fuel, and landed on the sea. The mystery is *why* they became so completely lost and confused.

It seems odd that this tragedy should have failed to alert the authorities that there was something frightening and dangerous about the stretch of ocean between Florida and the Bahamas – a chain of islands that begins a mere fifty miles off the coast of Florida. But then, the authorities no doubt took the view of many more recent sceptics: that the disappearance was a rather complex accident, due to a number of chance factors: bad weather, electrical interference with compasses, the inexperience of some of the pilots (four of them were trainees) and the fact that the flight-leader, Charles Taylor, had only recently been posted to Fort Lauderdale and was therefore not as familiar with the terrain as he might have been. As to the Martin Mariner, an explosion reported at 7.50 that evening, twenty-three minutes after the Mariner had taken off, could have been due to petrol fumes and a lighted cigarette. . . .

Similar explanations were adopted to explain a number of similar tragedies during the next two decades: the disappearance of a Superfortress in 1947, of a four-engined Tudor IV in January 1948, of a DC-3 in December 1948, of another Tudor IV in 1949, of a Globemaster in 1950, of a British York transport plane in 1952, of a Navy Super Constellation in 1954, of another Martin seaplane in 1956, of an Air Force tanker in 1962, of two new Stratotankers in 1963, of a flying boxcar in 1965, of a civilian cargo plane in 1966, another cargo plane in 1967, and yet another in 1973. . . . The total number of lives lost in all these disappearances was well in excess of two hundred.

Oddly enough, the first person to realize that all this amounted to a terrifying mystery was a journalist called Vincent Gaddis; it was in February 1964 that his article 'The Deadly Bermuda Triangle' appeared in the American *Argosy* magazine, and bestowed the now-familiar name on that mysterious stretch of ocean. A year later, in a book about sea mysteries called *Invisible Horizons*, Gaddis included his article in a chapter called 'The Triangle of Death'. His chapter also contained a long list of ships which had vanished in the area, beginning with the *Rosalie*, which vanished in 1840, and ending with the yacht *Connemara IV* in 1956. In the final chapter, Gaddis entered the realm of science fiction, and speculated on 'space-time continua [that] may exist around us on the earth, interpenetrating our known world', implying that perhaps some of the missing planes and ships had vanished down a kind of fourth-dimensional plughole.

Soon after the publication of his book, Gaddis received a letter from a man called Gerald Hawkes, who told of his own experience in the Bermuda Triangle in April 1952. He was on a flight from Idlewild Airport (now Kennedy) to Bermuda when the plane suddenly dropped about two hundred feet – not in a nose-dive, but as if falling down some strange

The U.S. Navy supply ship *Cyclops*, whose disappearance without even a distress call remains one of the most baffling mysteries in the annals of the Navy.

The British South American Airways Tudor IV 'Star Tiger' en route to Bermuda – and oblivion.

lift-shaft in the air; then the plane shot back up again. 'It was as if a giant hand was holding the plane and jerking it up and down,' and the wings seemed to flap like the wings of a bird. The captain then told them that he was unable to find Bermuda, and that the operator was unable to make radio contact with either the US or Bermuda. An hour or so later, the plane made contact with a radio ship, and was able to get its bearings and fly to Bermuda. As they climbed out of the plane they observed that it was a clear and starry night, with no wind. The writer concluded that he was still wondering whether he was caught in an area 'where time and space seem to disappear'.

Now all pilots know about air pockets, where a sudden change in pressure causes the plane to lurch and fall, and about air turbulence which causes the wings of a plane to 'flap'. What seems odd about this case is the total radio blackout.

This was an anomaly that had also struck students of UFOs – or flying saucers – who had been creating extraordinary theories ever since that day in June 1947 when a pilot named Kenneth Arnold saw nine shining discs moving against the background of Mount Rainier in Washington State. The flying saucer enthusiasts now produced the interesting notion that the surface of our earth has a number of strange 'vortices', whirlpools where gravity and terrestrial magnetism are inexplicably weaker than usual. And if extra-terrestrial intelligences happened to know about these whirlpools, they might well find them ideal for collecting human specimens to be studied at leisure on their distant planet. . . .

Ivan Sanderson, a friend of Gaddis's and a student of earth mysteries, felt that this was going too far. His training had been scientific, so he began by taking a map of the world, and marking on it a number of areas where strange disappearances had occurred. There was, for example, another 'Devil's Triangle' south of the Japanese island of Honshu where ships and planes had vanished. A correspondent told Sanderson about a strange experience on a flight to Guam, in the west Pacific, when his ancient propeller-driven plane covered 340 miles in one hour, although there was no wind – about 200 miles more than it should have covered; checks showed that many planes had vanished in this area.

Marking these areas on the map, Sanderson observed that they were shaped like lozenges, and that these lozenges seemed to ring the globe in a neat symmetry, running in two rings, each between 30° and 40° north and south of the equator. There were ten of these 'funny places', about 72° apart. An earthquake specialist named George Rouse had argued that earthquakes originated in a certain layer below the earth's surface, and had speculated that there was a kind of trough running round the central core of the earth, which determined the direction of seismic activities. Rouse's map of these seismic disturbance areas corresponded closely with Sanderson's 'lozenges'. So Sanderson was inclined to believe that if 'whirlpools' really caused the disappearance of ships and planes, then they were perfectly normal physical whirlpools, caused, so to speak, by the earth's tendency to 'burp'.

Sanderson's theory appeared in a book entitled *Invisible Residents* in 1970. Three years later a female journalist, Adi-Kent Thomas Jeffrey, tried to put together all the evidence about the Bermuda Triangle in a book of that name, printed by a small publishing company in Pennsylvania. It was undoubtedly her bad luck that her book failed to reach the general public. For one year later Charles Berlitz, grandson of the man who founded the famous language schools, once again rehashed all the information about the Bermuda Triangle, persuaded a commercial publisher – Doubleday – to issue it, and promptly rocketed to the top of the American best-seller lists. It had been twenty years since the disappearance of Flight 19, and ten years since Vincent Gaddis invented the phrase 'Bermuda Triangle'. But Berlitz was the first man to turn it into a worldwide sensation, and to become rich on the proceeds.

Berlitz's *Bermuda Triangle*, while highly readable, is low on scholarly precision – it does not even have an index. One reason for its popularity was that he launched himself intrepidly into bizarre regions of speculation about UFOs, space-time warps, alien intelligences, chariots of the gods (*à la* Von Däniken) and other such matters. And among the weirdest of his speculations were those concerning the pioneer 'Ufologist' Morris K. Jessup, who had died in mysterious circumstances after stumbling upon information about a certain mysterious 'Philadelphia experiment'. This experiment was supposed to have taken place in Philadelphia in 1943, when the Navy was testing some new device whose purpose was to surround a ship with a powerful magnetic field. According to Jessup's informant, a hazy green light began to surround the vessel, so its outlines became blurred; then it vanished – to reappear in the harbour of Norfolk, Virginia, a thousand miles away. Several members of the crew died; others went insane. According to Jessup, when he began to investigate this story, the Navy asked him whether he would be willing to work on a similar secret project; he declined. In 1959, he was found dead in his car, suffocated by exhaust gas; Berlitz speculates that he was 'silenced' before he could publicize his discoveries about the experiment.

And what has all this to do with the Bermuda Triangle? Simply that the Philadelphia experiment was supposed to be an attempt to create a magnetic vortex, like those suggested by Sanderson, and that (according to

Jessup) it had the effect of involving the ship in a space-time warp that transported it a thousand miles.

Understandably, this kind of thing roused sceptics to a fury, and there were suddenly a large number of articles, books and television programmes all devoted to debunking the Bermuda Triangle. These all adopted the commonsense approach that had characterized the Naval authorities in 1945: that is to say, they assumed that the disappearances were all due to natural causes, particularly to freak storms. In many cases it is difficult not to agree that this is, indeed, the most plausible explanation. But when we look at the long list of disappearances in the area, most of them never even yielding a body or a trace of wreckage, the explanation begins to sound thin.

Is there, then, an alternative which combines commonsense with the boldness necessary to recognize that all the disappearances cannot be conveniently explained away? There is, and it rests on the evidence of some of those who have escaped the Bermuda Triangle. In November 1964 a charter pilot named Chuck Wakely was returning from Nassau to Miami, Florida, and had climbed up to 8,000 feet. He noticed a faint glow round the wings of his plane, which he put down to some optical illusion caused by cockpit lights. But the glow increased steadily, and all his electronic equipment began to go wrong. He was forced to operate the craft manually. The glow became so blinding that he was dazzled; then, slowly, it faded, and his instruments began to function normally again.

In 1966 Captain Don Henry was steering his tug from Puerto Rico to Fort Lauderdale on a clear afternoon. He heard shouting, and hurried to the bridge. There he saw that the compass was spinning clockwise. A strange darkness came down, and the horizon disappeared: 'The water seemed to be coming from all directions.' And although the electric generators were still running, all electric power faded away. An auxiliary generator refused to start. The boat seemed to be surrounded by a kind of fog. Fortunately the engines were still working, and suddenly the boat emerged from the fog. To Henry's amazement, the fog seemed to be concentrated into a single solid bank, and within this area the sea was turbulent; outside it was calm. Henry remarked that the compass behaved as it did on the St Lawrence River at Kingston, where some large deposit of iron – or a meteorite – affects the needle.

Our earth is, of course, a gigantic magnet (no one quite knows why), and the magnetic lines of force run around its surface in strange patterns. Birds and animals use these lines of force for 'homing', and water diviners seem able to respond to them with their 'dowsing rods'. But there are areas of the earth's surface where birds lose their way because the lines somehow

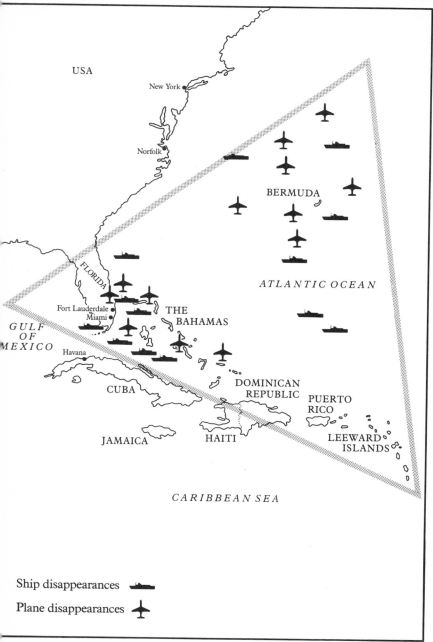

A map of 'the Bermuda Triangle'. The numerous instances of compass failure, radio blackouts, loss of electric power and disappearances are difficult to explain away.

cancel one another out, forming a magnetic anomaly or vortex. The *Marine Observer* for 1930 warns sailors about a magnetic disturbance in the neighbourhood of the Tambora volcano, near Sumbawa, which deflected a ship's compass by six points, leading it off course. In 1932 Captain Scutt of the SS *Australia* observed a magnetic disturbance near Fremantle that deflected the compass 12° either side of the ship's course. Dozens of similar anomalies have been collected and documented by an American investigator, William Corliss, in books with titles like *Unknown Earth* and *Strange Planet*. It was Corliss who pointed out to me the investigations of Dr John de Laurier of Ottawa, who in 1974 went to camp on the ice-floes of northern Canada in search of an enormous magnetic anomaly, 43 miles long, which he believes to originate about 18 miles below the surface of the earth. De Laurier's theory is that such anomalies are due to the earth's tectonic plates rubbing together – an occurrence that also causes earthquakes.

The central point to emerge from all this is that our earth is not like an ordinary bar magnet, whose field is symmetrical and precise; it is full of magnetic 'pitfalls' and anomalies. Scientists are not sure why the earth has a magnetic field, but one theory suggests that it is due to movements in its molten iron core. Such movements would, in fact, produce shifting patterns in the earth's field, and bursts of magnetic activity, which might be compared to the bursts of solar energy known as sunspots. If they *are* related to earth-tensions – and therefore to earthquakes – then we would expect them to occur in certain definite zones, just as earthquakes do. What effect would a sudden 'earthquake' of magnetic activity produce? One would be to cause compasses to spin, for it would be rather as if a huge magnetic meteor was roaring up from the centre of the earth. On the sea it would produce an effect of violent turbulence, for it would affect the water in the same way the moon affects the tides, but in an irregular pattern, so that the water would appear to be coming 'from all directions'. Clouds and mist would be sucked into the vortex, forming a 'bank' in its immediate area. And electronic gadgetry would probably be put out of action. . . .

Now, as we near the end of the twentieth century, we at last have the means of testing such hypotheses. With satellites circling the earth at a height of 150 miles, it should be possible to observe such bursts of magnetic activity with the same accuracy that earth tremors are recorded on seismographs. We should be able to observe their frequency and intensity precisely enough to plot them in advance. In which case, we shall not only have solved the mystery of the Devil's Triangle, but – perhaps more important – learned how to prevent such tragedies in the future.

THE *MARY CELESTE*

On 15 November 1872 the brigantine *Dei Gratia* slipped away from her berth in New York harbour on passage for the Mediterranean. She was carrying a cargo of kerosene which was to be unloaded at Genoa. But before that her master, David Reed Morehouse, had to put in at Gibraltar for more detailed instructions.

Morehouse had commanded his first ship at the unusually young age of twenty-one. Now in his mid-thirties, this bewhiskered Nova Scotian was a veteran of the Atlantic trade, and this crossing was to be as bad as any he could remember. Strong winds, heavy seas and often poor visibility plagued him and his crewmen until 4 December, a Wednesday. That morning the white-topped waves were replaced by a long, rolling swell. The clouds yielded to the sun for the first time, and prospects generally seemed to be improving.

The *Dei Gratia* was now 350 miles beyond Santa Maria, the most easterly of the Azores, and about 600 miles from Gibraltar. At noon the first mate, Oliver Deveau, took over the watch. A seaman named John Johnson relieved the helmsman.

Morehouse was on deck. Round about one o'clock, he noticed a sail five miles away on the starboard bow. As the vessel drew closer, he studied her through his telescope. His interest quickened: something about her seemed to be wrong. She was sailing badly with a tendency to yaw. The gap narrowed. Now he could see evidence that accounted for her behaviour. Her mainsail was furled, and she was under very short canvas. In view of the recent bad weather, this was not, perhaps, surprising. But the upper-fore-topsail appeared to have been blown away, and the lower-fore-topsail was in bad shape. Whilst the standing rigging looked to be in tolerably good repair, the running rigging had been carried away. A sail, which looked as if it had been taken in hurriedly, was lying in an unseamanlike manner on the roof of the forward deckhouse.

Such matters were enough in themselves to arouse his curiosity, but the really strange thing was that her deck was deserted. There was nobody at the wheel; nobody standing duty as look-out; no trace of anyone. Obviously she was in difficulties, and Morehouse ordered Johnson to steer towards her. Once he was within hailing distance, he shouted an offer of assistance. There was no reply. He turned to Deveau. He was to take two men with him; row across to the ship and investigate.

Deveau and his assistants spent the better part of half-an-hour on board. There was neither sight nor sound of any living creature. They began their search in the forward deckhouse, which served as the galley. There was no cooked food to be seen, though they found ample supplies of drinking water and sufficient stores to last six months. This, in itself, may not have been remarkable, but the fact that the deck was awash with several inches of water surely was.

Outside, a spar of wood had been lashed across the davits at the stern from which, normally, the longboat would have been suspended. A length of rope with a frayed end dangled over the counter. Of the other boat, there was no trace. The compass had been removed from the binnacle: and, whilst the main hatch was snugly in position, the fore and after hatches had been removed. A sounding-rod lay beside one of them, and Deveau measured the depth of water in the hold. It was three feet: nothing remarkable for a vessel of this construction – the pumps could have coped with it quite easily.

Down below he noticed that the seamen's oilskins, seaboots, and tobacco pipes were all present. The captain's bunk had not been made up: there was a small impression upon it – as if a child had lain there. The sheets and blankets were wet, but this was not surprising: the skylight had been left open.

On one of the bulkheads a chart recorded the ship's progress. On the desk, the logbook lay open. The last entry, dated 7 November, noted that force 7 winds had forced the crew to shorten sail. Nearby, the sighting of Santa Maria had been jotted down on a slate, but this had not been entered into the book. A quick calculation suggested that since the seventh the ship had continued on her course for several days – and then doubled back in a north-westerly direction. Finally, Deveau noticed that all the navigating instruments had been removed.

Deveau and the two sailors returned to the *Dei Gratia*. The damage, he told Captain Morehouse, was not serious: there seemed to be no reason why, crewed by himself and a couple of hands, she would not be able to follow the brigantine to Gibraltar. As he was quick to point out, there should be a tidy sum of salvage money waiting to be claimed.

Morehouse demurred. Conditions had been bad enough already, and there was no knowing what might lie ahead. He could well need a full crew. Deveau argued with him; and in the end Morehouse's business sense prevailed. Accompanied by Charles Lund and Augustus Anderson, Deveau made his way back to the abandoned ship. The boat passed close beneath her stern. Upon it were painted the words 'Mary Celeste, New York'.

It took Deveau and his men two days to repair the damage. On 13 December the *Mary Celeste* docked at Gibraltar after a trip in which, despite heavy rainstorms as she approached the Rock, she had given no trouble at all. She was promptly impounded until Captain Morehouse's salvage claim had been investigated by the Admiralty court. He and his men had hoped to be rewarded with something in the region of $80,000. They were to be disappointed. The assessors put the value of the *Mary Celeste* and her cargo at $42,643, and awarded them one-fifth of this amount – $8,528. It was generally agreed that this was a good deal less than generous.

Had cheque-book journalism been established at this time, Captain Morehouse and his crew might have fared very much better. Stories about the mystery of the *Mary Celeste* – some of them supposedly factual, and many of them frankly fictional – appeared in profusion. Most of them were inaccurate to a fault. For example, in the May 1884 issue of the *Cornhill Magazine*, a story by Arthur Conan Doyle entitled 'J. Habakuk Jephson's Statement' appeared. It was a mixture of reportage and a lavish helping of Conan Doyle's imagination. Whether by error or design, he named the ship *Marie Celeste*. The mistake, if such it was, has endured. Even nowadays, 'Marie' is more likely to be used than the correct 'Mary'.

The ship's crew has, times without number, been listed as thirteen – whilst seven was the actual figure. In one or two accounts the first mate has been given the role of a mass murderer who stalks sinisterly through the narrative. He kills all his shipmates – and then either commits suicide or else makes off to South America aboard another vessel. In fact, this officer was a perfectly respectable New Englander named Albert G. Richardson, who had fought as an infantryman in the Civil War before going to sea.

Those on board the *Mary Celeste* have variously been devoured by sharks; abandoned ship after collision with a giant squid; been eaten by presumably fastidious sea monsters that took care not to inflict too much other damage; been the victims of piracy; and even been in collusion with the *Dei Gratia*'s master in an elaborate plot to gain the salvage money.

Some years ago a group of schoolboys in Natal claimed that they had been in touch with the *Mary Celeste*'s captain during one of those essays in the occult where a tumbler spins round the table picking out letters. If this was so, the master mariner's memory must have been impaired by his experience. The gist of his story was that he and his companions had been watching the antics of a whale when the mainsail's boom swung across the deck and swept all of them except the helmsman overboard. This man promptly secured the wheel, launched a boat, and rowed out in an attempt to rescue the others. Unhappily, by the time he had scooped them out of the sea, the *Mary Celeste* had wandered on her way and they were unable to catch up with her.

Had the dead captain recalled events better, he would have known that

The half-brig *Amazon*, later re-named *Mary Celeste*, in 1861. *Below:* The *Mary Celeste* as she appeared when first sighted by the *Dei Gratia*, on 4 December 1872. Painting by Rudolph Ruzeika.

Captain David Reed Morehouse, master of the *Dei Gratia*, whose discovery of the *Mary Celeste* unfairly brought suspicion on him and his crew.

since the mainsail was furled, its boom could not have swung across the deck; that it would have been impossible for one man to launch the boat; and that the wheel, as discovered by the trio from the *Dei Gratia*, was not secured.

Before the First World War some papers were discovered in a North London house. They belonged, it was alleged, to a man who had actually been a survivor. Since his name did not appear on the crew manifest, they were obviously open to suspicion – and rightly so. The notion they put forward was that the captain had dived into the sea for a swim. Everyone else was perched on a precarious platform erected over the stern, watching him. This ill-constructed vantage point collapsed and they fell overboard. This was the cue for a family of sharks to appear on the scene. Having, presumably, good appetites, they made short work of their victims – though, unaccountably, they overlooked the narrator. Clinging to a spar of wood, he drifted for goodness knows how many hundred miles – until he was washed up on an African shore. If, as seems possible, this was a short story intended for publication, its very improbability must have made a rejection slip inevitable.

What, then, do we know about the *Mary Celeste*? Her keel was laid in Nova Scotia in 1860. When she was launched, she was named *Amazon*. She was rigged as a brigantine, and later changed to an hermaphrodite brig: i.e., to a two-masted sailing ship with a square rig on the foremast and a square topsail as well as a gaff mainsail on the mainmast. She was originally owned by a consortium of sailors and businessmen. She carried timber to London, corn from Baltimore to Halifax, and she made several voyages to the West Indies.

Some ships are considered to be lucky; others are not. The *Mary Celeste* fell into the latter category. Her first captain died shortly after his appointment. On her maiden voyage she collided with a fishing-boat and received a large gash in her hull. While she was undergoing repairs, a fire broke out and wrought even worse havoc. Her new master was dismissed, and she eventually set off across the Atlantic under yet another captain. This voyage was about as disastrous as any can be – short of actually foundering. In the Dover Strait *en route* to London, she crashed into a brig and suffered a good deal of damage. While this was being put right, captain number three was relieved of his command, and captain number four took over. If anyone hoped that this might be a change for the better, he was to be disappointed. On the return voyage, she ran aground off Cape Breton in Nova Scotia. Damage to the cost of $16,000 was inflicted; her owners went bankrupt; and she was sold by public auction. It was at this point, probably, that her name was changed to *Mary Celeste*. If it was intended

Captain Benjamin Spooner Briggs, master of the *Mary Celeste*.

to improve her fortunes, it failed. Her new owner followed his predecessor into insolvency.

In 1872 she was acquired by a syndicate named J.H. Winchester and Co., in which her master-elect, Captain Benjamin Spooner Briggs, owned eight of the twenty-four shares. Before bringing her into service, the syndicate spent $11,000 on alterations and repairs. Her poop was extended, an extra deck was added, and her tonnage was increased from 198.42 to 282.28.

By 5 November 1872 the *Mary Celeste* was tied up alongside Pier 50 in New York's East River ready to sail for Genoa. While loading the cargo – 1,700 barrels of alcohol – a gang of dockers had accidentally damaged the longboat beyond immediate repair. Captain Briggs agreed that the other boat, secured on top of the main hatch, was sufficient, and a spar was lashed across the stern davits.

Captain Briggs has been described as 'an intelligent and active shipmaster': stern when the occasion demanded it, but none the less popular with his men. His father and three of his four brothers had all made their careers at sea. The *Mary Celeste* was his fourth command. He was married to a capable woman who liked music. They had two children: a son who was at school, and spent much of his time living with Briggs's mother, and two-year-old Sophia. Mrs Briggs and Sophia were to accompany him on the voyage to Genoa.

The crew was composed of two mates, a steward-cum-cook (obviously good at his job: he was paid more than the second mate), and four seamen – all of them Germans. Three had impeccable references; the fourth was something of an unknown quantity – though Mrs Briggs, in a letter brought ashore by a pilot boat on the eve of departure, described them all as 'a pretty peaceable set'. She also wrote that 'We are enjoying our melodeon [harmonium] and have some good songs' – which suggests that, on this occasion at least, the *Mary Celeste* was not an unhappy ship.

On the afternoon of 5 November the *Mary Celeste* left her berth and headed down river. She was held up for two days off Sandy Hook by adverse winds and generally bad weather. By the 7th things had taken a turn for the better. Briggs gave the order to raise the anchor: the small ship set course towards the Azores on the first leg of her voyage. That was the last that anyone saw of her until she was sighted by Captain Morehouse.

The proceedings of the Admiralty court at Gibraltar dragged on for three months, and still failed to reach any conclusion about the cause of the mystery. Among its tasks was that of examining the ship in the hope of discovering any clues that had previously been overlooked. Among those who undertook this investigation were the commanding officers of four naval vessels, and it has to be assumed that they did their work thoroughly. They did not, however, reveal anything of much significance.

A valuable sword was discovered with what might have been (but weren't) bloodstains on its blade. There were also traces of what looked like blood (it was) on one of the rails. The ship's planking was in good order, apart from cuts on either bow about three feet above the waterline. However, they were not sufficiently severe to have put the ship in any jeopardy. Nine of the casks of alcohol on board had been either emptied or damaged, and there was evidence that the ship's boat had been launched in a hurry.

It was little enough upon which to base even a theory, though this did not discourage the theorists. Inevitably, the possibility of collusion between Captain Briggs and Captain Morehouse was considered – and, sensibly, dropped. Morehouse and the crew of the *Dei Gratia* also came under suspicion; but since there can be no prosecution without evidence, this line of thought was quickly dismissed.

The most colourful and contentious person present at the court was undoubtedly the assessor or – to give him his full title – the Attorney General for Gibraltar and Advocate General for the Queen in Her Office of Admiralty. His name was Frederick Solly Flood. Mr Flood has been described as arrogant, pompous, shrewd and excitable. He may have been all these things: he certainly had a vivid imagination that was prepared to put pretty well any theory on offer. One of his ideas was that the German crew had been at the alcohol. In a drunken frenzy, they had slaughtered their officers, Mrs Briggs and young Sophia. Then, having damaged the rigging to suggest that the ship had been in trouble from more natural causes, they had departed in the boat. Shortly afterwards they were picked up by a west-bound ship and taken to America. It made a good story, but there was not a shred of evidence to support it – especially after an analyst had stated that the stain on the sword was nothing more than rust.

A notion that was treated rather more seriously was that the fumes from the damaged casks had built up and caused an explosion. In panic, Briggs had given the order to abandon ship, and they had all been cast adrift on the ocean. It would have been more convincing if Captain Briggs had been the kind of man to lose his head in an emergency – and even more so had there been any evidence that an explosion had taken place. There was none.

A more probable hypothesis is that the *Mary Celeste* was struck by a waterspout – a phenomenon that is not uncommon in the area of the Azores. The difference between the atmospheric pressure and that inside the hull might have been enough to force off the hatch covers – after which, water would have poured into the holds. The presence of the sounding-rod gives substance to this idea. Possibly Briggs misjudged the severity. Conceivably, he and the rest of them took to the boat – but attached it to the stern in case the alarm proved to be false. The rope parted, and the *Mary Celeste* sailed on – leaving behind her unhappy occupants.

But this is all supposition. The truth will never be known. As for the *Mary Celeste*, her life as an unlucky ship continued. During the next twelve years she had almost as many owners. Finally, in December 1884, she ended her days on a reef off Haiti. The weather was good; the sea well charted. Suspicious, the authorities arraigned the captain and first mate on charges of defrauding the insurance company. The case was never brought to court. The captain died three months later; the first mate three months after that. Since the cargo was wickedly overinsured, their deaths probably frustrated justice.

WHAT HAPPENED ON 'LITTLE JEWEL'?

Old-movie buffs will remember the name, and perhaps the beautiful face, of Thelma Todd. A Massachusetts-born blonde, of considerable vivacity and uninhibited talent, she made the transition from part-time modelling to screen acting just as sound films were moving towards maturity. Her roles were not leading ones, but audiences always perked up when she appeared, as the dazzlingly pert foil to such top stars of the early 1930s as the Marx Brothers (in *Monkey Business* and *Horse Feathers*), and in some of the 'B' Westerns which had William Powell as the 'heavy' and were serving as the foundations of Gary Cooper's career. Distinguished company and a promising future for a girl, especially with a director, named Roland West, for an influential lover.

Some passages of their *affaire* were enjoyed aboard a luxurious ocean-going yacht which West had had specially designed and built for him in 1931. Nothing but the best for West: twin diesels, capacious fuel- and water-tanks for long cruises, vast ice-boxes to hold the big-game fish hauled in by him and his guests as they sat harnessed into the swivel-chairs aft – and an automatic pilot to take over the steering while everyone rested, or Mr West dallied with the delicious Miss Todd.

Doubtless it inhibited neither of them to remember that the vessel was named after Roland West's wife, Jewel. Since they had not yet ceased to be closely affectionate at the time of the yacht's christening, the diminutive 'Little Jewel' had been preferred, and, as an added touch of the exotic, inscribed on the bows and stern of the 69-foot, 70-ton craft in its Spanish form – *Joyita*.

In this floating pleasure-nest Thelma Todd gasped away the last moments of her life in 1935. The full circumstances never came to be known: carbon-monoxide poisoning was the inquest verdict. She had been in her thirtieth year.

The bereaved West sold *Joyita*, with some of Miss Todd's effects still aboard, to a private buyer. In 1941 she became US Navy property, requisitioned for patrol service at Pearl Harbor. She survived the great raid, only to meet serious disaster two years later when she ran aground off the Hawaiian Islands, necessitating considerable repair to her hull. 'Demobbed' at the war's end, *Joyita* was converted to a fishing vessel, most of her capacity transformed into cork-insulated holds for the catch. Her exotic days seemed truly finished – but she was destined to star in a tragedy with many of the elements of a film-play.

A further private buyer, in 1953, was an anthropologist of Scandinavian background but American nationality, Dr Ellen Katharine Luomala, a lecturer at the University of Hawaii in Honolulu. She wanted to do a good turn to a man who, if in no way connected with motion pictures, was of a type often depicted in a certain genre of them.

Lieutenant-Commander Thomas Henry ('Dusty') Miller, RNVR, had been born in Cardiff just before the First World War and had joined the merchant service at the age of thirteen. His subsequent war service had been in the Pacific, where he had decided to stay on as a civilian, freelance skipper of small craft, trading as Phoenix Island Fisheries. He was a personable ex-naval type, hard-drinking ashore (though never afloat), well known in island bars amongst male pals, though women were attracted by his dark looks and his devil-may-care manner.

He needed all his confidence, for work and money were not plentiful and, nearing his forties, he wanted a lucky break that would set him up for the future. Acquaintanceship and then something closer with Dr Luomala seemed to herald one – he was going through divorce proceedings to end an existing marriage – and their arrangement, that she should go on teaching anthropology while he used her little ship to supply Hawaii with fish from the Canton Islands, must have been regarded by them as an ideal one, pending marriage.

Things did not go according to plan. Three trips were enough to convince him that he could not trade at a profit: the Honolulu merchants paid less for his fish than it had cost him to catch and carry them. He tried extending his territory with a fourth voyage, this time taking his cargo to Apia, Western Samoa. When he opened *Joyita*'s hold, he found that the refrigeration had failed and much of the catch was already bad. He was glad to get rid of the lot for what little it would fetch.

Thelma Todd's perfumes had long been overlaid in *Joyita* by the stink of fish. All traces of the craft's former luxuries had vanished too, inside and out; she looked unkempt, and the many practical but unbecoming modifications for her present role had left her anything but shapely. It was not only her appearance which deterred the people whom Miller approached at Apia, on Dr Luomala's instructions, to get the best price he could for her vessel, pay his debts out of the proceeds, and come back to Honolulu. The engines, neglected from lack of funds to have them serviced and repaired, looked unlikely to carry her safely about the long, lonely stretches of the Pacific, where the least danger was that a breakdown could strand her on some island for weeks until spare parts could be obtained and fitted. An additional snag was that her papers were incomplete. Miller owed harbour dues and other debts at Pago Pago, the capital of the American-administered part of Samoa, and the US authorities had retained some of his ship's papers, to make sure he would eventually pay up.

For five months of 1955, *Joyita* lay at Apia, once German territory but a New Zealand mandate since 1920, and capital of Western Samoa. While the vessel deteriorated, so did her desperate skipper's morale. He was known and respected as an ex-naval officer and a good, hard skipper, and his persistent bad luck did not seem to be attributable to undue rashness or the failure of any crooked ventures, even if he was a type willing to take a risk. Some men were moved to see him having to do odd jobs, such as painting the verandah furniture of the Returned Servicemen's Association club, in order to subsist. Commander Peter Plowman, another ex-naval man and in the Fijian Government's employ, on learning that Miller had eaten nothing for two days save one small loaf of bread, took him home for a meal and lent him a little cash.

There was nothing long-term that could be done for him, though. Ex-servicemen who had opted for the lure and freedom of the Pacific islands rather than settle for conventional security were not scarce. One thing Miller would not do, though, was scrounge. He accepted any charity offered him, because he couldn't afford to refuse; but he hung grimly on to his one decent suit, and his letters to Dr Luomala did not reveal the extent of his plight.

Suddenly, his courageous determination seemed to be rewarded: a crisis had hit the Tokelau Islands, some 350 miles north-east of Samoa, and their recently appointed District Officer, a 29-year-old New Zealander named Pearless, had the idea of turning to Miller and his idle ship for help. There existed little in the way of regular sea services between the numerous and scattered Pacific islands and the Tokelaus were more inaccessible than most. Food was running short there. Copra, the islands' only export and source of income, was piling up awaiting collection, but no collection was scheduled. General medical supplies were dwindling too, and a man who had injured his leg badly was threatened with gangrene and needed an operation. A mercy-mission by Royal New Zealand Air Force flying-boat could not be risked; an earlier attempt to aid the islanders by air had resulted in the flying boat ripping its hull on coral as it taxied in the lagoon.

Miller had taken Pearless to the Tokelaus in *Joyita* once before, and they had become friends. An application by the Commissioner to charter the vessel on an annual contract to provide a regular link, which would have given Miller just the security he needed, had been officially turned down, largely due to those missing ship's papers. Now there was an emergency. Other vessels were not readily available. Pearless, who had come to Apia with his problem, but could not get back with the supplies and medical men he needed, together with some officials who had been waiting for long enough to get out to the islands, made another application to enlist Miller's aid. This time he succeeded. An island trading concern agreed to a single there-and-back charter for *Joyita*. It was arranged that she should sail from Apia at about noon on Sunday 2 October 1955.

A crew was needed, and Miller knew where to look for good men who had sailed under him in earlier hopeful days. Most important was Chuck Simpson, known around the islands as 'Captain Jah'. He was a big, tough American-Indian, who had settled down with a Samoan wife and a job in an Apia garage. It was a relief that Simpson agreed to sign on as mate. He was qualified, by experience and hard-necked character, to share his skipper's responsibilities, while, as an American national, he satisfied a regulation that a vessel owned by an American – Dr Luomala – must have at least one officer of that nationality aboard.

Two Gilbert Islanders, Tekoka and Tanini, were willing to join their old skipper as bosun and engineer respectively. There was a lot to be done to prepare the two 225-horsepower marine diesels for the voyage, so Miller was thankful to be able to sign an assistant engineer, a young part-Samoan named Henry McCarthy with a mechanical flair and experience gained from the US Marines in the war years. McCarthy's mother, who had heard gossip about *Joyita*'s condition, was not keen for him to go, but his eagerness to seize the chance was too much for her.

A doctor from Apia Hospital, named Parsons, and a dispenser, Hodgkinson, were to go out to attend the injured Tokelauan. Probably as a
stipulation in agreeing to the charter, the trading concern of E.A. Coxon
& Co. wanted passages for two of their representatives with business to do
on the islands. This posed a difficulty for Miller, for *Joyita* was not insured
to carry passengers: he could not have afforded the premium, but, anyway,
her thick cork insulation, put in by the firm which had converted her to a
fish carrier, made her as unsinkable as a lifeboat. He took the precaution,
though, of signing the traders as supercargoes. When a further opportunity
arose to take seven Tokelau Islanders, including a woman and two children, who had been stranded in Samoa awaiting a passage, he turned a
blind eye to regulations; their fares would be welcome.

In funds at last, Dusty Miller took aboard 2,640 gallons of diesel fuel.
The supplier, who let him have it on credit, evidently did not ask why he
wanted so much fuel for a trip requiring much less. The big water-tanks
were also filled right up, and much more food was stowed than a total of
25 people would need for a voyage of only 270 miles to the port of Fakaofo.
The rest of the cargo consisted of empty sacks to hold the waiting copra,
to pay for which one of Coxon's employees carried £1,000 cash.

Tanini, assisted by Henry McCarthy, worked long hours in the below-
decks heat to try to get the engines into trim. The starboard one was
satisfactory, but clutch trouble persisted in the other and was still not
cured by the Sunday departure day.

On that day Mr Bentham, superintendent of Apia Radio, sent a message
down to Miller, whom he had been expecting to hear from before now
about arrangements for radio contact. It was not compulsory for a skipper
to do anything about it, but surprising that a professional like Miller hadn't
bothered. Mr Bentham's message was that the radio station would listen
for calls from *Joyita* at 10 a.m. and 4 p.m. daily, and that he would stand
by for a pre-sailing test. There was no response. Only after *Joyita* had
sailed did the trading-company director visit Bentham to say that her call
sign was WNIM, and that Miller had agreed to contact Apia at the
arranged times.

Soon after Sunday noon, *Joyita*'s diesels coughed and roared into life.
She cast off and began to make for the harbour mouth. Watching from his
house, Commander Plowman saw the port exhaust emit a puff of smoke.
He heard the engines shut down and, with *Joyita* beginning to drift slowly
towards a reef, saw an anchor cast over.

Plowman was concerned enough to report by telephone to the islands'
Commission, but no official steps were taken. Eventually some of the
Tokelauan passengers came ashore, to say that there would be a delay due

As the *Joyita* drifts off Samoa, some of her passengers are taken off. Five weeks later, hundreds of miles off course, she was found abandoned – a *Mary Celeste* of the Pacific.

Captain Thomas 'Dusty' Miller, who mysteriously disappeared from the *Joyita* with both crew and passengers.

to engine trouble. The charterer hurried out to the vessel, where the engineers were engaged again in their sweaty task. Miller dismissed his suggestion that the voyage should be called off until the port diesel had been thoroughly repaired and tested. It would right itself when running, he said. He was tense, no doubt on tenterhooks that some American official might hear that he was proposing to sail with his papers incomplete and unauthorized passengers aboard. That could spell his ultimate ruin.

Joyita was still anchored when night fell. Mr Bentham waited at the radio station until 7 p.m., thinking that Miller might at least use some of the waiting time to test his radio. No call came. When Bentham, Commander Plowman, and others associated with Miller and his mission looked out next morning, *Joyita* had gone. The harbourmaster's log showed that she had sailed at 5 a.m., and headed north. Apia radioed the information to Fakaofo, where a relieved populace spent an uncharacteristically energetic Monday making ready to receive her.

She did not arrive there. At the scheduled times during the next days, Apia Radio listened for her call, but heard none, and got no response to attempts to call her. On 6 October, with *Joyita* now well overdue on so short a passage, an RNZAF Sunderland flying-boat carried out a sweep from Fiji, flying high enough over the island-flecked blue sea to scan a range of ten miles to either side, visually and by radar. Visibility was good; there had been no unduly heavy weather lately. Not a trace of *Joyita* showed.

The air search continued for a week, while all shipping kept a lookout and Apia Radio and other stations called in vain. A theory sprang up among those who had learned of the gross oversupply of fuel, water and food taken on by *Joyita*, and who knew something of Miller's personal difficulties. They guessed that he had seen his chance of escape from Samoa, where hardship had trapped him. He had not made for the Tokelaus at all, but on to Honolulu, where his fuel supply would easily carry his ship. How he could have persuaded, or subdued, his companions in *Joyita* to go there with him was not spelled out; but Dusty was resourceful, tough and desperate. Either that, or the frail luck which had kept him going from hand to mouth for so long had run out in some form of disaster. The search was called off, and *Joyita* given up for lost.

On 10 November, over five weeks after she had left on a voyage which should have lasted two or three days, she was found, more than 600 miles from her stated destination and apparently headed in a totally different direction. She was headed nowhere, though, except where the tides were carrying her. The big engines were silent. No emergency sail hung from her two slender masts. She was listing heavily, and deeply waterlogged.

Most dramatically of all, when she was boarded from the Gilbert and Ellice Islands' supply ship *Tuvalu*, there was not a soul aboard her, alive or dead.

Her life-rafts were missing, which at first pointed to the obvious – she had been abandoned. Yet she was still afloat, and Dusty Miller, and probably some of his old crew hands, knew her to be unsinkable. She was all the security he possessed in the world. Surely, he at least would have stuck with her until the end.

Her sextant and log were missing – Miller would have made sure he kept those. The large supply of food was gone, which was perhaps not so strange, any more than the absence of the £1,000 cash and all her people's belongings. But why would escapers from a seemingly sinking ship have risked the safety of their rafts by burdening them with several hundred empty copra sacks and heavy cases of cargo of a kind useless to survivors? It was simply not possible that two dozen people and all those goods could have got away on three rafts.

Joyita's radio silence was more easily explained. Her aerial lead was broken, and the break painted over – another of Miller's calculated risks to avoid being forbidden to sail? However, the transmitter had been left tuned to the distress wave-length, so someone must have tried to get a message off. But no form of written communication had been left aboard for rescuers to find.

There was a more disquieting discovery – a doctor's stethoscope and scalpel, surgical needles and stitching, and some lengths of bloodstained bandage. Blood had been shed aboard *Joyita*, accidentally or by violence. The finding of two old knives, marked 'Made in Japan', added to the latter fear.

The evident cause of the waterlogging was inundation through a fractured cooling pipe in that defective port engine: mattresses were found packed around it. It still did not account for everyone having abandoned ship, overburdening themselves with all they could take out of her, or why her skipper would have vanished, too – unless he had been the one whose blood had stained those bandages.

The world's Press seized on this story of a *Mary Celeste* of the Pacific, and writers gave free rein to their powers of deduction and imagination. Pirates; a chance encounter with a hostile Japanese fishing fleet, or boats manned by soldiers who did not know the war was over; a submarine; involvement in running drugs or arms; mass hysteria and the murder of Dusty Miller, perhaps because he had refused to make for the Tokelaus, but had been determined to get to Honolulu instead.... It was all conjecture, and none of it stood up wholly to every test.

The official inquiry, accepting that *Joyita* had flooded and become im-
mobilized, had to confess:

Although your Commissioners find it possible to speak with a reasonable degree
of conviction as to the cause of casualty to the ship, they are quite unable to do
so with regard to the ship's personnel.

Joyita was eventually sold for a song to a planter, who had her repaired
and refitted. She quite promptly ran onto a coral reef and had to be
salvaged again. Recommissioned, she managed a year's Pacific trading in
1958–9 before grounding on another reef and then becoming inundated
while being towed to Fiji.

There she was beached, left to be picked clean by creditors and pilferers,
until she was found by an author, the late Robin (Lord) Maugham, nephew
to that writer of cynical tales of the Pacific and elsewhere, Somerset
Maugham. Fascinated by the hulk and her story, Robin Maugham bought
her, studied all the evidence, asked all the questions, and formulated his
own version of what had happened, which he published in 1962 as a book,
The Joyita Mystery.

It is a plausible tale, which cannot be proved nor disproved, and might
even be true. Many another adventure novelist could have used the same
characters and circumstances to create quite a different story, with perhaps
the twist ending that Dusty Miller survived and is alive today, ever-thank-
ful for the chain of circumstances which enabled him to disappear and
reclaim his life elsewhere.

MYSTERIES OF THE AIR

UFOs

Of all flying-saucer incidents perhaps the most sinister is that which ended with the death of Captain Thomas Mantell of the United States Air Force at Fort Knox, Kentucky. It is the story of a brave attempt to solve what had been called the mystery of the century, of a dramatic radio conversation that suddenly ceased, of an aircraft flown by a skilled pilot dropping helplessly to earth from 20,000 feet. It happened over Godman Field, Fort Knox, on 7 January 1948 – a portentous day for all who were stationed there at the time.

Yet it had begun quite normally with routine training in clear, sunny weather. The notion of flying-saucers was far from anyone's thoughts. But that was before the alarm was raised, before the jangling chorus of telephone bells sounded and harsh radio instructions crackled from Godman Tower, before the men of Fort Knox ran into the open and stood looking skywards with shaded eyes.

Up there at the hazy limit of visibility was something described as 'a huge ice-cream cone topped with red', which soon had four National Guard F-51 planes roaring off the tarmac to investigate. And from one of them as it dwindled into the sky came back the tense voice of Captain Mantell.

'There it is! Twelve o'clock high. It looks metallic ... a tremendous size!'

None of the other pilots reported seeing anything, but presently Captain Mantell radioed that 'the Thing' was climbing rapidly. 'I'm going to follow it up to 20,000 feet,' he said. 'If I get no closer, I'll abandon chase....'

On the ground they waited, then frantically tried to call him back. But nothing more was heard from Captain Mantell, and nothing was seen until his broken body was recovered from the wreckage of the plane which crashed a few miles away. Meanwhile the 'cone', still unseen by the other pilots, had disappeared. And just what happened up there is still in doubt. But there is a persistent belief in some quarters that Mantell got too close, saw too much, and was destroyed by some power unknown on earth.

Flying-saucers, in the sense that some people regard them today, had come into their own just over six months earlier. On 24 June 1947 Kenneth Arnold, an American businessman, was making a routine air trip in a private plane to Washington from his home in Idaho. The journey took him along a range of snow-capped mountains and suddenly he was surprised to see a formation of strange silvery craft apparently swerving in

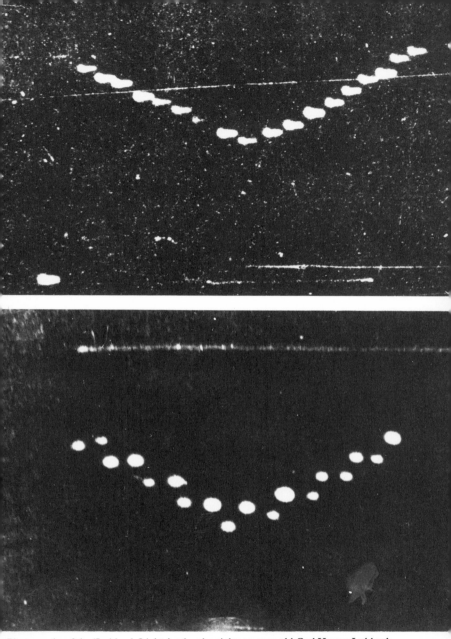

Photographs of the 'Lubbock Lights', taken by eighteen-year-old Carl Hart at Lubbock, Texas, on 30 August 1951.

and out of the mountain peaks. Not having seen anything like them before, he reported the experience as soon as he reached his destination. He described the objects as 'a chain of saucer-like things'.

At first Mr Arnold's sighting was not taken too seriously, but the word 'saucer' captured public imagination. Reports of other saucers were soon coming in from all over America and indeed from all over the world. What they were nobody could say and nobody knows for certain to this day. But the most attractive theory was that they were flying machines piloted by strange visitors from outer space.

Headlines flared. 'Is another world watching us?' they demanded. Cartoonists worked overtime and hoaxers rampaged the country. It was all a great joke – until the Fort Knox incident. Then flying-saucers, dignified by a new name – Unidentified Flying Objects or UFOs for short – suddenly became a world mystery if not a world menace.

Opponents of the notion that the saucers are craft from outer space insisted, and still do, that Mantell was not shot down by an alien death-ray but simply blacked out through lack of oxygen and crashed without regaining consciousness. And the UFO he was chasing? It might have been a 'skyhook' balloon, later whipped away in a high-altitude gale. Or it might have been a 'mock sun' caused by ice crystals in cirrus clouds which lay higher than Mantell's plane could reach.

But there was no clue to be found in Mantell's aircraft, and to this day nobody knows the answer for sure. The incident has a fundamental place in the whole flying-saucer mystery. Indeed it might well be argued that if Mantell had not died, the saucers would have died instead. As it was, his death boosted the mystery into a new phase in which every new sighting stirred up the old excitement.

UFOs are not peculiar to the modern era. People have been seeing odd things in the sky throughout recorded history. As far back as 1646, for example, a book was published called *Strange Signes from Heaven* which recorded sightings of many phenomena which could well come under the general heading of flying-saucers; and even in the Bible there are references suggesting that ancient peoples were puzzled by them.

So it seems that if flying-saucers are spaceships from another world, they are an unconscionable time making up their minds about us. But so firm is the grip that flying saucers now have on public imagination that however many are explained away, every new sighting stirs up the old excitement. One can see no end to it – and no universally accepted explanation – until interplanetary travel becomes an accomplished fact, and we can go far beyond the moon to see for ourselves what goes on out there.

The father of the UFO cult, if it be no more than a cult, was undoubtedly the late George Adamski, co-author of the book *Flying Saucers Have Landed*, published in 1953. He was the first man to claim that he had made contact with someone from another world. Adamski, born of Polish parents who emigrated to the United States in the 1890s, was an amateur astronomer living on the slopes of Mount Palomar where one of the world's biggest telescopes is situated and from the vicinity of which he did a fair amount of star-gazing himself with a six-inch private instrument.

On 20 November 1952, Adamski and a party of friends were enjoying a picnic lunch when, as the story goes, a large cigar-shaped object appeared over a mountain ridge. To Adamski its appearance meant one thing: that the unknown occupants of the object, plainly a spaceship, wished to make his acquaintance.

He asked two companions to drive him along the highway to a point where he could set up his telescope, which intuitively he had brought along for just such an encounter. Then, when the apparatus was ready, he sent his two companions away, asking them to watch carefully from a distance. A few seconds later, he afterwards claimed, he noticed a flash in the sky and almost immediately a small 'scout ship', evidently dispatched from the bigger aeroform, came gliding down from between two mountain peaks and settled out of sight behind a hillock about a mile away.

Within a short time, Adamski said, he became aware of a man standing about 500 yards away at the entrance to a ravine. Moving towards the man Adamski saw that he was wearing what appeared to be a ski-suit and had long sandy hair reaching to his shoulders. The newcomer seemed a pleasant sort of individual and Adamski quickly felt at ease with him even after it flashed through his mind that he was in the presence of a being from another world. Not surprisingly perhaps, the visitor did not speak English, but despite this formidable disadvantage he was remarkably skilful at making himself understood.

In fact, he and Adamski chatted together for a good hour, largely by means of signs and telepathy. Adamski was able to learn, for example, that the spaceman came from the planet Venus and that his attitude towards earthmen was absolutely friendly, although some concern was felt for our scientific progress, especially in atomic energy. The spaceman escorted Adamski to the hillock behind which his saucer was hidden and nothing untoward happened except when Adamski inadvertently stepped too close to the metal rim of the machine and got a slight electric shock. Despite his evident desire to be friendly, however, the Venusian declined the earthman's request to be taken for a ride. Presently, after stepping back into the vehicle, he soundlessly took off.

Adamski's friends, who had obediently kept watch, admitted afterwards

© Adamski

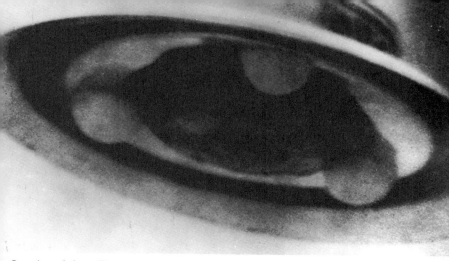

Opposite and above: The 'Venusian flying saucer', photographed by George Adamski through a six-inch telescope at Valley Center, Star Route, California, on 13 December 1952.

The five crew members of an R.A.F. Shackleton aircraft, who reported sighting an object believed to be a flying saucer two months earlier.

that they had seen him talking to someone in a brownish garment. They also claimed to have seen two sets of footprints in the sand, one of which was obviously their friend's and the other a smaller set which seemed not to go beyond the area in which he said the saucer had landed.

A sequel to the contact claim came a few weeks later when, according to Adamski, the saucer returned and hovered within a hundred feet of where he was standing in Palomar Gardens. It was on this occasion that Adamski managed to obtain some close-up saucer pictures, the veracity of which has been argued about ever since. The Adamski photographs, despite looking like lampshades, have in fact become standard saucer pictures recognized throughout the world. And nobody to my knowledge has ever managed to produce anything quite like them with faked devices.

The sensational nature of *Flying Saucers Have Landed* ensured that it would be a best-seller, and Adamski travelled the world as a philosopher and lecturer on the subject of UFOs.

When he came to London in 1964, I telephoned him at the small hotel where he was staying and was courteously granted an interview. I found him a modest, soft-spoken man with a gentle, patient face who answered every question without any attempt at evasion or the slightest show of hostility, and who was evidently prepared to go on answering as long as I was prepared to put the questions.

A lean, weather-beaten man with thick, iron-grey hair, he responded easily and without hesitation in support of his remarkable claim. And long before I left him, I knew I was beaten as far as tripping him into any incautious admission was concerned. I told myself that if he were deluded, he was the most lucid and intelligent deluded man I had ever met. And when, some years later, I came to write his obituary for a Sunday newspaper, I found it a melancholy task.

Like many other sceptics, I have always found the claims of George Adamski impossible to believe, just as I have found unacceptable the claims of others who have alleged experiences with 'our space brothers'. But if one accepts the notion, however remote, that some UFOs could be piloted spacecraft from other worlds, surely it should not be difficult to take a further step and accept that occasionally we are visited by space-travellers who want to make contact with us?

What then is the difficulty? Is it simply due to the knowledge that hoaxes have been perpetrated and will certainly be perpetrated again?

An event I investigated some years ago for my book *UFO* concerned the simultaneous discovery of no fewer than six flying-saucers positioned in line across the southern counties of England from Clevedon, near Bristol, to the Isle of Sheppey. There was nothing vague about these sightings.

The saucers were really there. Not only could they be clearly seen and photographed, they could also be touched, for they were all on the ground.

The uproar they caused lasted only a few hours, but in that time squads of police, a bomb-disposal unit, an RAF helicopter, and dozens of scientists turned out to investigate them – to say nothing of crowds of ordinary sightseers. The saucers may have been disappointingly small (measuring about four feet across and eighteen inches deep in the domed part), but they conformed clearly to the classical shape, and from each came an eerie bleeping as it lay gleaming whitish-silver in the grass.

It turned out, as the country later discovered, that these objects, far from being flying-machines piloted by 'little green men', had been made by students of Farnborough Technical College as a rag-day stunt and positioned overnight near roads and footpaths where they would be discovered early next morning. It was undoubtedly a good hoax, though possibly a little irritating to officials who were needlessly engaged in investigating the 'saucers' for the best part of a day.

Since the Second World War numerous organizations have come into being in different parts of the world to investigate UFO sightings and keep records. And there always seems to be plenty of work for them to do. Serious investigators are well aware how easy it is to fake sightings, and they remain constantly on guard against being caught out.

The outline of a saucer sketched on a window can be made to look pretty convincing against the sky beyond. You can hang a model by thread from the branches of a tree to achieve much the same effect. Or toss a flat hat, car-hub cover, ashtray or similarly shaped object into the air and snap it from low down against a tall building. But skilled photographers are not often taken in by these devices.

But what of people – and there seems to be a growing number – who claim experiences designated CE-III (close encounters of the third kind), in which they have spoken to visitors from other worlds and even been taken for trips in exotic interplanetary spacecraft?

One such case, a mystery for more than thirty years, is that of Cedric Allingham who startled everyone with a report that he had met a man from Mars while holidaying near Lossiemouth, Scotland, in 1954. In a book about the adventure, Allingham even published a hazy photograph of the Martian. What it amounted to was that while out bird-watching on a remote headland, Allingham saw a flying-saucer glinting in the sky and, when it landed, went fearlessly forward to greet the occupant. Just like Adamski's visitor, the man wore a kind of ski-suit. But his hair was short and dark, and he was using some kind of breathing apparatus with tubes leading up to his nostrils. According to Allingham they conversed by means of telepathy and drawings on a sketch-pad. The Martian seems to have been quite a jolly fellow, who managed to convey the impression that he had just popped over to planet Earth for the afternoon.

As science correspondent for the former London *Evening News*, I received an advance copy of Allingham's book for review and read it with increasing astonishment. But before I could find him for the purpose of an interview, I learned that he had gone abroad in ill-health and had suddenly died.

The alleged experiences of both Adamski and Allingham occurred well before the first research spacecraft were sent to Venus and Mars. In those days we had little idea what either planet was really like. Earthbound telescopes had revealed dark patches (thought to be vegetation) and faint lines (thought to be canals) on Mars. But it had not been possible to see through the thick cloud cover of Venus. It was not difficult to imagine that some sort of life, even intelligent life, could have developed on both planets. But now, alas, it is becoming increasingly clear that neither Venus nor Mars is capable of supporting life as we know it. And that applies also to other planets in the solar system.

Nevertheless, interest in UFOs shows little sign of abating. Media coverage of sightings may have dwindled, but hardly a day goes by without some new saucer mystery coming to the notice of investigators. For, as they happily point out, there are millions of other possible worlds, not only in our own galaxy, the Milky Way, but in the universe at large, where intelligent beings could have evolved and who may be trying to make contact with us or others like us.

TWO STARS FALL

Leutnant Bellstedt of the *Luftwaffe* was a simple aviator who did what he was told and never asked questions. A senior officer might be talking utter rubbish, but it would never have occurred to Bellstedt to correct him, or to wonder whether an alternative idea might be better, or anything like that. Indeed, so trusting and obedient was his nature that he probably never even entertained the idea that any of his superiors *could* talk rubbish. Wherever they pointed, he flew – and the seven other pilots in his squadron of JU88 fighter-bombers trailed along behind him.

Bellstedt's orders on that June day in 1943 were to fly to a map reference over the Bay of Biscay, and thereafter to provide protection for a couple of U-boats he would see beneath him. Had he taken the trouble to study the weather reports more carefully, he would have realized that this was Mission Impossible. The cloud mass was pretty well solid from sea level to 3,000 feet. Leutnant Bellstedt's likelihood of even finding the submarines was, to understate the matter, improbable. Such small details didn't bother this zealous airman. Neither he nor anyone else in his formation so much as glimpsed a U-boat. Whilst they were about it, Bellstedt decided, they might as well examine the sky to see whether there were any hostile aircraft which might be worth a burst or two of ammunition. There were none. The JU88s turned about and headed back in the direction of their base near Bordeaux.

Not all that far from the radio direction-finder on Cape Vilano, in Spain, the clouds parted and there, flying at an estimated 7,000 feet, was a civilian airliner. Bellstedt knew it well. It was the daily KLM flight from Lisbon to England: a DC3 that usually passed through this particular air space at about 12.10 hrs. Since the time was now 12.45, the aircraft was 35 minutes late. Bellstedt didn't wonder what had delayed it: he went by the book and radioed for instructions.

Usually the *Luftwaffe* ignored these ferry services run by three teams of KLM aircrew that had escaped from occupied Holland. On only two occasions in three years had they been molested; and on each occasion the DC3 had managed to escape into the cover of clouds. Nevertheless Bellstedt, who took nothing for granted, had to make sure. It was, perhaps, just as well for him that he did. On this occasion the instructions were terse and unambiguous.

'Shoot it down,' he was told.

Mustering his following into the correct order, he carefully lined up on the target and swooped. It was too easy, really; the DC3 was neither fast, nor small, nor armed. Racked by incendiary bullets, it quickly burst into flames and exploded. Before its remains tumbled into the sea, he thought he saw four men attempting to escape by parachute. Two of the 'chutes failed to open, a third caught fire, and the fourth seemed to unravel itself and blossom. Bellstedt was not entirely sure about this, but so it seemed to him. In fact, he was wrong. Nobody in the airliner had a parachute.

He put his JU88 into a steep dive and came down almost to sea level. He was not looking for survivors; nor even gloating over his kill. He simply wished to take a photograph to be sure that he received credit for his lethal industry. Leutnant Bellstedt was like that: meticulous.

Among those who embarked on KLM Flight 2L272 due to depart from Lisbon for Whitchurch, near Bristol, at 9.30 a.m. on 1 June 1943, at least two had misgivings. Kenneth Stonehouse, Reuter's man in Washington, is recorded in Ronald Howard's *In Search of my Father* as having told a Portuguese journalist, 'I'm not normally frightened, but somehow I feel bad about this air-trip. I wish I could go to sleep here and wake up at some English airfield.'

Bill Shervington, Shell Manager in Lisbon, had suffered an even more disturbing experience. He had actually dreamed that the aircraft was shot down. Whilst each, no doubt, would have liked to have cancelled his reservation, neither did. It was, perhaps, a matter of pride.

Leslie Howard, the famous actor and film director, had no such worries – or if he had, he kept them to himself. He had just completed an immensely successful tour of Spain and Portugal at the behest of the British Council. He had given talks about the stage and cinema in Britain, shown some propaganda documentaries and his own feature film *Pimpernel Smith* (about a professor of archaeology who rescues potential victims from Nazi Germany). Everything came to a stunning climax on the evening of 29 May, when his new movie, *The First of the Few* (the story of the Spitfire's inventor), was premièred in Lisbon. At a dinner afterwards, he was presented with a gold medallion for the best motion picture made in 1942.

Mr Howard was accompanied by his manager, a plumpish, bald gentleman named Alfred Chenhalls – who smoked cigars. From a distance he might conceivably have been mistaken for Winston Churchill despite a gap of fifteen years in their ages. Their plans for a return to Britain were uncertain. Originally it had been fixed for 29 May, but then Leslie Howard was persuaded to stay on in Lisbon for the showing of *The First of the Few*. The date of departure was postponed until 2 June. But, on the afternoon of the thirty-first, both men reconsidered. Chenhalls was anxious to get back to his office where a great deal of business was demanding attention; Howard was eager to be at the studios, where a motion picture he was producing – *The Lamp Still Burns* – was nearing completion.

Why, they wondered, hang on for another day? Surely they could return next morning. The BOAC office was informed of their wishes, but the clerk on duty reported that the aircraft was fully booked. In any case, he was not able to deal with such things. It would have to be referred to the air attaché at the British Embassy. As the clerk explained, it was a matter of priorities. This was a so-called luxury flight with only fourteen passenger seats. It was the attaché's duty to decide who should occupy them. As it turned out, there were no problems. The young son of a diplomat was making his way back to Britain from his temporary wartime home in the United States. He was accompanied by his nursemaid: there was no reason why they should not travel later.

Leslie Howard Missing in Plane Shot Down by Nazis

3 WOMEN, 2 CHILDREN AMONG 17 LOST : SEARCH FOR RUBBER BOATS IN ROUGH SEA

CABLES from Lisbon last night confirmed that Mr. Leslie Howard, famous film actor and Brains Trust broadcaster, was among 13 passengers, who included three women and two children, missing in the British Overseas Airways aircraft which was shot down by German planes between Portugal and Britain on Tuesday.

It is now known that the passenger plane was attacked over the Bay of Biscay. Signals from its Dutch crew of four picked up at noon on Tuesday said: " We are being attacked by other planes." Then – silence.

High seas were running when search was made for the missing aircraft. For many hours the Bay of Biscay was combed for rubber boats in which survivors might have escaped.

Only after prolonged search in rough weather was it officially broadcast that the plane was " presumed lost."

Right: Leslie Howard arriving at Southampton from New York on the *Aquitania* in August 1939. *Above:* How the British public first heard of Howard's fate. Was he the Luftwaffe's target, or an accidental victim?

The German authorities were uncertain about the role of the British Council. Unquestionably it had a propaganda purpose, but it seemed probable it served an intelligence function as well. From the former point of view, Leslie Howard's war record had already shown him to be a formidable protagonist. Was he also a member of the Secret Intelligence Service?

Undoubtedly his movements during the past four weeks had been watched, and his acclaim regarded with disapproval by German sympathizers. Even that last evening, when he was having a drink in the hotel's cocktail bar, an attractive Hungarian woman was thoughtfully sipping a martini nearby. She was thought to be (and a phone call confirmed that she was) an enemy agent.

1 June dawned. The show was over. Leslie Howard had carried out his mission. Shortly after 9 a.m. he and Alfred Chenhalls and the other passengers were walking across the tarmac of Lisbon's Portela Airport to board the DC3 en route to England. Suddenly Howard, who was endearingly vague about many things, remembered a package of nylon stockings that had been deposited with the customs authorities. They were gifts for friends in Britain: could somebody collect them?

When the messenger returned from the bonded area, he brought with him a message as well as the stockings. It was for another passenger – Father Arthur Holmes, Vice-President of the RC English College in Lisbon. It appeared that something very urgent had cropped up: Father Holmes must abandon his intended trip to England and report at once either to the British Embassy or else to the Papal Nunciature. Protesting that his baggage was still on board the aeroplane and couldn't they unload it (they could not – though he was assured that it would be returned on the next flight), Father Holmes departed. So did the diplomat's little boy and his nanny, who were actually in their seats before being told that their journey would have to be postponed.

Such matters delayed the take-off of the DC3 by 35 minutes. At last, with Leslie Howard, Alfred Chenhalls, the brooding Bill Shervington and the no less anxious Kenneth Stonehouse among the payload, the aircraft taxied to the runway and lifted into the sky. There was one empty seat on board – caused by the sudden exit of Father Holmes. The number of passengers was now thirteen.

The DC3 flew through bad weather up the coasts of Portugal and Spain, cleared Cape Vilano, and headed out over the Bay of Biscay towards its unholy rendezvous with Leutnant Bellstedt and his comrades. The last message received from its captain, Quirinus Tepas, was: 'From G-AGBB [the DC3's call-sign] to GKH [Whitchurch control]. Am being attacked by enemy aircraft.' The time was 12.54. After that: silence.

Why was this particular aeroplane singled out as a target for German aircraft? Chenhalls bore a superficial resemblance to Churchill, who was attending a conference at Algiers prior to the Allied invasion of Sicily. Had there been a case of mistaken identity? It seems unlikely. Churchill himself pointed out that 'It is difficult to understand how anyone could imagine that with all the resources of Great Britain at my disposal I should have booked a passage in an unarmed and unescorted plane from Lisbon and flown home in broad daylight.' It was also hard to see why the British Prime Minister should have been seen assiduously escorting a famous actor whose face was no less familiar. There were surely more important tasks to occupy his time.

Was, then, Howard the target? He was, after all, a potent instrument of Allied propaganda, and he was also suspected of being an Intelligence agent. Was it chance that brought the DC3 within the gunsights of Leutnant Bellstedt and his pilots, or was it intended? The weather made it impossible for the German fliers to pick up the pair of U-boats: and, in any case, information gleaned by the RAF suggested that there were *no* such submarines in that quarter of the Bay of Biscay. But if he was the intended victim, how – with so many changes of plan – had the *Luftwaffe* been informed that he was taking this particular flight? There must have been some last-minute phone-call – probably by a Nazi agent to the German Embassy.

Finally, there is the question of Father Holmes's message. Neither the British Embassy nor the Papal Nunciature had, in fact, asked him to call them, and nor was there any emergency at the College. Who, then, was responsible for (as things transpired) saving his life; and why was it done?

None of these questions was ever answered. There was, however, one good thing that resulted from the tragedy. Thereafter, all the flights across the Bay of Biscay were made at night. It was a policy that should have been adopted from the very beginning.

Two very famous entertainers lost their lives in air disasters during the Second World War; and in each case there was a mystery (that fine actress Carole Lombard also died in an air crash in 1942, but there were no peculiar circumstances: the pilot got it wrong, and flew into a mountain near Las Vegas). One was Leslie Howard; the other that maestro of perhaps the most beautiful sound that a popular light orchestra has ever produced, Glenn Miller.

Miller, born in 1905 at Clarinda, Iowa, was too old for military service; and, in any case, his eyesight was bad enough to make any medical test a fiasco. Nevertheless, in 1943 he was serving as a major in the United

States forces – largely on the insistence of General Eisenhower. The Allied invasion of Europe was imminent, and the Miller sound was considered to be an essential ingredient in any formula designed to create good morale. The result was that he was assigned to establish the American Band of the Allied Expeditionary Forces.

He arrived in London with Lieutenant Don Haynes, his administrative manager, and his illustrious sixty-piece orchestra soon after D-Day (6 June 1944). They were accommodated in a house in Lower Sloane Street. Hitler's bombardment of the capital by his notorious V-weapons had already begun. Instead of being comfortably tucked up in their beds, the musicians spent an anxious and sleepless night nursing their instruments in the cellar. Next day they were moved out of town to Bedford, which was just as well. Twenty-four hours after their brief sojourn, the building in London received a direct hit.

It may have been an inauspicious beginning, but the programmes they broadcast from the BBC on the AEF programme more than made up for it. 'Chattanooga Choo-Choo', 'In the Mood', 'Moonlight Serenade', 'Pennsylvania 65000', 'American Patrol' – the Miller favourites poured out daily over the air, and everyone loved them. Eisenhower once remarked that, next to a letter from home, a dose of Glenn Miller was the best thing he could think of to raise the spirits of his troops.

Whilst good enough company when the occasion demanded, there was something withdrawn, even melancholy, about Miller. Among the items in his kit was the model of a house he planned to build in California after the war. Perhaps it was a symbol of hope, though it doesn't appear to have served its purpose very well. As he once told a BBC producer, he had an uncomfortable feeling that he'd never see the western seaboard of the USA again.

The band played on; the soldiers and airmen crossed the Channel and went to war; and Miller and his musicians did what they could to turn the men's minds to more pleasant things. On one occasion, he promised a draft of departing servicemen that, if they could recapture Paris by Christmas 1944, he and his band would put on a show for them in the French capital. It was easy enough to say, but more difficult to carry out. The broadcasting men protested that Paris had no facilities for transmissions. Remain here, they said, and you'll be playing to an audience of millions; go there, and you'll be lucky if you reach a few thousand. It was almost, Miller thought, as if they were trying to prevent him from keeping his promise.

Eventually, a deal was concluded. By prodigiously hard work, the band managed to record enough programmes to cover six weeks (129 recordings

Glenn Miller during one of his wartime shows. His plane disappeared without trace.

in all). With so much in store, the show could still go on while Major Miller and his musicians fulfilled their engagement in France.

Conditions in Paris were terrible. There was not enough accommodation, almost no heating, hardly any lighting, and apparently nowhere in which to stage a performance on the scale he envisaged. Nevertheless, Glenn Miller was undaunted. By early December he had roughed out a plan by which Don Haynes would go on ahead and find lodgings, studios and a theatre. He would follow with the band a few days later. Bad weather aborted Haynes's departure. Miller became increasingly impatient. Eventually he decided to switch roles. He would lead the way and make the arrangements; Haynes would bring the orchestra over two days afterwards.

The weather remained awful. There seemed to be no way of getting to Paris – until, towards the middle of December, whatever fate governed the Miller destiny caused him to encounter an old friend, Colonel Norman Basselle. He told Basselle his problem; the Colonel considered matters for a moment or two, and then observed that the journey might not be impossible. Indeed, he said, 'I'll come with you.'

So it was that, in the late afternoon of 14 December 1944, Major Glenn Miller, Colonel Basselle, and an experienced transport pilot named Flight Officer John R.S. Morgan of the 35th Depot Repair Squadron assembled at an airfield a few miles out of Bedford. Their aircraft was a small Norseman (otherwise designated as a UC-64A): a high-winged monoplane powered by a radial engine.

The prospects did not look good. Fog had been rolling in all day. RAF training flights had been grounded, and the forecast offered no hope. If anything, conditions were likely to become worse. Nevertheless, there was no embargo on flying, and Morgan reckoned that anything, even this, was possible. They climbed into the cockpit; the engine coughed and caught; and the little aeroplane wobbled off, gathered speed, and climbed into the sky. In England, and over the North Sea and the Channel, the fog was becoming thicker than ever.

Two days later, travelling in a large, four-engined transport, Lieutenant Don Haynes and the orchestra landed at Orly airport on the edge of Paris. Haynes had expected to find Miller waiting to greet them. There was no sign of him. He dug out the duty officer and asked him where Miller was. The duty officer said that he had not the slightest idea. When, then, had he arrived in Paris – and where, indeed, had he touched down? Again the answer was a sad shake of the head. The duty officer knew nothing.

For the next day or two there was still hope. A thorough search was made for the Norseman on the assumption that Morgan might have been compelled to make a forced landing. No traces were ever found.

Despite its leader's absence, the band continued its broadcasts – living, as it were, off its stock of 129 recordings. Inevitably, however, rumours began to circulate. People, unable to contemplate the awful fact that he might be dead, made up all kinds of far-fetched theories to account for his disappearance. Eisenhower normally put an embargo on the publication of casualty lists over the Christmas period. This year there was a single exception. Major Glenn Miller was reported as missing.

The big show in Paris took place, for shows transcend missing persons and pretty well everything else. Miller's arranger waved the baton; but, despite his valiant efforts, it wasn't quite the same. And the question remained: what *had* happened to Glenn Miller? It is still there. As a member of the Ministry of Defence's Air Historical Branch said in late 1983: 'They've never found the answer. They never will.'

It seems probable that, whatever the cause, the Norseman came down into the Channel. One possibility is that, with its very limited radio equipment, the pilot lost his way and the aircraft ran out of fuel. Another is that the wings iced up, causing it to stall and fall from the sky. There is also, of course, the possibility of mechanical failure. But it is ironic that in a still-embattled Europe the one cause which is not a possibility is enemy action.

FLIGHT INTO YESTERDAY

The voice was high and frantic, the message loud and clear. 'We must be over you. We cannot see you,' called the pilot. 'Gas running low,' she continued. 'We are flying at an altitude of 1,000 feet.'

The radio-operator on the US cutter *Itasca* received the message at 7.42 a.m., he noted in his log-book. Sixteen minutes later the transmission restarted. The woman's voice sounded even more alarmed. 'We are circling you. We cannot hear you. Go ahead on 7,500, either now or on scheduled time of half-hour.' The operator tapped out the morse direction-finding signal on 7,500 kilocycles. Immediately the voice responded. 'We are receiving your signals, but are unable to get a bearing. Please take a bearing on us and answer by voice on 3,105.'

'*Itasca* calling. *Itasca* calling,' the operator obediently repeated into his microphone. He went on calling every five minutes.

It was 8.45 a.m. before he received an answer. The voice from the air cut in, 'We are in line of position 157–337. We are running north and south. We are listening on 3,210 kilocycles.'

Changing his frequency, the radio-officer repeated his message. The anxious men in the radio-room strained their ears for the reply. None came. Her transmission at 8.45 a.m. on 3 July 1937 comprised the last words heard from Amelia Earhart. It was the last anyone ever heard of her – the last definite news that is.

Amelia Earhart, the famous American woman pilot, was on one of the final phases of a world flight, circling the globe at the equator. She and her navigator, Captain Fred Noonan, took off from Lae, New Guinea, at 10.00 a.m. on 2 July on a flight of 2,556 miles to Howland Island, a tiny dot in mid-Pacific, the last stepping-stone to Hawaii and the United States: a flight of twenty hours.

Anchored off Howland lay the US coastguard-cutter *Itasca*, stationed to help Amelia find the very small island. Throughout the night the *Itasca* had kept radio watch. There was a lot of static and most of Amelia's words were lost in transmission. Tension in the radio-room mounted until, at 6.15 a.m., her voice was heard clearly. 'About a hundred miles out,' she reported. The officers relaxed. All seemed well. The International Date Line, which runs between New Guinea and Howland, meant that Amelia and Fred were flying into yesterday. As 8 a.m. approached, the ship's officers crowded on deck, searching the sky with their eyes, and listening.

By 8.45 a.m. they knew the Electra was off-course. Amelia Earhart might still find Howland, or some other island. If the plane came down in the sea, the empty fuel tanks would keep it buoyant for hours, perhaps for days. Amelia might be anywhere in 400,000 square miles of sky or sea. The only clue to her position was the statement that she was in line of position 157–337. But what did that cryptic message mean? It was not a radio bearing; it could be a sun bearing. But that possibility did not help the searchers, for they did not know her geographical point of reference.

The continued radio-silence was the greatest mystery of all. If the Electra was still airborne, her radio signals should still be heard. The Electra, the Navy men knew, carried a radio transmitter capable of sending messages up to 1,000 miles. On the sea's surface, its radio would be silent, its aerial ineffective.

'Amelia Earhart missing,' Captain Thompson of USS *Itasca* radioed Washington. A battleship and an aircraft-carrier ordered to assist you, the Navy Department replied. The greatest air–sea search ever mounted for a missing aircraft was put into operation. Seven Navy ships, and the carrier's planes, swept an area of 151,556 square miles. The weather was fine and clear, the sea moderate, but it was like looking for a needle in a haystack. No trace of the Electra was found, no floating debris, no smashed pieces on land. The search was called off on 19 July, and the US Navy

Amelia Earhart, photographed at the cockpit in 1922 (*left*), and being cheered by children in the East End of London in 1928, after becoming the first woman to fly the Atlantic.

pronounced Earhart and Noonan 'lost at sea'. America mourned her greatest heroine.

The leg of the journey on which Amelia and Noonan had come to grief was the most intimidating of the entire project, a daunting challenge of flight and navigation over two and a half thousand miles of open water to seek a landfall on a derisory target only two miles long and half a mile wide, with a maximum elevation of twenty feet about sea level. Though saddening, it seemed no great surprise that even such brilliant and experienced aviators should have failed to survive its dangers.

But the matter did not end there. Fresh evidence nearly thirty years later suggested the possibility that Intelligence agencies in the US had attempted to exploit the glittering reputation of Amelia Earhart by involving her in a planned act of espionage which was to lead to her death. To understand the story and its significance one must consider two seemingly unrelated factors – the political and diplomatic relationship between the United States of America and Japan in the 1930s, and the achievements and reputation of Amelia Earhart.

At the peace conference of 1919 Japan had been granted a mandate, subject to the ultimate control of the League of Nations, over the Marianas, the Carolines, and the Marshall Islands in the Pacific. Article four of that mandate laid down that: 'The military training of the natives, otherwise than for the purpose of internal police and the local defence of the territory, shall be prohibited. Furthermore, no military or naval bases shall be established, or fortifications erected in the territory.'

Throughout the 1920s and 1930s the United States Government and its various intelligence departments were well aware of the increasing threat to their country's security as these limitations were blatantly ignored by the Japanese, who were building sea-plane bases and fortifications throughout the islands, notably on Truk and Saipan, where they had established what was virtually a military and strategic headquarters. America, however, was reluctant to protest and powerless to intervene. She could not bring pressure to bear in the League of Nations, for she was not a member of that assembly; she could not risk direct confrontation in the face of Japanese intransigence, for in the aftermath of the First World War the mood of the American electorate was profoundly isolationist. Moreover, with a presidential election in the offing, Franklin Delano Roosevelt had no intention of committing political suicide.

This era of Japanese–American tension, suspicion, and mutual surveillance was also one of the great eras of flight, the age of record-breakers. The world's finest aviators – and Amelia was certainly one of these – were accorded the adulation now reserved for pop stars. In 1921, at the age of 23, she had flown solo; a year later, climbing to more than 14,000 feet in a tiny biplane, she had set the first of her many world records for women. In 1928, as navigator to pilot Wilmer Stultz, she had become the first woman to fly the Atlantic; and four years later, on 20 May 1932, she had claimed her place amongst aviation's immortals as the first woman to achieve the same feat single-handed, piloting a Lockheed Vega monoplane from Newfoundland to Londonderry in 14 hours and 56 minutes.

She was feted by royalty, including King George V and the Prince of Wales, and became a personal friend of President Franklin D. Roosevelt and his wife Eleanor; she was adored by the public far beyond the bounds of her native America. Tall, lean, athletic and rangy, with a boy-short haircut and a wide and generous smile, she was everyone's darling, feminist without being strident, independent without arrogance, and, as a bonus, possessed of a truly striking facial and physical resemblance to America's hero of the air, Colonel Charles Lindbergh, from whom, inescapably, she inherited the tabloids' sobriquet 'Lady Lindy'. She was well born, well educated, a forthright and accomplished public speaker, an experienced social worker. All of these qualities and accomplishments combined to make her a very valuable potential servant of the United States Government.

When the suggestion of a round-the-world trip was made, Purdue University, in recognition of Amelia's services as a visiting lecturer, pledged 50,000 dollars towards the cost of providing a suitable aeroplane, a twin-engined, ten-seater Lockheed Electra; but it was some authority far richer and more powerful than Purdue that planned and funded the transformation of the machine into what Amelia fondly dubbed her 'flying laboratory'. The passenger-seats were ripped out to make space for extra fuel tanks and for the installation of a navigation centre lavishly equipped with the latest products of American technology. Most significant was the decision, not made public, to remove the original engines and to replace them with much more powerful units that provided the aircraft with range and speed capabilities far in excess of the figures shown in the log-book and in the flight plan for the final voyage. On its licence the Electra listed as its function 'long distance flights and research'. All the information now available seems to point to the fact that the Electra was deliberately equipped for the task of aerial surveillance. The target of such surveillance could only be the Japanese.

Originally the flight was planned and publicized as a journey from east to west; during the weeks before take-off the direction was reversed, though nothing was said of this in public, and no announcement that the

The Lockheed Electra, nicknamed the 'flying laboratory', passing the Golden Gate Bridge at Oakland, California, in March 1937. Four months later she and her navigator, Fred Noonan (*right*), went missing in the Pacific – officially 'lost at sea'. But were they captured and executed by the Japanese as spies?

project was actually under way was made until Amelia and Noonan were already airborne and beyond the reach of the Press or other interested spectators. On Howland Island three runways had been constructed for the sole purpose of receiving the Electra, a remarkable governmental expenditure upon what was ostensibly a private venture. The US Navy ship *Swan* and the USS *Ontario* were positioned along the route as guard-ships, and the coastguard cutter *Itasca* was stationed alongside Howland to transmit and receive homing signals.

The precise distance between Lae and Howland Island is 2,556 miles; the Electra with its extra tanks had a range of over 4,000. All stages of the journey as far as Lae had been flown at speeds never exceeding 150m.p.h.; with its new engines the aeroplane was capable of travelling at 220. Yet in one of her last radio messages to *Itasca* Amelia stated she was running out of gas. When these facts are considered together, a logical conclusion is that the aviators had not adhered to their stated intention of flying direct from Lae to Howland, but had in fact first headed north to overfly *en route* the Japanese airfields and fleet-servicing facilities on the Truk complex in the Central Carolines, a fast-developing area of military preparation.

During a preflight briefing Amelia had said that should she fail to find Howland Island she would head for the American-occupied Gilbert Islands and either ditch in shallow water or make an emergency landing on a beach. No trace of her or of her aeroplane was ever found in or near the Gilberts, despite an exhaustive air–sea search.

On 27 May 1960, twenty-three years later, the San Mateo *Times* printed a letter from a Mrs Josephine Akimaya, who claimed that in 1937, as a girl living in Saipan, she with many other natives had seen a white man and a woman 'very tall, very boyish-looking, with close-cut hair and wearing men's clothes' taken to military police headquarters by Japanese guards who described them as American flyers and spies, and who later announced that as such they had been executed.

For the next six years an enterprising radio news reporter, Fred Goerner, with the backing of the Columbia Broadcasting System, the Scripps' League, and Associated Press, carried out an astonishing programme of investigative journalism involving no fewer than four prolonged visits to the Pacific islands and literally thousands of hours of research. He recorded countless interviews with anyone he could trace; the interviewees ranging from the great Fleet Admiral Chester W. Nimitz, commander of the US Pacific Fleet during the Second World War, to elderly villagers on Saipan. The account of this assignment, related in his book *The Search For Amelia Earhart*, tells of frustration at every turn, of evasion, and at times of blatant lying by officers, both service and civilian, of the United States Government, determined in the face of steadily mounting evidence to deny involvement in an illegal act of peacetime intrusion into another nation's territory. Admiral Nimitz, it must be added, was guiltless of such duplicity, and in fact gave Goerner tacit encouragement to continue his searching. As an officer who despite his age was still on active duty, Nimitz could say little; but Goerner received indirect confirmation that the Admiral thought he was on the right track.

As to the actual fate of Earhart and Noonan, Goerner's conclusions, based upon a mass of evidence too lengthy to be detailed in a brief account, may be summarized thus. From Lae they set course north to the Carolines, not west to Howland. Their mission was unofficial but vital: to overfly the Truk complex and reconnoitre its fleet-servicing capabilities and the positioning of its airfields. By late afternoon they were over Truk Lagoon, and would have observed the airfields on Etten and Moen Islands and the vast repair docks. As they set course for Howland, the weather changed and tropical thunderstorms burst around them. Confused by totally unfamiliar weather conditions during the last stages of the flight, they were convinced that they had overshot Howland when they were in fact many miles short of it. Their emergency navigational correction had then been wrong and had brought them not to the Gilberts, but to Mili Atoll in the southeastern Marshalls. There they had crash-landed in shallow water. On or about 13 July 1937 a Japanese fishing-boat took them off the island. They were probably transferred to the seaplane tender *Kamoi*, and taken by stages to Saipan. Having overflown Japan's most secret and important bases in the Pacific, their fates were sealed. Noonan was summarily beheaded; and Amelia died after prolonged imprisonment – probably of dysentery.

The official verdict remains, however, and is never likely to be revised, that Amelia Earhart and Captain Fred Noonan were lost at sea somewhere between Lae and Howland.

HINDENBURG: THE MYSTERY INFERNO

The radio reporter's name was Herb Morrison. He was employed by a Chicago station, though on this sixth day of May 1937 he was covering an event at Lakehurst airfield, New Jersey. The occasion was the arrival of the airship *Hindenburg* after its first Atlantic crossing of the year.

At four o'clock that afternoon, the giant zeppelin was sighted to the south of the field. It was already ten hours behind schedule and people were becoming impatient. Morrison was told it would make fast at the mooring-tower round about six. But even for this it was late. A thunderstorm had drifted down from the north and had lingered over Lakehurst for an hour before sweeping away, grumbling, in the direction of Philadelphia.

Herb Morrison filled in the time with chatty background information. Then, as the immense silver cyclinder, 830 feet long, approached the tower, he began his commentary. The interest of his listeners quickened. They heard him describe a sudden gust of wind that swung the airship sharply to port. In their minds' eyes they could see the helmsman make a rapid correction. Everything still seemed to be all right until, a few seconds later, Herb Morrison's voice suddenly changed key and took on a note of panic.

'It's bursting into flames and falling on the mooring mast!' he cried. 'This is terrible! This is one of the worst catastrophes in the world. Oh, the humanity and all the passengers! I told you – it's a mass of smoking wreckage. Honest, I can hardly breathe. I'm going to step inside where I can't see it. It's terrible. I ... I ... folks, I'm going to have to stop for a moment because I've lost my voice. This is the worst thing I've ever witnessed.'

At this point Herb Morrison broke down. In just over half a minute, fire had consumed the largest flying-machine the world has ever seen. Thirty-five of the ninety-seven passengers and crew were either dead or dying.

The wreckage continued to blaze for another three hours. The age of the airship was dead. It had perished in the body of Germany's greatest zeppelin.

In 1919 two ex-Royal Air Force officers, John Alcock and Arthur Whitten Brown, accomplished the first non-stop flight across the Atlantic. Their machine was a modified Vickers Vimy bomber. Despite its satisfactory performance, Brown wrote that if ever such undertakings were to become commercial propositions, they would have to be carried out by rigid airships.

Brown's prognosis turned out to be correct – at least until 1937. Nevertheless, there were several setbacks. American experience with airships turned out to be costly in lives and materials. British prospects, for a while, seemed to be more promising. In the same year as Alcock and Brown's flight, the R34 flew the Atlantic and back; in 1930 the R100 made a successful crossing to Canada. But then, in the same year, the R101 crashed on its maiden flight to India, killing forty-eight of the fifty-four people on board. Among the dead was Lord Thompson of Cardington, the British Air Minister. Thereafter Britain concentrated on heavier-than-air machines.

The only nation which seemed to have mastered the secret of airship travel was Germany. Even before the First World War, zeppelins were making trouble-free domestic flights. In the autumn of 1928 the *Graf Zeppelin* made its debut. Named after Count Zeppelin, the originator of these ships of the sky, it could carry 20 passengers and 12 tons of freight at a maximum speed of 95 k.p.h. By the end of 1936 it had flown 1 million kilometres, and completed 16,000 flying hours covering 578 flights. Most of them had been to Brazil – though on one or two occasions they had been across the storm-ridden North Atlantic skies. No less impressive was the fact that not a single passenger had been killed or injured in the history of German civil aviation.

The *Graf Zeppelin* had a monopoly of transatlantic air traffic, whether to North or South America. To exploit this advantage, it was decided to build another, much larger airship specifically for the crossing to New York. It was to be almost double the size of the earlier ship, and designed to fly at a far greater speed – 150 k.p.h.

All previous zeppelins had relied on hydrogen. Whilst it provided the maximum lift, it had the danger of being highly inflammable. To introduce greater safety to the newcomer, which was designated L129, the designers decided to incorporate helium as well. Each bag, and there were sixteen of them, would have a cell of hydrogen in the centre, surrounded by the much less volatile gas. Helium, indeed, was more likely to kill a blaze than to start one. There was, however, a snag. The only source of supply was the United States of America. Everything depended upon the agreement of the United States Government.

In 1933 Adolf Hitler had succeeded the senile von Hindenburg as Chancellor of Germany. The persecution of the Jews had begun, and the Führer, as Hitler chose to describe himself, was beginning to make warlike noises. When these utterances reached America, it seemed reasonable to assume that the new airship might one day be taken over by the *Luftwaffe*. Zeppelins had, after all, originated the aerial bombardment of cities in the First World War. In view of this, the United States became adamant: no helium was to be supplied.

It was a severe setback. The only consolations were that the superior buoyancy of hydrogen on its own enabled nine more passenger cabins to be constructed, and that the specifications had made allowances for some

Previous pages: The giant dirigible *Hindenburg* flying over Manhattan for the last time, on 6 May 1937, on its way to Lakehurst, New Jersey.

Above: As the *Hindenburg* prepares to land, flames suddenly burst from the top of the airship.

Top: The largest flying-machine the world had ever seen, the epitome of swift, comfortable transport, collapses in flames.

Above: The smoking wreckage.

such situation. Hardly a scrap of wood was used in the ship; instead, everything was manufactured from an alloy named duralumin. Even the small piano in the lounge was made of it.

Just the same, as the R101 disaster had shown so tragically, the hazards were considerably increased. Indeed, anyone who flew in L129 might have felt a lot less than comfortable if he or she had known that some of the R101 materials were actually incorporated in the new zeppelin's construction. After the British airship had plunged to its blazing doom on a hillside near Beauvais in France, the salvaged remains were auctioned. The highest bid came from the zeppelin company's works at Frankfurt. It suggests a curious insensivity, or else lack of imagination, on the purchaser's part.

By the beginning of 1936 the new airship had been completed and named *Hindenburg* – considerably to the disgust of Adolf Hitler, who would have preferred his own name to be used. To ensure that his displeasure should not be forgotten, he always referred to the ship as L129. Nevertheless, as even the Führer had to admit, it was a beautiful creation and a splendid boost to Germany's prestige. The passenger accommodation included a dining-saloon, a lounge, a smoking-room, luxurious cabins, showers galore, and a promenade deck. During 1936 the *Hindenburg* made ten trips to New York and seven to Rio de Janeiro. Each was completely free from trouble, and it looked as if the performance of the *Graf Zeppelin*, which was still running a service to Rio, had at last been surpassed.

Although bookings at the start of 1937 were disappointing, business seemed likely to improve as the year progressed. The coronation of King George VI was due to take place in London on 12 May and, later, the Paris Exposition was sure to be well attended. Such was the mood of optimism that a sister to the *Hindenburg*, to be called *Graf Zeppelin II*, was already under construction. When, on 3 May 1937, the *Hindenburg* departed from the Rhine–Main airport near Frankfurt on the season's inaugural flight, the crew – normally 40 – was increased to 61. The extra hands were trainees intended for *Graf Zeppelin II*.

By no means all the omens were good. The German Ambassador in New York, Dr Luther, had received a disturbing letter from a German expatriate woman living in Milwaukee. The gist of it was that the *Hindenburg* would be destroyed by a time-bomb, and that all mail loaded aboard should be carefully searched. Dr Luther was not an alarmist, but he took the warning sufficiently seriously to pass it on to the German Air Ministry.

Other people, too, had forebodings, though less specific. The boxer, Max Schmeling, had booked a passage on the *Hindenburg*. At the last minute, however, he cancelled it and travelled by ship.

Captain Ernst Lehmann, the senior captain on board, was described as 'quiet, sensitive, perhaps even a little dreamy'. On this occasion he was also in a state of depression, for the Lehmanns' son had just died suddenly at the age of twenty-one. To make matters worse, his wife had consulted a clairvoyant in Vienna. Frau Lehmann was told that her husband would perish in a blazing airship.

Among the passengers was a *Luftwaffe* officer, Colonel Fritz Erdmann. Minutes before the *Hindenburg* slipped away from the mooring mast, he experienced what he described as 'a terrible feeling'. It was so strong that he begged to be allowed to say goodbye to his wife once more. Afterwards, a number of people noticed that he was in tears.

Possibly as a result of Dr Luther's prodding, the airship was searched with more than common thoroughness before departure; and, although the passengers did not realize it, Gestapo officers rather than customs officials went through the baggage. Despite this, however, it would not have been difficult to smuggle a small incendiary device on board. Nor were all the travellers scrutinized. A late arrival, carrying a suitcase and a parcel, was almost certainly overlooked.

At eight o'clock that evening the *Hindenburg* slipped away from the tower and, amid the blare of a band pumping out patriotic airs down below, ascended gracefully into the darkening sky. Rain that had been falling stopped; the cloud base lifted. Colonel Erdmann was still unhappy. His companions, on the whole, were cheerful – though it hadn't escaped their notice that the airship was booked to only half its capacity. Had others, like Max Schmeling, suffered misgivings and preferred to patronize ocean liners?

There was little turbulence on the crossing, though 50-knot headwinds slowed the ship down. Even when, at 6 p.m. on 6 May, twelve hours behind schedule, the *Hindenburg* approached the mooring mast at Lakehurst, a thunderstorm delayed matters by a further sixty minutes.

Dr Eckener once observed that he thought the *Hindenburg* had been born beneath an unlucky star. He now seemed to be correct. Even at the last minute, a gust of wind slammed her off-course. The helmsman responded with a turn that was probably too tight, and which could have snapped one of the bracing wires. If it did, it would have slashed a hole in a gas cell. This was not in itself dangerous – though even the smallest spark would have ignited the escaping hydrogen.

Two hundred men were waiting on the ground to grab the mooring ropes. On board, the crew was going calmly about its business. The only suggestion that anything might be amiss came from the leading rigger. There seemed, he reported, to be something wrong with number four cell. But he had no time to elaborate, and no time for another look.

Accounts of the explosion vary. One man on the ground noticed 'a small burst of flame'. Another saw a ball of flame beneath the ship. *The Times* correspondent described a 'bomb-like explosion [that] sent out clouds of red and billowing smoke'. It was heard fifteen miles away.

It all happened in thirty-two seconds. One moment the *Hindenburg* was floating elegantly in the sky; the next it had fallen in flames nose-downward to the ground. The marvel, perhaps, lies not in the number that were killed, but in the tally of those who escaped despite the seven million cubic feet of incandescent hydrogen about them. One elderly lady actually walked out of the exit as if at the end of a normal trip. Captain Lehmann survived the crash, but the clairvoyant in Vienna was right: he died afterwards in hospital. Colonel Erdmann's misgivings were justified. He perished in the flames. The leading rigger also died, which denied the subsequent court of inquiry the opportunity to hear about his concern for cell number four.

What, then, went wrong? Hitler, in one of his rare references to the Almighty, described it as 'an act of God'. Indeed the Nazis took trouble to ensure that the crew told the US court of inquiry as little as possible. Partly due to this attitude of non-cooperation, its findings were indecisive. Electrical causes, a major structural failure, a broken propeller, and sabotage were among the mooted causes. St Elmo's fire (a luminous electrical discharge in the atmosphere), combined with a leaking gas-bag, was hazarded as another possibility.

But could it have been sabotage? Was the letter from the woman in Milwaukee really a well-informed warning? There were many who hated the Nazis, and one of the riggers in the crew was known to have a Communist girl friend. He was a withdrawn character; a young man who never mixed with the others and who struck people as lonely. His name was Erich Spehl, and he was regarded with suspicion – to such an extent that a Gestapo officer, disguised as an airship hand, was assigned to keep an eye on him. He certainly had the ability and the opportunity, though nothing was ever proven. Nor did Spehl survive.

The idea of sabotage becomes more attractive when we consider the one hour's delay occasioned by the thunderstorm. If some sort of device had been set for seven o'clock, everyone should have been safely on the ground. The *Hindenburg*, an unwitting symbol of Nazi might, would have been destroyed, but nobody would have been hurt. As things were, that sudden change in the weather may have killed thirty-five people – and altered the course of aviation history.

GHOSTS AND THE OCCULT

THE GHOSTS OF BORLEY

The residents of Borley do not solicit your interest, nor tout for your cash, on the strength of their hamlet's notoriety. There are no souvenir shops, no blatant signboards, no pub named the Spectre, as there is at another English village with a similar sort of reputation. Where many another place – perhaps in countries other than England – would have made commercial use of such long years of publicity and continued speculation, this tiny settlement, remote in the flat green borderland of Essex and Suffolk, preserves its privacy so far as it is able, in the tradition of a region noted for what might almost be termed secretiveness. Yet the very name of Borley lives in most people's minds as the site of what was chillingly termed 'the most haunted house in England'.

It no longer stands, that original Borley Rectory. It burned down to a shell at the end of February 1939. A handsome private house has replaced it, and other new ones cover what was its garden – none of them troubled by those influences which so disturbed the site's past and made it known to the world. Perhaps the fire exorcized them, as some witnesses thought they saw happening. Perhaps. . . . But Borley is all 'perhaps'.

Its prominence goes back more than a century, to a time when ghosts were commonplace and few ancient buildings, especially ones with religious associations, were without their rumours of haunting. Many of these, however, were manufactured by smugglers, who operated far inland and preferred people to stay fearfully indoors after dark rather than glimpse their comings and goings. The decline in smuggling, and the spread of gas- and electric-lighting, outdoors and in, extinguished more spectres than any services of exorcism.

But there was no gas at Borley in 1862 when the Rev. Henry Dawson Ellis Bull and his family moved into Borley Place, the Tudor house adjoining the church. Vague tales of the usual ghostly monk and nun, the phantom coach with headless driver and suchlike did not worry them. There had been no monastery or nunnery on the spot for certain. Rev. Bull was a worldly man, wealthy and tweedy, fond of his gun and other sports (with fourteen children he was not inappropriately named), and materialist enough, in the mid-Victorian fashion, to prefer to build a tasteless house across the road for his new rectory. He gave it twenty-three rooms, to accommodate his large family, their frequent guests and a plentiful staff of servants. He added more rooms in due course, and a stable-block with grooms' quarters.

One other structure was erected: a garden pavilion, where pleasant summer evenings could be spent looking out across the lawns. If any resident ghost were to be seen in the locality, it was the nun who flitted about those lawns, though only by daylight, and the Bulls seem to have regarded the spectacle as a form of entertainment. Unexplained disturbances, though, such as objects being moved and even thrown, occurred indoors from time to time, causing at least one servant to give in her notice.

Rev. Bull died a widower in 1892. His son Harry, who succeeded him as rector of Borley, preferred to live in the older house, leaving his unmarried sisters to inhabit the ugly modern rectory. Now that they were no longer children, and had lost innocent acceptance, the Misses Bull found the nun a more disquieting sight. She seemed to glide along, in her flowing black robes, with her head bowed and a pained look on what could be seen of her face. When they ventured to engage her in conversation, she vanished.

One of the sisters awoke once to see a man standing by her bed; he proved to be spectral too; tall and in dark clothes. They began to believe the local legend of a monk and a nun from nearby establishments having fallen in love and eloped, only to be brought back and bricked up together in a wall. Their unlikely conveyance on their escapade was said to have been the coach, whose driver's lack of a head did not discommode him from carrying on his work in a spectral capacity.

The Rev. Harry Bull married in 1911 and died in 1927. The rest of the family dispersed, leaving behind them no notes of warning or guidance for the new rector, the Rev. Guy Smith, who arrived with his wife more than a year later, having lived in India and knowing nothing of Borley Rectory. They found it ugly, dilapidated, cold, inadequately serviced in all respects, and a thoroughly undesirable residence. When parishioners, who showed a marked disinclination to cross the threshold, told them it was haunted into the bargain, they could almost be amused at the appropriateness of it.

It ceased to be in the least bit funny when they began to experience things themselves: sudden loud rappings, dragging footfalls in empty rooms, the service bells ringing all at once, and lights where none should be. The nun appeared, and, as a last straw for Rev. and Mrs Smith, the phantom coach rocketed through the hedge and across the lawn, before vanishing.

Rev. Smith, a *Daily Mirror* reader, wrote to that newspaper to seek help. The *Mirror* sent a reporter, together with the best-known psychic investigator of the time, Harry Price, the man whose name was to become enduringly linked with Borley Rectory. Price first visited Borley in June 1929 and asked searching questions of the clergyman who had turned to the Press for the succour which faith ought to have been able to supply. Rev. Smith answered firmly that his faith held strongly enough, but that the evidence of his and his wife's eyes and ears had to be believed, and needed investigating in the common interest.

His assertion was backed up by a display of phenomena which had the reporter scribbling busily: small objects flew about; keys jerked themselves free of keyholes; a red glass candlestick hurtled down a staircase and smashed in splinters.

Price's investigations took some days, and naturally attracted other Press attention. The *Daily Mail* sent a man down, too; but he watched Price, as well as the manifestations, and became suspicious. After a pebble had hit him on the head, he managed to feel one of Price's jacket pockets, all of which always bulged with odds and ends of his eccentric calling, and found that it was full of stones and fragments of brick. No doubt in view of the risk of libel, the *Mail*'s editor decided not to print that detail.

Price suggested a séance, in the so-called Blue Room upstairs in the rectory, a particular centre of disturbance. He, his secretary, Rev. and Mrs Smith, and the *Mirror* reporter were joined by two of the Misses Bull, who had been persuaded to add their influence. A veritable fusillade of rappings seemed to emanate from a dressing-table mirror. By a code of tappings, which the 'spirit' agreed to use, its identity was convincingly established as that of the late Rev. Harry Bull.

His sister Ethel questioned him about family matters, but he had no significant message to pass. The sitting was enlivened by little sparks flashing about the room and a cake of soap rising from the washstand and hitting the side of a metal water-jug so hard that it left a deep dent. Later that evening all the keys to all the hall doors fell out of their holes simultaneously. Yet, many years later, after Harry Price had published the details in his first book on Borley, Mrs Smith wrote to the *Church Times* denying emphatically that either she or her husband believed the house to have been haunted. They attributed the disturbances to the rats, which, along with other features of the building's neglected state, had caused them to leave after less than a year in July 1929.

Borley Rectory stood empty for seventeen months, until there arrived the Rev. Lionel Foyster, a relative of the Bulls. He was fifty-one, with an attractive wife, Marianne, thirty years his junior, and a baby daughter, Adelaide.

The Borley spirits wasted no time in showing the newcomers what they could do; so much so that Rev. Foyster immediately opened a diary, beginning with an account of his wife's hearing her name called by a doleful male voice. Shortly afterwards she told him she had seen a pale man in a dressing-gown on the stairs. He had a large, Kitchener-style moustache, and she recognized him as the deceased Harry Bull.

Mr Foyster's diary began to fill rapidly, with reports of service-bells rung by no human hand, and things flying about or disappearing, only to turn up elsewhere. A number of hymn books settled themselves on the plate-warming rack over the kitchen range. Worst of all, flying objects, including a hairbrush, a doorknob and a hammer, struck and injured his wife.

Lionel Foyster decided that the time had come for an exorcism. He called in two other Anglican priests to help him, and they all went about the vastnesses of the rectory, burning incense, sprinkling holy water, and reciting prayers and intoning:

I conjure thee, unclean spirit, by the holy mysteries of the Christian religion to afflict this house no more. Tremble, O Satan, thou enemy of the faith, thou foe of mankind, who has brought death into the world, who has deprived men of life, and has rebelled against justice, thou seducer of mankind, thou root of evil....

Things turned comparatively quiet for a few days. Then, as Mr Foyster lay in bed feeling unwell one morning, he heard his wife's cry of alarm and her footsteps running up to the room. She was almost too distraught to tell him what had happened – in the kitchen passage, a great shadowy form, like an enormous bat, had touched her shoulder with a wing or hand, and the force had been like that of a blow with an iron bar.

The Foysters stayed on, nevertheless, coming to terms with the manifestations so far as they could. Guests of theirs witnessed some of the goings-on, and wondered how they could stick it. Sir George and Lady Whitehouse, with their nephew Edwin, who later became a Benedictine priest, were staying at Borley Rectory when something new occurred: pieces of paper started appearing, bearing the name 'Marianne' in a childish scrawl. In 1931 identical inscriptions appeared on walls.

These served to turn the limelight onto the attractive Marianne Foyster, whose possible association with what her husband termed the 'goblins' came under much scrutiny in later years. Marianne was thought by some to have mediumistic powers; but she claimed subsequently that, of all the Borley phenomena, the one she had never seen was the nun. There was enough without her, though, to keep Mr Foyster at his diary until, after fifteen months and 50,000 words, an arthritic hand, combined with the sheer amount of repetitious material, caused him to give it up.

The Foysters left Borley in 1935. It was the end of the house as a rectory: no one wanted to inhabit it, the Church authorities had come to consider it unsuitable. It lay empty, and the mind can only conjecture what eerie goings-on continued within its echoing gloomy spaces – that is, presuming anything went on at all. But there was a renewal of activity there in May 1937 – for this time its tenant was Harry Price.

Borley Rectory, 'the most haunted house in England'.

Harry Price (*left*), the investigator, with the Rev. Lionel Foyster and his family.

A brick suspended in mid-air during the demolition of the Rectory in 1943. This was the last of many such manifestations.

He did not live at the rectory – his home was 150 miles away – but he
kept visiting it to conduct his researches over varying periods. He adver-
tised for a panel of intelligent, unbiased observers to help him, and drew
up a code of practice to be followed:

> If you see an apparition, remain still, and no *not* approach it. Note carefully its
> shape, clothing, degree of solidity or transparency, size, clothing (if any) and other
> relevant details. Should it speak, enquire its name, origins, reason for haunting,
> and any possible assistance that may be given to it. See Instruction Number
> Eleven for particular procedure with regard to the 'Nun's Walk' in the Rectory
> grounds.

Instruction Number Eleven did not have to be invoked, for the nun made
no appearance. A letter M seemed to some observers to materialize before
them. The most interesting new phenomenon arose at one of a number of
séances held in the decaying surroundings. Miss Helen Glanville, daughter of
Harry Price's collaborator Sidney Glanville, was using a planchette, the little
board which moves to and fro on wheels under the sitter's hand, causing
an attached pencil to write down things which are presumed to emanate
from a communicating spirit (a presumption nowadays largely rejected).

Miss Glanville's contact was a female entity who identified herself as
Marie Lairre. She had been a nun with a French order at Le Havre in the
seventeenth century, but had left there to marry Henry Waldegrave, a
member of the influential Roman Catholic family whose house, Borley
Manor, had occupied the site on which the rectory was subsequently built.
The family had been patrons of Borley church, in which their fine tomb
can still be seen. Marie Lairre's sensational disclosure, through the planchette, was that her husband had murdered her in the old house, by
strangling.

Harry Price leaped at this timely piece of corroborative evidence for the
book he was writing, *The Most Haunted House in England*. By the time it
appeared, though, Borley Rectory was no more, and again the planchette
seemed to have had something to say about it.

At a session with it, on 28 March 1938, Helen Glanville heard from a
male spirit calling himself Sunex Amurex that the house would burn down
that very night. He was wrong – by eleven months. At midnight on 27
February 1939 fire broke out in the hall, where a new owner, Captain
W.E. Gregson, who had renamed the house Borley Priory, was sorting
piles of books. A stack of them fell (or was it pushed? – Gregson had
experienced his share of strange happenings already) and knocked over a
paraffin lamp. The blaze got beyond control, and by the time the Sudbury
fire brigade's engines had arrived the whole roof had fallen in. Villagers

watching the fire helplessly had been petrified to see an apparently trapped young woman at an upstairs window – but there was no woman in Captain Gregson's household, not even a servant.

No body was found in the ruins. The villagers were not surprised. At the height of the blaze they (including the local policeman) had seen two cloaked figures walk out of the flames and leave the scene. One had obviously been a young girl; the other was 'formless'.

Those who dismiss the planchette board generally claim that its movements are determined by the user's subconscious mind. But there were details of the communications through Miss Glanville which could scarcely have come from hers. In telling of her murder by her husband, Marie Lairre had added that he had buried her under the cellar floor of the old house, from which it could naturally be inferred that the former nun would know no rest, unshriven in unconsecrated ground.

Sunex Amurex had got the date of the fire wrong; but there had been a fire, and it had destroyed Borley Rectory, as he had predicted. He had said it would break out 'over the hall'; it had started in the hall. Asked by Miss Glanville if it would put an end to the hauntings, he had said it would not, but would lead to the proof of their cause. That proof would be the discovery of bones under the ruins.

Price's book appeared and predictably became a best-seller. For one reader, it confirmed his own theories about a case which had long fascinated him. He was Dr John Phythian-Adams, Canon of Carlisle, who hastened to write to Price, laying out his hypothesis and suggesting excavations under Borley Rectory ruins.

Two years passed before anything could be done about it: there was a war on; East Anglia, with its many bomber airfields, was a notable target for raids; and there was no labour to be had to go poking about for ancient remains. Borley was often written about, though – those sceptical of Harry Price and his methods, which many suspected extended to rigging the effects he wanted, saw that he was making almost a private industry out of the place. Overseas servicemen who had heard of it were among those who went looking for ghosts, and it would have been surprising if some had not claimed to have seen mysterious shapes moving about in the ruins.

With the ruins further damaged by gales and becoming dangerous, they were pulled down, and in August 1943, under Harry Price's supervision, excavations began, concentrating on the old well under the foundations. Only trivial household items were found, until the digging was extended along the passage between the well and the cellar entrance. There, three feet below the surface, they found human bones, including part of a skull. A pathologist identified it as having been that of a woman aged about thirty. Later a dental surgeon was able to show that she must have had a painful abscess of the jaw, which reminded people of descriptions of the ghostly nun's dismal expression.

The remains were given Christian burial in the churchyard at Liston, some miles away. Harry Price was at the graveside. He was a devout churchman, most unlikely, it was thought, to have buried those remains where he wanted them found, a task which in any case would have been virtually impossible without detection. But he did very well for himself again with another book, *The End of Borley Rectory*, published in 1946, two years before his death.

The story of Borley's hauntings has not ended with the rectory's end. It is too potent to be allowed to fade, and is an automatic candidate for inclusion in any collection such as this present one. And there remain those who claim that the ghosts have not necessarily vanished. The nun has reputedly been seen many more times, in a variety of costumes. A former BBC director, who had perhaps never heard of Price's dictum about not approaching too close, got near enough to find that 'she' was a column of dancing midges, moving slowly along the so-termed 'Nun's Walk'. He and a colleague dug there, and found what they expected – an underground stream whose course the midges had been following.

The BBC were back officially in the late 1970s, with recording apparatus. Borley church had become the newest focus of ghost-hunters in recent years, so the reporters set their recorders up there, for all-night running, and left them. The results were impressive to some hearers, not so to others, consisting of a few scratching noises, a seeming groan, something like a sigh, all of which might have been merely the natural stirrings of an ancient, empty building.

Harry Price faked some things and exaggerated others: that is not an uncommon failing on the part of people who believe in something and passionately wish to convince others. But strange things had been happening at Borley Rectory long before he came onto its scene, and several different families of residents had experienced them. However much is rejected as being of too doubtful provenance, there remains as much again that cannot be explained away.

As much as the locals there would perhaps wish the matter forgotten, so that the earnest ghost-hunters and the awed sightseers alike might go away for ever, Borley is certain to remain an evocative name for ever.

THE GHOSTS OF VERSAILLES

Their story was so strange that they hesitated to tell it. They had even, at first, been reluctant to confide in each other what they had seen, or thought they had seen. Yet the two ladies were of such flawless respectability and such high intelligence, one the Principal of St Hugh's College, Oxford, the other headmistress of an important school for girls at Watford, a few miles from London. Miss Anne Moberley was the daughter of the distinguished scholar George Moberley, headmaster of Winchester College, who later became Bishop of Salisbury; she had been born too early (1846) to receive a proper education, which was not then afforded to women, but with the instinct of a natural scholar she educated herself to such a standard that she was given the honorary degree of Master of Arts by Oxford University and appointed Principal of one of its three women's colleges.

Miss Eleanor Jourdain was younger, born in 1863, the daughter of a vicar. At Lady Margaret Hall, Oxford, her brilliant scholastic career was crowned by an honours degree in modern history and a doctorate of the University of Paris. Her special subject was French literature, and in 1900 her Paris flat was used as a modest finishing school for her English pupils. She was not, she always insisted, very well acquainted with French history, nor was her friend Miss Moberley, who in the summer vacation of 1901 was staying with her at the flat.

Energetic Victorians that they were, they decided one day to explore the vast gardens of Versailles, the magnificent palace built for the Sun King, Louis xiv. The days of its glory were past. Since, in October 1789, the French royal family had fled back to Paris, terrified by the threats of the revolutionary mob, it had become no more than a museum surrounded by a park, used very occasionally as an international conference centre. The magnificent buildings, the statuary and fountains, Grand Canal, Swiss Lake, orangery, all were lifeless memorials to a splendour long gone.

The distances between one part of the palace and another were great, but the two English ladies wore stout boots and were not afraid of exercise, close and cloudy as the day was. It was their first visit to Versailles; they were determined to see as much as possible. They inspected the Grand Trianon, once the home of King Louis's flaunting mistress Madame de Montespan, remarked on its grandeur, and tramped on towards the Petit Trianon, small and domestic by comparison, but sufficiently imposing to the English visitors.

Louis xv had built it for his mistress Madame de Pompadour, and the unlucky Madame du Barry had entertained there, but its closest associations were with Marie Antoinette, who in the days before her tragic fall had enjoyed playing at milkmaids with her ladies in its model village, forgetting the pomp of Court in mock-rustic pleasures.

The way to the Petit Trianon was straightforward, according to the Baedeker map which, like all conscientious English travellers, they carried everywhere. But Miss Jourdain suggested that instead of going straight there they take a more picturesque path. It led them by some farm buildings, derelict and apparently deserted except for a woman who was shaking a white cloth out of a window. Various agricultural implements, including an old plough, were lying about.

Miss Jourdain was beginning to think that they should have taken the main road to the Petit Trianon after all. She was afraid they were slightly lost and felt depressed in spirits, as Miss Moberley also seemed to be. Why had not her bi-lingual friend asked the way from the woman at the window, she wondered? Perhaps it was from reluctance to trouble a stranger.

Soon they met someone to ask. Two gardeners were at work; Miss Moberley noticed their curious uniform, of a green colour, and their three-cornered hats, and remembered afterwards that the spade one of them was using was pointed, and that they had a wheelbarrow. Asked the way to the Petit Trianon, the gardeners directed them straight ahead, speaking in what they thought 'a casual and mechanical way'.

Before they left the gardeners, Miss Jourdain noticed a woman and a girl standing on the threshold of a nearby cottage. She was interested in the unusual style of their dress: each wore a fichu over the shoulders, the ends crossed over and tucked into the bodice of the dress. The girl could be no more than fourteen, yet her skirt was ankle-length; in England it would have been much shorter. She was taking a jug from the woman. Miss Moberley made no comment on the pair, or their odd clothing.

The gardeners' directions led them towards a small round garden pavilion or summer-house on the edge of woodland. A man was seated inside it, alarming both ladies by his sinister appearance. Dressed like a stage villain in a black cloak and soft hat shading his face, he seemed to look through them, rather to their relief, as both were repelled by his pock-marked, swarthy face, and a sort of evil look about him.

Suddenly they heard running footsteps, and even more suddenly the runner was standing beside them. Unlike the man in the summer-house, he was 'distinctly a gentleman', thought Miss Moberley, handsome of feature, with dark curly hair; he wore a dark cloak and his shoes were buckled. He spoke to them urgently, rapidly, but all they could make out were the words '*Mesdames, Mesdames,*' (or could it have been '*Madame*'?)

Miss Anne Moberley (*left*) and Miss Eleanor Jourdain (*right*), reliable witnesses to the haunting of the woodlands at the Petit Trianon, Versailles (*below*).

'*il ne faut pas passer par là. Par ici – cherchez la maison!*' ('Ladies, Ladies, you mustn't go that way. This way – seek the house!') Miss Jourdain, with her trained ear for spoken French, thought his accent curious. He smiled – an odd smile – and disappeared as though into thin air, though they heard the sound of his hurried footsteps after he was gone. Again, they said nothing to each other about him.

Crossing a little rustic bridge, beside which was a small waterfall, they found themselves in the garden overlooked by the long windows of the classical Petit Trianon. On the terrace that surrounded the building a lady was sketching; a tourist perhaps, Miss Moberley thought, for a moment resenting her presence as one tourist does resent another. Her dress was long – and yet somehow not the right length for contemporary fashion – and, like the women and girl at the cottage, she wore a fichu over her shoulders and bosom, of a light green colour. She raised her head as the Englishwomen passed, showing a pretty enough face, but not, thought Miss Moberley, an attractive one. She was not young.

Miss Jourdain paid no attention to the artist, yet, very oddly, twitched her skirt away as they passed her. Miss Moberley was by this time in the grip of a most unpleasant sensation, as though she were in a dream, surrounded by an unnaturally still, oppressive atmosphere. It was not broken by the appearance, though a door in a one-storeyed wing to the left of the house, of a young man. His manner was jaunty, thought Miss Moberley, as though he were a footman, but he wore no livery; she disliked the way he looked at them, disrespectful to the point of being mocking. He directed them accurately enough, however, to the entrance of the Petit Trianon.

There, much to their pleasure, they found themselves in the midst of a wedding party. Into this cheerful occasion they were welcomed, and readily joined in the festivities, feeling now 'quite lively again', as Miss Moberley afterwards said. When they felt they had stayed long enough they left the grounds and went back to the Hôtel des Réservoirs for tea.

Perhaps the strangest thing in this strange story is that a week passed before Miss Moberley asked Miss Jourdain 'Do you think that the Petit Trianon is haunted?' and Miss Jourdain answered 'Yes, I do.' Either the ladies were not given to small talk or making unnecessary conversation, or each was uncomfortably aware of having seen something not easily explained – or, worse, of having imagined it. Learned women, in 1901, were a sufficiently rare breed to cherish their reputation for sanity and good sense. However, the silence was broken, and they began to exchange notes.

Their 'sightings' had not been identical. Miss Moberley had not seen the women and girl at the cottage, Miss Jourdain had not seen the sketcher on the terrace, though she thought she had felt someone near, and had

19.

1904

Returning for the first time to the Petit Trianon in 1904 & finding that "the kiosk" was no longer there, I made this hurried drawing of it from recollection - as seen in 1901.

Authorities shew us that there was "a naissance de la rivière" in that position above the lake. Mique states that he placed, in 1780, "une petite d'architecture" above the 1st grotto. Desjardins says that the Queen rejected a "ruin" copied from one at Baalbec. Note p. 90. "D'après la 44e planche des ruines de Baalbec," Elle représente un édifice circulaire d'un dessin très élegant. Voy. Les ruines de Baalbec - par Robert Wood, Londres, 1757 in-folio, fig.

We looked up this "planche" in the Bodleian Library, & finding that it had resemblence to our kiosk (both were round, had low walls, pillars, & a roof with a slightly Chinese effect) thought that it might have been copied with modifications. A "ruin" stands for the copy of an older building.

In an old map procured in 1909, the name "le kiosque" represents some thing exactly in this part of the garden & that we instinctively gave it the ancient name.

A sketch of the 'kiosk' or summer-house as the two ladies recalled it three years later in 1904. The lower sketch approximates to the building which was there in the time of Louis XVI.

pulled her skirt away. But they agreed about the oppressive, gloomy atmosphere of the place, the unnatural stillness of the air. Miss Moberley told her friend that the woodland beyond the summer-house where the pockmarked man had been sitting had looked 'like a wood worked in tapestry ... with no light and shade, and no wind stirring the trees'. Miss Jourdain agreed. 'I began to feel as though I was walking in my sleep,' Miss Moberley added. 'The heavy dreaminess was oppressive.'

Their curiosity was thoroughly roused. At the risk of looking ridiculous, and of wasting valuable time, they decided to investigate the things they had seen as thoroughly as possible, first lodging at the Bodleian Library in Oxford separate accounts of what they had experienced, so that they could not later be accused of making it all up as they went along.

They consulted all the documents and records which would tell them about Versailles in the past and at the present day. The costumes they had seen, they agreed, had been of the eighteenth century, about the time of the Revolution, and pictures confirmed this. Contemporary plans, maps and descriptions revealed no trace of the scenery they had observed: but old ones described all those features – the small wood, the summer-house, the waterfall were there in the time of Louis xvi.

They returned to Versailles, but were unable to retrace their steps. Everything had changed, even to the appearance of the Petit Trianon, and nowhere did they see anyone dressed in eighteenth-century fashion. They turned to history-books for an explanation, and to *Légendes de Trianon* by Julie Lavergne, based on information handed down to her.

There they learned of an incident which had happened in October 1789. As Queen Marie Antoinette sat sketching in her 'English garden' before the Petit Trianon, a messenger came in haste to warn her that a mob of revolutionary women from Paris were marching on Versailles. She must go back to the palace, he said, but not by the way which would lead her towards them. This story was remembered by a girl called Marianne or Marion, a gardener's daughter, who would have been about the same age as the girl Miss Jourdain had seen at the cottage door. The Queen obeyed, and escaped the fury of the mob; but nothing could save her from the fate that overtook her four years later, when her head and the King's fell beneath the guillotine. Portraits confirmed the likeness of the sketching lady to Marie Antoinette. She, too, had not looked young in 1789, though she was only thirty-four: the anxieties of the coming revolution had stolen the bloom from her face.

Miss Moberley and Miss Jourdain were interested and pleased to learn that their experience was not unique. Others had seen the Queen sketching, and the gardener in a tricorne hat, and the old landscape features of the gardens. It was said that Marie Antoinette was always seen there in the month of August.

The two ladies worked out an explanation of their 'ghost story' most ingeniously. They had not seen ghosts, but had received impressions, they said. On 10 August 1792 the Tuileries were stormed, and the royal family imprisoned in the Temple. Could not the force of the Queen's horror and despair have imprinted itself on the Petit Trianon, where she had once been happy, and produced images of her and those about her there, on the anniversary of her first step towards the guillotine? The day on which the two English ladies had 'seen' her had been her last at Petit Trianon.

Therefore, they reasoned, the running messenger had seen the Queen, not them, and had said '*Madame*', not '*Mesdames*'. The strange accent Miss Jourdain had noticed would have been Austrian, as the Queen employed many attendants from her native land. As for the sinister man with the pock-marked face, they identified him as the Comte de Vaudreuil, a former friend of Marie Antoinette's whom she had come to look on as her evil genius.

And the young man with the insolent manner, who had conducted them to the entrance of the Petit Trianon? They could not easily account for him; perhaps he was a person of the present time. But the door from which he had emerged had been blocked up for a century. The costume of the gardeners, and the implements they were using, were those of the 1780s.

The Moberley–Jourdain story has never been proved or disproved. No 'sightings' of the Versailles ghosts have been reported since theirs, and many suggested explanations have been put forward, such as that they may have interrupted the shooting of a film. But there is no record of any costume film of that date, and even in those very early days crowds of people in modern dress would have been evident, including a camera-man and probably a violinist rendering music appropriate for influencing the emotions of the actors.

Miss Moberley and Miss Jourdain were well-balanced people of unusually high intelligence, not interested in personal publicity – which at that time would have amounted to something like notoriety. When their experiences, told by themselves, were published, it was under the title *An Adventure*. Perhaps it was just that: an extraordinary yet credible adventure in Time.

STRANGE ANTICS IN A TOMB

On a headland above Oistin's Bay, Barbados, the island in the Caribbean, stands a church, and by its side a cemetery in which reposes a tomb, a strongly constructed stone vault which has stood empty and abandoned since 1820. It is built of large stone blocks, firmly cemented together, and it is recessed two feet deep into the solid limestone rock. Its floor space measures 12 feet by 6 feet, reached by several steps, and its entrance was once closed by a large slab of blue marble, sealing the vault until it was required to be opened to take another coffin.

Between the years 1812 and 1820 this fortress of the dead was entered by some unauthorized person or by some 'thing' who, or which, scattered and disarranged the coffins reposing therein. Each time the vault was reopened, the coffins were found in confusion, yet the walls were intact and the heavy stone door securely in place. This series of apparently inexplicable occurrences led an old lady to remark that she didn't believe in ghosts, but she was afraid of them.

The mystery of the Barbados tomb is as much a puzzle today as it was to the citizens of the island in 1820 when the Chase family, who owned the vault, abandoned it in fear and despair and reburied their ancestors in another part of the churchyard. The removal of the six coffins brought the manifestations to an end. No one has offered a feasible solution to the strange antics which so suddenly beset the tomb, but one fact may be significant: they occurred only during its occupancy by the Chase family, and the bones of a previous tenant were left undisturbed.

The tomb was built in 1724 by the Hon. James Elliott and on 14 May the body of his wife, Elizabeth, was placed in it. He does not seem to have been buried in it himself and it was not re-opened until 1807 when it was found empty. What had happened to the bones of the long-deceased Elizabeth is not revealed. The last remains of Mrs Thomassina Goddard were interred in it, and the following year the vault passed into the possession of the Chase family.

When, on 22 February 1808, the vault was opened to receive the tiny coffin containing the remains of Mary Ann Maria Chase, the infant daughter of the Hon. Thomas Chase, Mrs Goddard's coffin was found undisturbed, and both coffins were in their place when the vault was re-opened on 6 July to take the body of another Chase daughter, Dorcas, whose age is not recorded. Everything was normal, and so it remained until the vault was opened again on 9 August 1812 to receive the body of Thomas Chase himself. A startling sight greeted the mourners. The coffins of Chase's two daughters stood on end against the north-east wall, bottoms upwards. Careful examination of the vault revealed nothing to account for its desecration. The children's coffins were replaced beside that of Mrs Goddard which lay undisturbed, and Thomas Chase's heavy lead-enclosed coffin was carried in by eight men and deposited on the floor. The mourners withdrew and stone-masons cemented the entrance slab into position.

Four years went by until 22 September 1816, when the small coffin of Samuel Brewster Ames was brought to the vault. The stone slab was removed and the mourners peeped in. A gruesome sight met their gaze. All the coffins, save that of Mrs Goddard, were in confusion. Her wooden coffin had disintegrated and the others were scattered about and up-ended. No one knew what to make of it: the coffins were put back in their original positions, the walls, roof and floor of the vault were sounded, and the mourners left in bewilderment. Again the masons cemented the entrance slab into position.

Barely two months later it became necessary to re-open the tomb. The body of Samuel Brewster, who had been killed in a slave-rising in April and temporarily buried elsewhere, was brought to it on 17 November. Unfortunately, none of the people intimately involved – the members of the Chase family who repeatedly found their vault desecrated – left any description of their reactions or opinions, but we may assume that they stood waiting on that November day in trepidation and dread as the labourers hacked away the cement sealing the entrance.

The slab was drawn aside, and the members of the family peered inside. The previous confusion reigned; the coffins were propped against the walls, crossing and overlapping each other. Only the remains of Mrs Goddard lay undisturbed. The Chase coffins were restored to their rightful positions and Mrs Goddard's bones, which had fallen out of her decayed coffin, were wrapped up and deposited against a wall. The mourners withdrew; once again the masons sealed the vault.

The inexplicable desecration of the tomb excited 'great astonishment' in the island, states an early chronicler of these mysterious events, Sir Robert H. Schomburgh, who goes on: 'No signs were observed that the vault had been opened without knowledge of the family.' The Chase family was naturally anxious to discern the truth and diligent inquiries were set on foot to learn if any unauthorized person could have entered the tomb. But a careful examination disclosed that this was impossible. Its walls were sound and strong, the entrance slab secure.

Three years went by until 17 July 1819, when the death of another member of the family, Thomassina Clarke, required the vault's re-opening. By now the gruesome story was known all over the island and the

Governor, Lord Combermere, being in the vicinity, took the opportunity to attend the funeral himself. When the entrance slab was drawn back, the old confusion was again revealed. Mrs Goddard's remains alone were undisturbed. Thomas Chase's weighty coffin stood against another wall, and the others were scattered about in sacrilegious disarray.

Mrs Clarke's coffin was brought in and all six coffins were rearranged, those of the three adults on the floor, which they occupied fully, with the infants' coffins on top. Under Lord Combermere's eye, fine sand was strewn on and around the coffins to disclose footmarks if anyone entered, and the entrance slab was replaced. It was cemented into position and to it the Governor affixed his seal, in the presence of several witnesses, who included the Rector of the parish, the Rev. Thomas Orderson, and two local worthies, Robert Bowcher Clarke and Rowland Caton.

For the next episode, which took place on 18 April 1820, we can read Sir Robert Schomburgh's account. He states:

Lord Combermere was residing in 1820 in the neighbourhood of the church, and having been told of this mysterious circumstance, he made unexpectedly an application to the Rector to have the vault re-opened, when, to the astonishment of all present, the coffins, to the number of five or six, were found scattered about, and one of the largest thrown on its side across the passage, so that, had the door not opened outwards, an entrance could not have been effected except by removing the slab on the top, which is of immense weight. The private marks made on the previous occasion were undisturbed, and, as this was the fourth occurrence of a similar disturbance without the cause being explained, the family resolved on removing the bodies from the vault, and some of them were interred in the parish churchyard.

'All I know is that it happened, and I was an eye-witness of the fact,' records the Hon. Nathan Lucas.

Sir Algernon E. Aspinall, in his *Pocket Guide to the West Indies* (1954), goes on to relate: 'The vault was filled in and closed, as, after this occurrence, it was feared that it might give rise to undue excitement among the population, whose nerves were naturally worked up to a high pitch of tension by this gruesome episode.'

Such are the facts of the case; the rest is speculation. Our knowledge of the circumstances is derived from the reports written by the Rev. Thomas Orderson, and he left several accounts, which unfortunately do not entirely agree, and the sketch he made of the position of the undisturbed coffins differs from the drawing made by the Hon. Nathan Lucas.

What possible explanation can there be for the strange antics of the coffins in the Chase vault? The significant fact seems to be that the desecration concerned only members of the Chase family. For once the rule

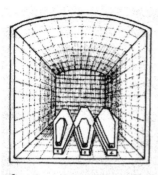

Situation of the Coffins when the Vault
was closed July 7th, 1819
in the presence of the Reverend
Thomas H. Orderson.

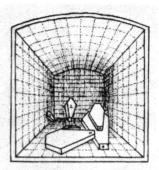

Situation of the Coffins on April 18th,
1820, when the Vault was reopened
in the presence of the Rt Honble Lord
Combermere, R.B. Clarke, Esq -,
Rowland Cotton and Honble. N -
Lucas

The drawings made by the Hon. Nathan Lucas, showing the positions of the coffins when the Chase family vault was closed in July 1819 and when it was re-opened nine months later.

The Chase vault, empty since it was abandoned in 1820.

that natural explanations must be preferred to the supernatural seems to be at fault. The suggestion that the desecration was the work of natives was eliminated early on, due both to the superstitious dread which would have deterred them from tampering with a tomb and because no forceful entry had been made.

The disturbances which occurred during a period of six years could not have been the work of any human agency. That easy solution is rejected by all investigators, though certain 'facts' seemed to support it. Arthur Reece, writing in *Once a Week* on 11 March 1864, states that Thomas Chase was a man of strong and possibly cruel character, who might have made enemies amongst the natives, and Reece says that both he and Dorcas Chase died by their own hands, the daughter having starved herself to death due to her father's cruelty, 'whereupon the other corpses were desirous to expel her'. Mr Reece does not, however, support his statements by reference to any contemporary authority.

Only two other 'natural' explanations remain. According to one theory, the coffins were disturbed by earthquakes, which at first glance seems a most probable solution. But think of this: if earth tremors caused the disturbances, it means they were confined to a space of seventy-two square feet, for they were not felt elsewhere, and they occurred repeatedly at, and only at, that small spot.

Flooding, which might have floated the coffins about, is an equally unrewarding solution. No water-marks were noticed and the position of the vault at the top of a headland makes flooding unlikely. If it had occurred, it must have been of an intensity to raise the coffins above ground level, far higher than the two feet the vault is recessed into the solid rock. Nathan Lucas, who witnessed the opening in 1820, tells us: 'There was no vestige of water to be discovered in the vault; no marks where it had been, and the vault is in a level churchyard, by no means in a fall, much less in a run of water.'

We are left only with the supernatural. Sir Arthur Conan Doyle suggested that the disturbances were the work of forces desiring the speedy decomposition of the bodies of the Chase family, and they had a particular animus against lead coffins, a point difficult to consider as the question of which coffins were encased in lead is in confusion. If this is the true solution, these 'forces' achieved their object by the transfer of the coffins to earthen burials, and it may be significant that the manifestations ceased once the coffins were reburied.

There is just one clue to the mystery: only the Chase family were interfered with. But it is a clue which fails to carry us any farther because we know next to nothing about the family's history. They were people, it seems, who caused the hatred of someone or some 'thing', who or which wreaked his, her or its vengeance upon their bodies. What caused the disturbances in the vault is a mystery which remains to excite our imagination. One guess is as good as another, it seems.

MADAME BLAVATSKY: MYSTIC OR FRAUD?

When that remarkable lady Helena Blavatsky died in 1891, most people regarded her as an outrageous old fraud who had been thoroughly exposed. Yet thousands of her followers all over the world remained convinced that she was an 'avatar' – or messiah – who had been crucified by a materialistic age for daring to speak the truth. It is true that this situation is fairly commonplace where 'messiahs' are concerned. What makes Madame Blavatsky so different is that many of her followers have been highly literate, intelligent people, and that now, almost a century after her death, they are still convinced that she was genuine. She remains a mystery woman, to whom the passage of time has provided no answer.

Fame came late to Madame Blavatsky, and before it arrived her life was chaotic, difficult and adventurous. Helena Petrovna Hahn was born in Russia in 1831, the daughter of a princess who was also a celebrated novelist. Her mother, Helena Hahn, was an ardent feminist, and she seems to have found her nervous and highly strung daughter intolerable. Little Helena made up for lack of love by overeating, and became thoroughly obese. At the age of sixteen, to spite a much-hated governess (her mother being dead by this time), Helena got herself engaged to a landed gentleman named Nikifor Blavatsky, who was twenty-four years her senior. The family called her bluff and forced her to go through with the marriage; at the altar, when the priest told her that she should honour and obey her husband, she replied positively: 'I shall *not*!' And soon after, terrified by his attempts to put an end to her virgin state, she ran away from home.

What happened between 1849, when the eighteen-year-old girl left home, until 1873, when she arrived in New York as a woman of 42, is a matter that has puzzled her biographers; the latest of these, Marion Meade, has succeeded in finding out a great deal; yet even so, she is unable to spin out her findings to more than thirty-five pages. And she admits frankly that the question of how Helena supported herself after she left Russia remains a mystery. But we know that she rode in a steeplechase in Constantinople when she was twenty, with the aim of making money, and that

the horse fell on her and crushed her chest, causing a scar. She also seems
to have become a paid companion to various wealthy women. She went to
Cairo and became a snake-charmer, then to Paris, where she became a
member of the retinue of a wealthy Russian princess, with whom she
travelled to London. Then she somehow crossed to America, and went on
to Japan and India. She later claimed to have visited Tibet, but most
biographers seem to doubt the truth of this statement.

What *is* certain is that, some time in the 1850s, she caught a glimpse of
her true vocation when she heard about the fantastically successful movement known as Spiritualism.

This had all started in the year 1848, when loud knocking noises were
heard in the home of the Fox family in New York State. Neighbours came
in to listen to the thunderous bangings, and one of them asked the unseen
knocker whether he was a spirit. A code of knocks established that the
entity was the ghost of a pedlar who had been murdered in the house. The
two daughters of the family, Kate and Margaret, seemed to be able to
persuade the 'ghost' to make knocking noises whenever they liked; and
one day the spirit announced that it had come to proclaim the dawn of a
new era. 'You must proclaim this truth to the world.'

Groups of people met in gatherings that came to be called 'séances', and
when Kate or Margaret was present, unseen fingers played guitars, objects
floated around the room, and tables moved up and down on two legs. In
no time at all other people discovered that they possessed the same powers
as the Fox sisters; some could even make the spirits materialize in the
room and talk to the audience. These people who seemed to be able to act
as intermediary with the 'spirit world' came to be known as 'mediums'.
The spirits proclaimed that their purpose was to prove there was no such
thing as death – that life went on on another plane. Millions of people
were eager to hear the message; 'Spiritualism' swept across America, then
across Europe.

And at this point we must raise a basic question: *is* Spiritualism a de-
lusion held by gullible people? Nobody who has seriously studied the
subject – even the most 'tough minded' sceptics – can wholly accept such
a view. There have, indeed, been plenty of fraudulent mediums. And we
may well doubt whether even the genuine mediums somehow 'prove'
that there is a spirit world. Many modern researchers are inclined to the
view that the phenomena of Spiritualism are some strange manifestation of
the unconscious mind, and they could well be right. Perhaps human
beings possess powers of which most of us are unaware – powers like
telepathy and clairvoyance. (How many of us have had a sudden odd
conviction that we are going to get a letter from Auntie Florence today,

and the letter actually arrives?) One thing is clear: that the people who want to dismiss all 'occult' phenomena as fraud are merely being silly and shallow.

Now Helena Blavatsky had good reason to know this, for there is reliable evidence that she was a natural 'medium' long before the word was invented. As a child, she 'saw spirits'. And one day when she was sitting with a pen in her hand, gazing blankly into space, her hand began to write in excellent German – a language she could only speak poorly. Neither was the handwriting in the least like Helena's. The 'communicator' named herself as Tekla Lebendorff, the aunt of an officer in the regiment of Helena's father. Her father was intrigued, and used his influential connections to check government archives. To his astonishment, everything Tekla Lebendorff had said was true – her date and place of birth, number of children, date of death.

Yet stranger things were to come. One day Helena went to the home of the officer who was Tekla's nephew; he told her that his aunt Tekla was not dead – he had received a letter from her only the other day. Yet the information dictated by the 'spirit' who called itself Tekla was otherwise accurate. If the 'spirit' was not Tekla Lebendorff, then who on earth was it? This is, we must admit at once, a question to which there is no satisfactory reply.

But the one thing that seems clear is that Helena *was* a medium. One day she tried to climb up to a picture on the wall, placing one table on top of another; the tables slipped, and she fell with a crash. She woke up on the floor, unhurt, to find that the tables were back in their proper place. But a handprint high on the wall revealed that she had really climbed up there.

So when Helena heard about Spiritualism, she felt at once that fate might be throwing her a life-belt. She was a homeless wanderer with no special talent. But if the Fox sisters and dozens of other mediums could become famous – and make a more-than-adequate living – then so could Helena Blavatsky. She hastened to seek out the most famous medium of the day, Daniel Dunglas Home; but the effete, delicate Home found this female whirlwind too much for his nerves, and offered little help. So Helena once more became a wanderer, and in July 1873 she landed in New York determined to seek fame and fortune.

In fact she almost starved; New Yorkers were not really interested in an overweight Russian woman whose chief accomplishment seemed to be an ability to cause knocking noises and the tinkling of unseen bells. Then, just as she was losing hope, her luck turned. A newspaper sent to interview her a serious, bearded gentleman named Henry Steel Olcott, who was a lawyer as well as part-time journalist. Olcott was bowled over by the extraordinary woman with the Russian accent and enormous eyes. He wrote about her so warmly that other newspapers interviewed her. She told them about her trip to Tibet, her lifelong search for spiritual knowledge, and how she had met certain secret 'Mahatmas', spiritual adepts who would one day rule the world. They called themselves the Luxor Brotherhood. It was the Luxor Brotherhood who told Olcott that he should leave his wife and devote himself to Madame Blavatsky and Spiritual Truth. He did so, although there was never any sexual involvement between herself and Olcott (she claimed to be incapable of sex because she had a 'kind of crooked cucumber' in her vagina).

She began to write a vast work; Olcott used to sit opposite her and watch her hand fly across the pages, apparently guided by some invisible entity. The work was called *Isis Unveiled*, and when it appeared in New York in September 1877, it became an unexpected best-seller, and made Helena famous.

According to *Isis Unveiled*, man is not the first intelligent dweller on earth – in fact, he is the fifth 'root race'. The first consisted of fire-mist, while the fourth lived in Atlantis, which was destroyed thousands of years ago.... Sceptics will dismiss – and indeed, have dismissed – all this as the invention of a clever woman who wanted to found a religion. Yet even the most superficial reading shows that *Isis Unveiled* is totally unlike various other 'Bibles' concocted by self-proclaimed messiahs in ponderous imitation of the Old Testament. It is a work of enormous learning, and its ideas are breathtaking and imaginative. If it is a fraud, it is a fraud of near-genius.

By the time *Isis Unveiled* appeared, Madame Blavatsky and Colonel Olcott had already launched the society with which her name has become identified: the Theosophical Society. It had a motto: 'There is no religion higher than truth', and the success of *Isis Unveiled* brought in hordes of new members. Yet now that she had achieved acceptance and fame, Helena Blavatsky began to feel increasingly unhappy in America, with its crass materialism and noisy vulgarity. She hungered for older and more refined cultures. So when she heard that a new religious movement, with ideas similar to her own, had been founded in India, she decided to have done with the Americans.

The trip itself was something of a disaster, with sea-sickness and endless problems, but when she arrived in Bombay in February 1879, she felt it had all been worth it. She was received with joy by the devotees of the new movement, the Arya Samaj, who were flattered that the West was at last taking the culture of India seriously. And although various disagree-

The mysterious Madame Blavatsky – medium, 'messiah' or fraud?

ments with the Arya Samaj soon developed, the Theosophical Society itself took root and became an undoubted success. Her mediumistic powers seemed to increase, and she gave some startling displays, one of which included a rain of roses which fell from the air.

A new disciple named Alfred Sinnett asked if he might be permitted to correspond with the 'secret Mahatmas' who lived in some remote part of the Himalayas; Madame Blavatsky agreed to convey a letter to them. A few days later Sinnett found on his desk a reply from a 'Mahatma' who signed himself Koot Hoomi. Sinnett and another disciple, A.O. Hume, conducted a lengthy correspondence with Koot Hoomi which eventually filled a volume.

Yet just as it seemed that Madame Blavatsky had established herself as one of the most remarkable religious teachers of the nineteenth century, disaster descended like an avalanche. An acquaintance of earlier years named Emma Coulomb heard of Madame Blavatsky's fame and came to Bombay to become her housekeeper. It was Helena's greatest single mistake. Madame Coulomb was a sour, trivial-minded woman, who soon came to loathe her employer. She stored up endless grudges. In 1884 Madame Blavatsky took a trip to Europe, during which time she went to London. The newly formed Society for Psychical Research asked her if she would be willing to be 'investigated' by them, and she unhesitatingly agreed, so they sent out a brilliant young man named Richard Hodgson. And Emma Coulomb now decided to get her own back with a vengeance. She denounced Madame Blavatsky to Hodgson, claiming that all the phenomena were fraudulent. The Coulombs demonstrated how 'Mahatma letters' were made to fall from the air, and Hodgson tracked down the shop which had sold the saucers and vases which had appeared as 'apports' from the Tibetan masters. An apparently solid 'shrine' in which messages from the masters appeared was discovered to have a secret sliding panel connected with Madame Blavatsky's room.

Hodgson's report was devastating, and in one single night the edifice that Madame Blavatsky had constructed so painfully seemed to collapse. She rushed back to India, determined to sue for damages, but her lawyer persuaded her not to: a 'medium' is always at a disadvantage in a court of law. Her enemies – Christian missionaries who detested the Theosophical Society – carried the war into her own camp by issuing a writ for libel. Madame Blavatsky was forced to flee ignominiously back to Europe.

And that, in effect, was the end of her. In 1887 she settled in London, where the poet W.B. Yeats became one of her disciples. He found her delightful, humorous and down-to-earth. (Her cuckoo-clock hooted at him one day when he was alone in the room with it, although it was not working.) She was still surrounded by the faithful, and the Theosophical Society continued to flourish, for her disciples had no doubt that it was the Coulombs who had lied and cheated and brought about her downfall. (There is much to be said for this view – Coulomb was a carpenter, and could have constructed the 'hidden door' in the shrine.)

Although she was dying of Bright's Disease, she wrote, day and night, a work even vaster than *Isis Unveiled* – it was published, in a greatly edited form, after her death, under the title *The Secret Doctrine*. And finally, with complications of heart disease, kidney disease and rheumatic gout, she died on 8 May 1891. The Society was taken over by a disciple, Annie Besant, and has continued to flourish to this day.

Perhaps the simplest and most obvious solution to the riddle is that Madame Blavatsky was a genuine medium but a less-than-genuine 'messiah'. Few people can seriously accept the existence of Koot Hoomi and the other Mahatmas. Yet no one who takes the trouble to read her books can accept that she was simply a fake. They are too full of amazing insights and genuine wisdom. Her views deeply influenced a remarkable young German scholar named Rudolf Steiner, who went on to create his own Christianized form of Theosophy, known as Anthroposophy. And Steiner presents a similar riddle to Madame Blavatsky: a man of profound spiritual insight, whose views on education and farming are now accepted as being long before their time, yet whose strange tales of Atlantis, Lemuria and earlier races sound like science fiction.

It is not even true that most intelligent people find the 'Mahatmas' unacceptable. A few years ago I edited a volume called *Men of Mystery* – about various 'adepts' and occultists – and the chapter on Madame Blavatsky was contributed by the eminent judge Mr Christmas Humphreys. I was intrigued to discover that this remarkable and brilliant man had no doubt of the real existence of the Tibetan masters. And I have met others, whose intelligence I respect, who held the same view. As to myself, I confess that the more I have studied her work, the more I have become convinced that she cannot be dismissed as a kind of super-confidence woman. At the very least it must be conceded that she was – as her biographer John Symonds has remarked – 'one of the most remarkable women who ever lived'.

REINCARNATION

The belief in reincarnation – that we have lived many lives – is more widely accepted in the East than in the West. Yet oddly enough, one of the most powerful and convincing cases dates from America in the 1870s.

On 11 July 1877 a thirteen-year-old girl, Mary Lurancy Vennum, had an epileptic fit and became unconscious for five days. When she woke up, she told her family that she had seen heaven, and talked to a brother and sister who had died. From then on she had regular mild fits or trances, in which she seemed to go into a state of ecstasy. At other times she appeared to turn into other people, including a young man who called himself Willie Canning, and a sour old woman, Katrina Hogan. Neighbours said that the girl ought to be confined in an asylum, and Lurancy's parents were inclined to agree.

They were dissuaded by a friend, Asa Roff. Sixteen years before, the Roffs had lost their sixteen-year-old daughter Mary after a number of similar 'fits'. Now the Roffs sent for a doctor they knew, E.W. Stevens. When he arrived, Lurancy was in one of her peculiar trances, and Willie Canning and Katrina Hogan appeared in quick succession, the latter treating Stevens with some hostility. But Stevens succeeded in placing Lurancy in a hypnotic trace, and the moment this happened 'Katrina' vanished and Lurancy spoke in her own voice. She explained that she had been 'taken over' by evil spirits. Stevens, who also knew something about Spiritualism, suggested that, in that case, she needed a 'spirit guide' or control. (A 'control' is an entity who takes over a medium in trance, and acts as 'master of ceremonies'.) Lurancy replied that she knew of a spirit who would be willing to act as her control – Mary Roff. And Asa Roff, who was also present, explained that Mary was his dead daughter. 'Yes, ask her to come. She'll help you.'

The next day Lurancy Vennum became another person, the girl who claimed to be Mary Roff. Lurancy's father sent a message to the Roffs' home, and Mrs Roff and her daughter hurried round to the Vennums'. As they came along the street, Lurancy, who was looking out of the window, said excitedly: 'Here comes my ma and sister Nervie!' And when they came in, she flung her arms around their necks and cried.

'Mary' went back home to the Roffs, and any doubts they might have had were quickly dispelled as the girl recognized all her old friends and neighbours, and remembered dozens of incidents dating from her lifetime. One day Mrs Roff found an old velvet head-dress that Mary used to wear; at that moment Mary came in from the yard and said immediately:

'Oh, that's my old head-dress that I used to wear when my hair was short.'

Dr Stevens, fascinated by all this, asked her endless questions to test that she really *was* Mary Roff – for, after all, Lurancy lived nearby and might have learned many things by overhearing them. He soon became convinced that this explanation would simply not fit the facts – Mary gave proof on a hundred occasions that she knew every detail of the dead Mary Roff.

They asked her how long she could stay; she replied: 'Till some time in May.' Later she gave the date as 21 May. And on that date, she went around saying goodbye to friends and neighbours, hugged and kissed her family, and walked over to the Vennums'. And by the time she arrived there, Mary Roff had vanished and Lurancy Vennum was back again. From then on, the 'fits' ceased. But Mary Roff continued to drop in occasionally. . . .

Our first reaction, of course, is to wonder whether Lurancy's unconscious mind had picked up all the information about the dead Mary Roff. Closer study of the case makes this unlikely. It was investigated by Richard Hodgson, the 'tough-minded' member of the Society for Psychical Research who denounced Madame Blavatsky; Hodgson ended up totally convinced that this was a genuine case of the 'paranormal'. Lurancy, for example, had never been in the Roffs' home; yet as soon as 'Mary' walked in, she began to recognize all kinds of objects from her childhood. Dr Stevens was a careful and conscientious observer, and his account of the case strongly suggests that Mary Roff returned from the dead and lived on earth for four months.

Reincarnation is, of course, part of the religious belief of Hindus and Buddhists, and some of the most remarkable and convincing accounts of reincarnation come from India. In the early 1930s the case of a girl called Shanti Devi excited worldwide attention. Kumari Shanti Devi was born in Delhi on 12 October 1926, and when she was four, she began to talk about a town called Muttra, a hundred miles away. She claimed that she had lived there in a yellow house, and that her husband had been a man called Kedar Nath Chaubey. The principal of the local school was so intrigued by all this that he examined Shanti, and asked where her husband lived; Shanti gave him an address. The principal wrote to Kedar Nath, and to his astonishment received a reply verifying that he was a widower, whose wife – a girl called Ludgi – had died ten years earlier. He confirmed in detail many things that Shanti had related.

However, a hundred miles was a long way to travel, so Kedar Nath wrote to a cousin in Delhi and asked him to call on Shanti Devi's family.

The cousin, Kanji Mal, arrived at the door, and was instantly recognized by Shanti. He went away totally convinced. The result was that Kedar Nath hurried to Delhi. Shanti, wildly excited, flung herself into his arms. She then answered in detail all kinds of questions about her life with him. All Kedar's doubts vanished. This was undoubtedly his former wife. But what on earth could he *do* about it? He could hardly take a ten-year-old girl back to his home ... So, sad and perplexed, he returned to Muttra. A few days later, Shanti was taken to Muttra by her parents, together with three scientific investigators. And from the moment she arrived, no one had the slightest doubt that she was genuine. Among the crowd on the station platform she recognized an elderly man as her brother-in-law. Then, in a carriage, she directed the driver, and showed an intimate knowledge of the town – also pointing out a number of houses that had been built since she died. She directed the carriage to the house in which she had lived with Kedar, then to another house into which they had moved later. She led them to an old well, which had now been filled in, and showed the spot in one of the rooms where she had buried a hundred rupees in the earth floor. The men dug, and found only an empty jewel-box – at which point Kedar Nath admitted with embarrassment that he had found the box and spent the money. Later, Shanti recognized her former parents and her brother in the crowd. All this was placed on record, and caused such a stir that it was reported in newspapers all over the world.

Cases like that of Shanti Devi – and there were many others – were studied by Professor Hemendra Banerjee of Rajasthan University. And in America Dr Ian Stevenson of the University of Virginia began an exhaustive scientific study of such cases, his first results being published in 1966 under the cautious title of *Twenty Cases Suggestive of Reincarnation*. His cases come from India, Ceylon (now Sri Lanka), Brazil and Alaska, and all are full of documented evidence. A single one will give a sample of his astonishing material.

In 1954 a three-year-old boy called Jasbir Lal Jat died of smallpox. Before he could be buried the next day, the corpse stirred and revived. It was some weeks before the child could speak, but when he did his parents were astonished that his personality had changed completely. He announced that he was the son of a Brahmin family (a higher caste than his 'present' family) who lived in the village of Vehedi, and he refused to eat food unless it was cooked by a Brahmin. He said that he had been poisoned by some doctored sweets, and had fallen off a cart, smashed his skull and died. Jasbir's family were, understandably, sceptical, assuming that his illness had affected his mind. But they began to reconsider in 1957 when a Brahmin lady from Vehedi came to Jasbir's village, and he instantly recognized her as his aunt. Jasbir was taken back to Vehedi and, like Shanti Devi, led the party round the village, showing a detailed knowledge of its lay-out, and recognized members of his family. His name, in his previous existence, had been Sobha Ram. The accusation about the poisoned sweets was never satisfactorily cleared up – Sobha Ram was said to have died of smallpox – but Dr Stevenson's detailed account leaves no doubt that Jasbir knew too much about Vehedi and the life of Sobha Ram for any deception to have taken place.

The oddest point about this case, of course, is that Jasbir was already three and a half when he 'died', and was taken over by the 'spirit' of Sobha Ram – *who died at the same time.* The logical explanation, therefore, would seem to be that Jasbir really died, and that the spirit of Sobha Ram grabbed the body before 'brain death' occurred and fought his way back to life. This raises some fascinating questions about the whole relation between spirit and matter, life and death. . . .

Stevenson points out that most of the really convincing cases of reincarnation take place in cultures that already accept reincarnation as a fact. This, as we have already seen, is not always so. In 1910 a five-year-old girl named Alexandrina Samona died in Palermo, Sicily, and her mother was wild with grief. Soon after, she had a dream in which her dead child assured her that she would return in the form of a baby. Later that year Adela Samona gave birth to twins, one of whom was the double of Alexandrina, and who was therefore given her name. (The other was a totally different personality.) When the new Alexandrina was ten, her mother took her on an outing to the town of Monreale, where Alexandrina had never been before. Yet the child insisted that she *had.* She described various things she had seen in the town, and said that she had been there with her mother and a woman with 'horns' on her forehead – whereupon Signora Samona recalled that a few months before the death of the first Alexandrina they *had* been to Monreale, accompanied by a neighbour who had unsightly cysts on her forehead. Other details recalled by Alexandrina also proved correct. This case gave rise to widespread interest, and was reported together with lengthy depositions of everyone concerned, leaving little doubt about the basic accuracy of the facts.

In recent years there has been a steadily increasing interest in reincarnation, dating from 1956 when a book entitled *The Search for Bridey Murphy* became a best-seller. A hypnotist named Morey Bernstein placed a Colorado housewife, Virginia Tighe, in a trance, and asked her questions about the period before she was born (a technique known as 'regression'). Mrs Tighe declared that in the nineteenth century she had been an Irish girl named Bridey Murphy, who lived in Cork – she gave extremely detailed information about her life there. The case caused a sensation, which collapsed abruptly when an American newspaper ran an 'exposé', declaring that Mrs Tighe had had an Irish aunt who told her endless stories about Ireland, and that as a child she had lived opposite a woman called Bridey Corkell, with whose son she was in love.... Yet on closer investigation it is impossible to dismiss the Bridey Murphy case as unconscious self-deception. To begin with, the newspaper that did the exposé was the one that had failed to gain the serial rights on Bernstein's book, which had gone to a rival. It emerged that Virginia had never met her 'Irish aunt' until she was eighteen, and that she was certainly never in love with Mrs Corkell's son – who turned out to be the editor of the Sunday edition of the newspaper that denounced her. But the general public are not interested in such fine points as these; as far as they were concerned, Bridey Murphy had been proved to be a fake.

Other hypnotists, like Arnall Bloxham (an Englishman) and Joe Keeton, began to try the techniques of 'regression', and produced astonishing information that seemed to prove that patients *could* recall their 'past lives'. One of Bloxham's subjects gave an impressive account of being a naval gunner at the time of Nelson; while another, a housewife, recalled many past lives, including one of being a Jewess involved in an anti-semitic pogrom in York. Her knowledge of ancient history proved to be astonishingly detailed (as Jeffrey Iverson has recounted in his book *More Lives than One?*). A professor identified the church she had described – in the crypt of which the hunted Jews took refuge – as St Mary's, the only problem being that St Mary's had no crypt. A few months later, workmen renovating the church discovered the crypt.

Now book after book appeared with powerful evidence for reincarnation. In *The Cathars and Reincarnation*, Dr Arthur Guirdham described a patient called 'Mrs Smith' who had dreams and visions of being alive in thirteenth-century France, as a member of a persecuted sect called the Cathars, who were finally exterminated by the Inquisition. Guirdham had himself been interested in the Cathars because he had also had strange dreams about them. Now, stimulated by Mrs Smith's detailed 'dream knowledge' of the period, he investigated Catharism with the aid of French scholars, and found that she was correct again and again; when she and the scholars disagreed, it was usually she who turned out to be correct. In *Second Time Round* Edward Ryall described in detail memories of a previous existence as a West-Country farmer who lived during the reign of Charles II, and took part in the battle of Sedgemoor. In *Lives to Remember*, Peter Underwood and Leonard Wilder described hypnotic experiments with a housewife, Peggy Bailey, and detailed memories of three of her previous lives.

Yet obviously the problem here is one of how far we can accept the evidence of people who have become convinced that reincarnation is a reality. To many sceptics Arthur Guirdham's case is undermined by his admission that he was also a Cathar in a previous existence, and – by a strange coincidence – the lover of the previous Mrs Smith. The reader of A.J. Stewart's *Died 1513, Born 1929* is bound to experience a certain incredulity to learn that, in her previous existence, Miss Stewart was James II of Scotland.

In 1981 the sceptics found a formidable champion in Ian Wilson, whose book *Mind Out of Time?* is a devastating analysis of some of the cases of reincarnation. I myself am quoted approvingly because of an experiment I conducted on BBC television in which a housewife was made to hallucinate as an evil clergyman by means of post-hypnotic suggestion. Wilson goes on to show how easily our unconscious minds can deceive us, citing many cases in which people have convinced themselves that long-buried memories of some book they once read are actually memories of past lives. He points out, for example, that the man who thought he had been a gunner in one of Nelson's ships had read C.S. Forester's Hornblower novels as a child and could easily have picked up his 'facts' from them. His final considered assessment is that most cases of reincarnation are actually examples of the strange psychological illness known as 'multiple personality'.

Wilson's scepticism is salutary and bracing. But the book suffers from the defect of most attempts to 'explode' a particular belief: it seems to ignore some of the most convincing evidence. Anyone who is interested in reincarnation immediately turns to the index to see what he makes of the Lurancy Vennum case – and discovers that, for some odd reason, he does not even mention it. Discussing Stevenson's cases, he objects that so many involve young children, and points out that children often fantasize about being somebody else. But he only has one brief and indirect reference to the astonishing case of Jasbir Lal Jat, and prefers to pick holes and find minor errors in less well-documented cases.

And then Wilson seriously undermines his own arguments by citing one of the most remarkable cases of recent years – that of the Pollock twins. In May 1957 two sisters – Joanna and Jacqueline Pollock, aged eleven and six – were killed by a car that mounted the pavement. In October 1958 Mrs Pollock had female twins, who were called Jennifer and Gillian. Jennifer had a scar on her forehead in exactly the place her dead sister Jacqueline had had one. When the twins were only four months old, the family moved away from Hexham to Whitley Bay. But when the twins were taken back three years later, they behaved as if they had known it all their lives, recognizing the school, the playground and the old house where their sisters had lived. When Mrs Pollock decided to open a locked cupboard in which she had kept the dead children's toys, the twins immediately recognized them item by item, naming all the dolls. One day Mrs Pollock was shocked to find them playing a game in which one twin cradled the other's head saying, 'The blood's coming out of your eyes. That's where the car hit you.' But the Pollocks had been careful never to tell their children anything about how their sisters had died.

So although Mr Wilson points out that the evidence is by no means watertight – because John Pollock himself believes in reincarnation – he leaves most readers with the impression that it is quite strong enough for any reasonable person. And when, at the end of his discussion of the Bridey Murphy case, he admits reluctantly: '. . . when the dubious and the downright spurious has been discarded, there remain signs of some not yet understood phenomenon at work,' most readers will be inclined to comment: 'You can say that again!'

MONSTERS

SOMETHING QUEER IN THE LOCH

Millions of people have heard of the Loch Ness Monster, thousands have seen it, hundreds hunted it and dozens photographed it. Yet the mystery remains. In the search for truth hundreds of thousands of pounds and many man-hours have been spent; surely, then, with the assistance of all kinds of modern technology the 'Monster', or monsters, should have been found by now.

The fact is that few people realize how large Loch Ness is: a veteran 'monster hunter' has pointed out that you could submerge the whole of the human race in the lake without trace. It is the third largest fresh-water lake in Europe, twenty-four miles long and a mile wide, and lies in the Great Glen, that slanting line of four lochs – Linnhe, Lochy, Oich and Ness – running across Scotland from Fort William at the south-western end to Inverness in the north-east. At the south-western end of Loch Ness, at the entrance to the Caledonian Canal itself, lies Fort Augustus, built after the Jacobite rising in 1715. Until 1933 the only road by the loch ran along the southern shore between Fort Augustus and Inverness; for several miles it turns away from the loch and, where it runs along the shore, the view of the water is often obscured by trees and shrubs.

In 1933 a new road was opened running right along the northern shore of the lake. During its construction undergrowth beside the water was cleared, and for the first time travellers had an unobstructed view along the length of the loch. It is this last point which explains the statement that is often made to the effect that the monster was first seen in 1933. In fact, as we shall see, stories of a strange being in the loch go back more than a thousand years.

Apart from its sheer size the loch offers another problem to explorers. Its shores plunge steeply, overshadowing the dark waters, often affecting observers with a sense of gloom. From the rivers and mountain streams which run into the loch, peat is carried down to stain the water a reddish brown. It becomes so opaque as to make underwater vision difficult and photography virtually impossible, even a few feet below the surface.

Finally, the loch is very deep, reaching almost 1,000 feet close to the romantic ruins of medieval Urquhart Castle, while there are deep pools in numerous other parts. Around the shore areas of marsh and undergrowth make access to the lake difficult and some parts are rarely visited.

These are some of the facts which explain why 'Nessie' is so rarely seen and is so hard to find. In the fifty years since the new road was built much of the undergrowth on the lakeside has grown up again, covering the bare

Mr Alexander Ross, piermaster at
Drumnadrochit (*above*), and Miss Janet
Fraser, of the Half-Way Tea House,
Aultsaye – two of the many witnesses
who claim to have seen the monster in
the loch in 1933.

open shores and once again making chance sightings more difficult. Although in those fifty years technology has advanced to help mere observation, the chances of being in the right place at the right time to observe this elusive monster in its murky habitat remain extremely slender.

It should be noted that the thousands of words written, pounds expended and man-hours dedicated to the search for the monster have come not from the tourist (for few of these, even if they do believe in the existence of the monster, expect to be lucky enough to see it, while the local people, apart from a few 'novelty' shops, do little to capitalize on it), but from individuals whose imagination has been captured by the evidence and who have been sufficiently convinced to try to discover the truth. It is largely to the research undertaken by these people that we owe our knowledge today.

Long before the media existed, when, indeed, few people could even read and write, a scribe named Adamnan wrote the life story of St Columba, who is credited with the conversion of the Picts. According to this biography St Columba, in his travels through the provinces of the Picts in about AD 565, came to the river Ness and (despite the fact that on his arrival on the shore he found some local people burying a man who had been snatched out of the water and 'viciously bitten' by some aquatic monster while he was swimming) sent one of his companions to swim across the river and collect a boat moored on the opposite side. St Columba's trusting and intrepid messenger had barely reached the middle of the stream when a monster, disturbed by the swimmer, rushed upon him with 'a great roar and open mouth'. The saint, however, promptly ordered the monster off ('Go back at once!') and the terrified monster fled 'more quickly than if it had been dragged on by ropes'.

This delightful story of the saint and poet may well have a touch of the Irish in it, but is unlikely to be a total invention. Indeed in the centuries which followed, tradition had it that a 'water horse' lived in the loch (as in other Scottish lakes) and a seventeenth-century traveller talks of a floating island that appeared and disappeared; while for generations local children were warned not to play too close to the water.

As the years passed, stories of some creature in the lake persisted and a number of these were collected by a local historian and published in the local Press towards the end of the nineteenth century. But the possible existence of a strange animal was regarded by the local people as something it was better to keep quiet about, even though the crew and passengers of the steamer which daily plied the length of the loch occasionally saw something which they described variously as being like a salamander, a huge eel and a horse-like creature with a mane.

By the turn of the century reports were becoming more widespread. Fishermen and others crossing the lake on several occasions saw a hump looking like the bottom of an upturned boat which, however, made off at speed on being approached. One observer even described an enormous animal which scared him out of his wits by surfacing beside his boat. Indeed it is an interesting characteristic of all accounts of close sightings of this animal that the observers have been virtually paralysed by astonishment and awe. In 1889 two brothers, fishing near Urquhart Castle, saw a 'huge form' rise from the calm waters of the loch and make off at speed. The terrified brothers rowed for the shore in equal haste. A few years later another couple of local fishermen saw a large creature lying motionless on the surface of a deep pool at the mouth of the river Moriston. After a while one of the men flicked his line at it and the animal instantly swam off. These two men described the beast as having a head like an eel, a tapering tail and being between thirty and forty feet long.

For many years these fishermen's tales were regarded as just that. It was, as usual, the media – in the shape of two local newspapers – who were responsible for drawing aside the veil, and it coincided with the opening up of the lake shore and the view along the loch. It started in 1933 with a local correspondent reporting a story of a sighting of the animal by the owners of a lakeside hotel at Drumnadrochit (the hoteliers asked, by the way, to remain anonymous) and it resulted in a surprising flood of information about previously unrecorded sightings, both old and new. These helped to fill the columns of the papers for many months, and for the first time brought the monster to the attention of the world beyond the borders of Inverness-shire.

There were, however, several serious attempts made to collate and investigate the various stories with a view to establishing the truth. A man named Rupert Gould, who had already published a book about sea serpents, assiduously collected information about forty-seven sightings, illustrated by drawings and photographs, and presented various theories to explain Nessie's identity. A list of the various sightings of the monster would be tediously repetitious. Most of them, however, described a humped beast; frequently a long neck and snake-like head was mentioned; some observers described small horns, others a kind of mane. Its colour was grey, or reddish-brown; it had flippers or flipper-like feet and a fish- or snake-like tail. Two observers described it as frog-like in appearance.

Gould's book was published in 1934 at the height of the excitement about Nessie. World reaction, predictably, ranged from laughter, to scepticism, to fascination. Gould, however, had turned up a clutch of interestingly similar stories which could not lightly be dismissed.

There were also several stories of the animal having been seen ashore – the first emanating from people who had been children in the 1870s. Other witnesses who had seen the animal ashore described a monstrous dark-grey object with a skin like an elephant, a long neck and feet or flippers. When disturbed, the animal moved rapidly back into the water and, on the evidence of one observer who startled the creature as it was crossing the lakeside road in front of his car, it gave a 'sharp bark like a dog as it disappeared into the water'.

Sightings, sometimes fortuitous, sometimes by hopeful tourists with patiently trained binoculars, continued to occur spasmodically but regularly during the next few years. But more important affairs intervened and Germany's less friendly monster ousted Nessie from the pages of the world's Press – except for the occasion when Italy (desperate for *some* modicum of success) claimed to have bombed the loch and killed the famous denizen.

The wife of the then manager of the Caledonian Canal, Mrs Constance Whyte, knew better, and being interested in Scottish history she proceeded to unearth the old stories and investigate the new. She published her findings in 1951 – and attracted the attention of Maurice Burton, a scientist and writer who felt that the monster demanded more attention. Mrs Whyte continued with her researches and published a book entitled *More Than A Legend*, which once again revived the interest of both laymen and scientists: one of these was an aeronautical engineer called Tim Dinsdale, who became so interested that he eventually gave up his career to devote himself to the enigma.

With the revival of interest the lunatic fringe, of course, also got into the act. Large rewards were offered by zoos and circuses to anyone who could capture Nessie dead or alive. A well-known whisky firm offered a cool million pounds for its capture. The hoaxers came out again, planting the jaw-bones of a long-dead whale and launching plastic 'monsters'. Pianists played seductive music at the water's edge; an airship hovered over the lake peering into the depths; a bacon joint was dragged through the water; a mock 'female' monster, smelling delectably of fish-oil, was towed along the loch (and mysteriously vanished); there was an abortive plan to strap cameras onto dolphins; and a yellow submarine, manned not by the British Beatles but by an American team, emerged from the depths with the crew sadly complaining that nobody had told them that you couldn't see further than twelve inches.

Over the years the theory that the monster just *could* be some kind of plesiosaur, long thought (like the coelacanth) to be extinct, had been gaining ground. However, said the scientists, it was more likely to be a grey

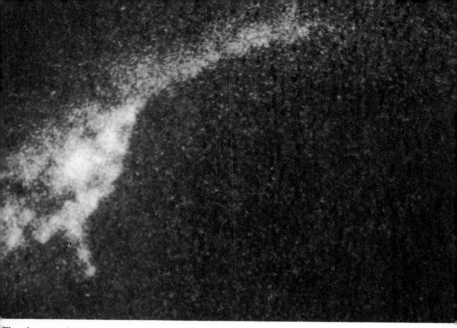

The photograph taken in 1976 by Dr Robert Rimes, President of the Academy of Applied Science, showing a creature with a long neck, a tiny head, a bulbous body and flipper-like appendages.

The monster photographed on the surface by Anthony Shiels on 21 May 1977, from Urquhart Castle.

seal, a giant eel or even a killer-whale which had found its way through the narrow entrance from the sea into Loch Ness. Then it could be one or more otters or a deer swimming in the loch. It could even be inanimate: an ancient tree trunk suddenly released from some clinging mud-bed to bob briefly to the surface, or a mat of vegetable fibres raised to the surface by the gases of decomposition which then escaped to allow the rotting weeds to sink again.

None of this quite explained the problem, however, and when in 1960 Dinsdale was fortunate enough to capture a ciné-film of a distant moving object which caused a sensation when it was shown on BBC's *Panorama* programme, the sceptics were noticeably shaken. At last science, combined with proper organization, got under way. Properly financed and planned expeditions prepared to go to work, and the ponderously named Loch Ness Phenomena Investigation Bureau was formed to sponsor exploration on a continuing basis. This organization set up a number of permanent observation spots around the loch, provided information for passing tourists and residents, and asked for any information however nebulous. It went to work in a reasonably organized fashion with teams of lookouts, mounted cameras and so on but, in the end, failed to produce anything more concrete than the evidence gathered over past years.

Others joined the hunt. H. G. Hasler, founder of the Transatlantic Race, brought a sailing ship (which, being silent, he thought would have a better chance than a noisy engine-powered boat) to the loch and fitted it with hydrophones. These picked up odd clicking and tapping noises here and there, and the crew also saw inexplicable disturbances and eddies and even small humps in the water. But there was still no more tangible result.

Other expeditions, from Cambridge and Birmingham universities for example, also logged numerous strange eddies, humps and objects resembling long necks. All were carefully investigated. It was established that wakes from passing boats, even half-an-hour after the boats had disappeared from sight, could, to the naked eye, look like humps in the water; birds swimming in line could look like a hump or, taking off, like a long neck. Two 'monsters' were definitely identified as an otter and (probably) a large salmon. Seals, swimming deer and floating debris added to the confusion, but positive identification was meticulously carried out. Many of the reported 'sightings' were eliminated; nevertheless, after two years of work the Cambridge expedition wrote:

> We cannot say with conviction that the Loch Ness monster does not exist. Indeed, the small pieces of evidence we have all suggest that there is an unusual animal in the loch. However, we consider that the 'monster' is much smaller than many people have claimed and that the huge humps are wake effects.

Films, including Dinsdale's, were analysed by experts at the Joint Air Reconnaissance Intelligence Centre; they were unable to identify the subjects filmed with any known object or animal. In the opinion of these experts one of the films analysed appeared to show two objects moving along close together, thus supporting a previous supposition drawn from eye-witness reports that there was more than one monster in the lake.

The Loch Ness Phenomena Investigation Bureau (which no longer exists, although a permanent exhibition of photographs and other evidence does) aroused the interest of several well-known figures, including Sir Peter Scott who is on record as saying that although the existence of the Loch Ness Monster does seem impossible, it is, in fact, probably true.

The search for a monster in the loch continues, although the interest of voluntary subscribers and investigators has temporarily died away. Although many of the 4,000-odd 'sightings' can be naturally explained in one or other of the ways mentioned above, it is virtually impossible to dismiss them all in this fashion. After all, there's nothing unique about Nessie. In other Scottish lakes, in Ireland, Scandinavia, Canada, Patagonia, and Australasia stories of lake monsters are common. The existence of sea serpents whose description is so like the 'identikit' of Nessie as to make them close relatives has long been taken for granted by deep-sea sailors. Huge eels are commonplace. It is difficult to discard entirely the evidence of all those thousands of people who, long before Nessie became a part of popular legend, had seen some strange aquatic animal in the loch.

Personally, in this mundane technological age in which 'long-leggedie beasties' can't possibly exist unless they can be measured by one means or another, I am entirely in sympathy with a local resident near Foyers who, describing a remarkable patch of disturbed, foaming water which he had seen, commented: 'If that wasna the monster, then there's something mighty queer in the loch.'

THE ABOMINABLE SNOWMAN

When Eric Shipton, the Everest explorer, was flying back from Karachi in 1951, he was startled when a stewardess told him that crowds of reporters would be waiting to see him at the airport. It would be another two years before Sir Edmund Hillary and Sherpa Tensing reached the summit and turned Everest into front-page news. It was not until he landed in London that Shipton discovered what all the excitement was about: a footprint in the snow. When crossing the Menlung Glacier, Shipton's team had observed a line of huge footprints; Shipton photographed one of them, with an ice-axe beside it to provide scale. It was thirteen inches wide and eighteen inches long, and its shape was curious – three small toes and a huge big toe that seemed to be almost circular. The footsteps were those of a two-legged creature, not a wolf or bear. The only animal with a vaguely similar foot is an orang-utan, but it has a far longer big toe.

Ever since European travellers began to explore Tibet, they had reported legends of a huge ape-like creature called the *metoh-kangmi*, which translates roughly as the filthy or abominable snowman. The stories cover a huge area, from the Caucasus to the Himalayas, from the Pamirs, through Mongolia, to the far eastern tip of Russia. In central Asia they are called Meh-teh, or Yetis, while tribes of eastern Asia refer to them as Almas. The earliest reference to them in the West seems to be a report in 1832 by B.H. Hodgson, the British Resident at the Court of Nepal, who mentions that his native hunters were frightened by a 'wild man' covered in long dark hair. More than half a century later, in 1889, Major L.A. Waddell was exploring the Himalayas when he came across huge footprints in the snow at 17,000 feet; his bearers told him that these were the tracks of a Yeti. And the Yeti, according to the natives, was a ferocious creature which was quite likely to attack human beings and carry them off for food. The best way to escape it was to run downhill, for the Yeti had such long hair that it would fall over its eyes and blind it when going downhill.

In 1921 an expedition led by Colonel Howard-Bury, making a first attempt on the north face of Everest, saw in the distance a number of large, dark creatures moving against the snow of the Lhapta-la Pass; the Tibetan porters said these were Yetis. And in 1925 N.A. Tombazi, a Fellow of the Royal Geographical Society, almost managed to get a photograph of a naked, upright creature on the Zemu Glacier; but it had vanished by the time he sighted the lens. And so the legends and the sightings continued to leak back to civilization, always with that slight element of doubt which made it possible for scientists to dismiss them as lies or mistakes. Shipton's photograph of 1951 caused such a sensation because it was taken by a member of a scientific expedition who could have no possible motive for stretching the facts. Besides, the photograph spoke for him.

At least, so one might assume. The Natural History Department of the British Museum did not agree, and one of its leading authorities, Dr T.C.S. Morrison-Scott, was soon committing himself to the view that the footprint was made by a creature called the Himalayan langur. His

One of the footprints, thirteen inches wide and eighteen inches long, that Eric Shipton discovered at Menlung Glacier in 1951.

Sir Edmund Hillary in 1960 with an alleged Yeti scalp. *Right:* Khumbo Chumbi, an elder of the Sherpa village which has had the scalp in its possession for 240 years.

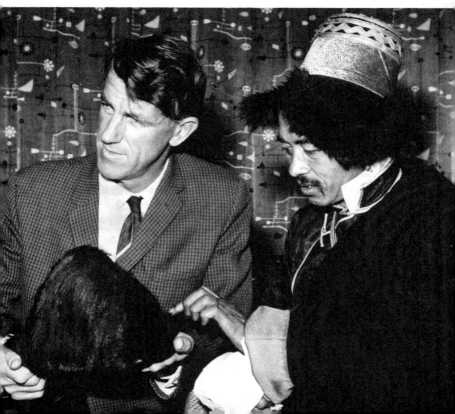

assessment was based on a description of the Yeti by Sherpa Tensing, who said it was about five feet high, walked upright, had a conical skull and reddish-brown fur. This, said Dr Morrison-Scott, sounded quite like a langur. The objection to this was that the langur, like most apes, walks on all fours most of the time; besides, its feet have five very long toes, quite unlike the four rounded toes of the photograph. Morrison-Scott's theory was greeted with hoots of disdain, as it undoubtedly deserved to be. But that brought the identitification of the strange creature no closer.

A more imaginative view was taken by the Dutch zoologist Bernard Huevelmans in a series of articles published in Paris in 1952. He pointed out that in 1934 Dr Ralph von Koenigswald had discovered some ancient teeth in the shop of a Chinese apothecary in Hong Kong – the Chinese regard powdered teeth as a medicine. One of these was a human-type molar which was twice as large as the molar of an adult gorilla, suggesting that its owner had stood about twelve feet tall. Evidence suggested that this giant – he became known as Gigantopithecus – lived around half a million years ago. Huevelmans suggested that Shipton's footprints were made by a huge biped related to Gigantopithecus. But few scientists considered his theory seriously.

In 1954 the *Daily Mail* sent out an expedition to try to capture – or at least photograph – a Yeti. It spent fifteen weeks plodding through the Himalayan snows without so much as a glimpse of the filthy snowman. But the expedition gathered one exciting piece of information. Several monasteries, they learned, possessed 'Yeti scalps', which were revered as holy relics. Several of these scalps were tracked down, and proved to be fascinating. They were all long and conical, rather like a bishop's mitre, and covered with hair, including a 'crest' in the middle, made of erect hair. One of these scalps proved to be a fake, sewn together from fragments of animal skin. But others were undoubtedly made of one piece of skin. Hairs from them were sent to experts for analysis, and the experts declared that they came from no known animal. It looked as if the existence of the Yeti had finally been proved. Alas, it was not to be.

Sir Edmund Hillary was allowed to borrow one of the scalps – he was held in very high regard in Tibet – and Bernard Huevelmans had the opportunity to examine it. It reminded him of a creature called the southern serow, a kind of goat, which he had seen in a zoo before the war. And serows exist in Nepal, 'abominable snowman' country. Huevelmans tracked down a serow in the Royal Institute in Brussels. And comparison with the Yeti scalp revealed that it came from the same animal. The skin had been stretched and moulded with steam. It was not, of course, a deliberate fake. It was made to be worn in certain religious rituals in Tibet;

over the years its origin had been forgotten, and it had been designated a Yeti scalp.

All this was enough to convince the sceptics that the Yeti was merely a legend. But that conclusion was premature. Europeans who went out searching for the snowman might or might not catch a glimpse of some dark creature moving against the snow. But their tracks were observed – and photographed – in abundance. A Frenchman, the Abbé Bordet, followed three separate lots of tracks in 1955. Squadron Leader Lester Davies filmed huge footprints in the same year. Climber Don Whillans saw an ape-like creature on Annapurna in June 1970, and Lord Hunt photographed more Yeti tracks in 1978.

In Russia more solid evidence began to emerge. In 1958 Lt-Col Vargen Karapetyan saw an article on the Yeti – or, as it is known in Russia, Alma – in a Moscow newspaper, and sought out the leading Soviet expert, Prof. Boris Porshnev, to tell him his own story. In December 1941 his unit had been fighting the Germans in the Caucasus near Buinakst, and he was approached by a unit of partisans and asked to go and look at a man they had taken prisoner. The partisans explained that Karapetyan would have to go along to a barn to look at the 'man', because as soon as he was taken into a heated room, he stank and dripped sweat; besides, he was covered in lice. The 'man' proved to be more like an ape: naked, filthy and unkempt; he looked dull and vacant, and often blinked. He made no attempt to defend himself when Karapetyan pulled out hairs from his body, but his eyes looked as if he was begging for mercy. It was obvious that he did not understand speech. Finally, Karapetyan left, telling the partisans to make up their own minds about what to do with the creature. He heard a few days later that the 'wild man' had escaped. Obviously this story could have been an invention. But a report from the Ministry of the Interior in Daghestan confirmed its truth. The 'wild man' had been court-martialled and executed as a deserter.

It was in January 1958 that Dr Alexander Pronin, of Leningrad University, reported seeing an Alma. He was in the Pamirs, and saw the creature outlined against a cliff-top. It was man-like, covered with reddish-grey hair, and he watched it for more than five minutes; three days later he saw it again at the same spot. For some reason, good Marxists poured scorn on the notion of a 'wild man'; but the evidence went on accumulating, until Boris Porshnev began to make an attempt to co-ordinate the sightings. The impressive body of evidence he has accumulated is described in some detail in Odette Tchernine's impressive book *The Yeti*.

If the abominable snowman really exists, why should he be confined to Tibet and central Asia? The answer which is emerging from a huge patchwork of research is that he is not. There is also much evidence from the American continent – from Ecuador and Venezuela to Canada. And some of the most impressive evidence comes from northern California, where the 'wild man' is known as Bigfoot, a term invented by the Press in the 1920s. In Canada he is known as the Sasquatch. A typical Bigfoot sighting took place in Oregon, when three loggers saw a man-like figure watching them. It was massively built and covered from head to foot in dark hair; but it was definitely man-like rather than ape-like. As they approached, it vanished into the forest. All descriptions of Bigfoot – and there are hundreds – make him sound exactly like the Yeti.

In 1967 Roger Patterson, a photographer, came close to producing definitive evidence for Bigfoot when he had his cine-camera to hand at Bluff Creek, northern California, and saw a huge creature skulking in the woods. He filmed for several frames before the animal went out of sight. The film was shown complete in a television programme that formed part of Arthur C. Clarke's 'Mysterious World', and was certainly impressive. The better frames show that the creature is feminine, with large breasts and buttocks, and it moves with a swinging, free gait that makes it hard to believe that it is a man in a King Kong costume – a conclusion nevertheless supported by both American and Russian scientists who have examined the film. Comparisons with human beings standing in the same places establish that the creature was about six and a half feet high.

Footprints found at Bluff Creek are 14 to 15 inches long. Hundreds of such footprints have been studied in areas where Bigfoots and Sasquatches have been sighted. A typical print is from 16 to 18 inches long, and has a double ball which is unlike the single ball on a human foot; the depth of footprints suggests that it weighs anything between 300 and 1,000 lb.

Those who claim to have been close to Bigfoot, or to have entered areas where he has recently been hiding, usually report the same extremely strong smell that Karapetyan described. And an encounter with the creature in the Guacomayo Range of Ecuador reveals that Bigfoot suffers from body odour whether he is in hot or cold climates. Count Pino Turolla, an Italian archaeologist, was exploring a deep cave with a companion in December 1970 when he noticed a strong animal odour. The tunnel entered a large cave, and the men paused to light cigarettes. Suddenly, they were petrified by a deafening roaring noise, and a boulder crashed down close to them. As a huge, lumbering form crossed the beam of their flashlights, both men fled back to the daylight. But at some point Turolla picked up a flat disc, which in the daylight proved to be a jade amulet carved with a stylized face; he believes that this suggests that the creatures inhabiting the cave were primitive men rather than apes.

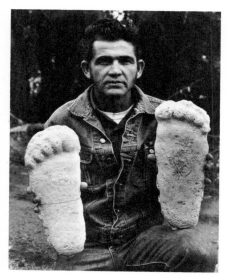

Bob Gimlin holding 14½-inch casts from tracks made by the Bigfoot filmed by Roger Patterson at Bluff Creek, California, in 1967.

A frame from the ciné film taken by Roger Patterson. The Bigfoot corresponds very closely to the Yeti. Is this Neanderthal man?

To summarize: the evidence for the existence of the Yeti, or Alma, or Bigfoot, or Sasquatch, is very strong indeed; hundreds of sightings make it unlikely that it is an invention. If, then, we assume for a moment that it really exists, what is it?

Dr Myra Shackley, lecturer in archaeology at Leicester University, believes she knows the answer. She is convinced that the Yeti is a Neanderthal man. And this is also the conclusion reached by Odette Tchernine on the basis of the Soviet evidence.

Neanderthal man was the predecessor of modern man. He first seems to have appeared on earth about a hundred thousand years ago. He was smaller and more ape-like than modern man, with the well-known receding forehead and simian jaw. He lived in caves, and the piles of animal bones discovered in such caves suggest that Neanderthal woman was a sluttish housewife, and that his habitation must have stunk of rotting flesh. He was also a cannibal. But he was by no means a mere animal. Colouring pigments in Neanderthal caves suggest that he loved colour; he certainly wove screens of coloured flowers. And since he buried these with his dead, it seems certain that he believed in an after-life. Mysterious round stones found in his habitations suggest that he was a sun worshipper.

Our ancestor, Cro-Magnon man, came on earth about fifty thousand years ago; it was he who made all the famous cave paintings. Neanderthal man vanished completely over the next twenty thousand years, and the mystery of his disappearance has never been solved. The general view is that he was exterminated by Cro-Magnon man (William Golding's novel *The Inheritors* is a story of the encounter between the two).

The psychologist Stan Gooch advanced a startling thesis in his book *The Neanderthal Question*: that Neanderthals were not entirely exterminated, but that their women occasionally bore children to Cro-Magnon males. The descendants of these products of cross-breeding became the Jews. (It should be noted that Gooch is himself Jewish.) Gooch believes that Neanderthal man was more 'psychic' than Cro-Magnon man, and that such psychic faculties as present-day man now possesses are inherited from these Neanderthal ancestors.

Whether or not we can accept Gooch's theory, it seems reasonable to suppose that Neanderthal man may have survived, driven into the wilder and less hospitable places of the earth by his conqueror. Myra Shackley has travelled to the Altai mountains of Mongolia and collected evidence for the existence of Almas. 'They live in caves, hunt for food, use stone tools, and wear animal skins and fur.' And she mentions that in 1972 a Russian doctor met a family of Almas. In fact, Odette Tchernine cites a number of such stories. Professor Porshnev discovered again and again evidence among mountain people that they knew of the existence of 'wild men'; the Abkhazians still have stories of how they drove the wild men out of the district they colonized. Tchernine refers to these wild men as 'pre-hominids'.

Porshnev himself investigated a case of a female Alma who had been caught in the Ochamchir region in the mid-nineteenth century. Hunters captured a 'wild woman' who had ape-like features and was covered in hair; for several years in captivity she was so violent that she could not be approached, and food had to be thrown to her. They called her Zana. Porshnev interviewed many old people – one was 105 – who remembered Zana. They told him how she had become domesticated, and would perform simple tasks like grinding corn. She had a massive bosom, thick muscular arms and legs, and thick fingers; she could not endure warm rooms but preferred the cold. She loved to gorge herself on grapes in the vineyard, and also enjoyed wine – she would drink heavily then sleep for hours. This may explain how she became a mother on several occasions, to different fathers. Her children usually died because she washed them in the freezing river. (Presumably, having half-human characteristics, they lacked her tremendous inherited endurance of cold.) Finally, her newborn children were taken away from her, and they grew up among the people of the village. Unlike their mother, they could talk and were reasonable human beings. The youngest of these died as recently as 1954 (Zana died about 1890). Porshnev interviewed two of her grandchildren, and noted their dark skin and negroid looks. Shalikula, the grandson, had such powerful jaws that he could pick up a chair with a man sitting on it. Here, it would seem, is solid, undeniable evidence of the existence of 'wild men'.

Dr Shackley admits that it is her ambition to find one. It is a strange thought that if she, or any other scientist, could do this, we might be privileged to stare into the face of the creature who vanished so mysteriously thirty thousand years ago.

The ruins of Borley Rectory.

SELECT BIBLIOGRAPHY

DEATHS AND DISAPPEARANCES
Scientific and Medical Evidence in the Christie Case, Francis Camps (Medical Publications Ltd, 1953).
Ten Rillington Place, Ludovic Kennedy (Gollancz, 1961).
The Two Stranglers of Rillington Place, Rupert Furneaux (Panther Books, 1961).
Frogman Extraordinary, J. Bernard Hutton (Spearman, 1960).
The Fake Defector, J. Bernard Hutton (Spearman, 1970).
Martin Bormann, James McGovern (Arthur Barker, 1968).
The Bormann Brotherhood, William Stevenson (Arthur Barker, 1973).
Motoring and the Mighty, Richard Garrett (Stanley Paul, 1971).
Gehlen, Spy of the Century, E.H. Cookridge (Hodder and Stoughton, 1971).
Death of a President, William Manchester (Harper and Row, 1967).
Best Evidence, D.S. Liston (Collier Macmillan, 1982).

HISTORIC AND PREHISTORIC ENIGMAS
Anastasia: The Life of Anna Anderson, Peter Kurth (Jonathan Cape, 1983).
I am Anastasia: The Autobiography of the Grand Duchess of Russia (Michael Joseph, 1958).
The File on the Tsar, Anthony Summers and Tom Mangold (Jove/Harcourt Brace Jovanovitch ed. 1978).
The Hunt for the Czar, Guy Richards (Peter Davies/Sphere, 1972).
The Princes in the Tower, Elizabeth Jenkins (Hamish Hamilton, 1978).
Richard III, Charles Rose (Methuen, 1981).
Richard III, Paul Murray Kendall (Allen and Unwin, 1955).
The Murder of Napoleon, Ben Weider and David Hopgood (Robson Books, 1982).
Assassination at St Helena, Sten Forshufvud and Ben Weider (Mitchell Press Ltd, Vancouver, 1978).
A Land, Jacquetta Hawkes (The Cresset Press, 1951).
The World's Last Mysteries (The Reader's Digest, 1977).
The Habsburg Twilight: Tales from Vienna, Sarah Gainham (Weidenfeld, 1979).
A Nervous Splendour: Vienna 1888/1889, Frederic Morton (Weidenfeld, 1979).
I Was to Be Empress, Princess Stephanie of Belgium (London, 1937).
The Road to Mayerling, Richard Barkeley (New York, 1958).
The Quest for Arthur's Britain, G. Ashe (Pall Mall Press, 1968).
Arthur's Britain, L. Alcock (Allen Lane, 1971).
By South Cadbury is that Camelot . . ., L. Alcock (Thames and Hudson, 1972).
The Bourbon Tragedy, Rupert Furneaux (Allen and Unwin, 1968).
The Shadow King, H.R. Madol (London, 1930).
Sutton Hoo: The Excavation of a Royal Ship Burial, C. Green (Merlin Press, 1969).
The Treasure of Sutton Hoo, B. Grolskopf (Robert Hale, 1971).
The Turin Shroud, Ian Wilson (Gollancz, 1978).
Verdict on the Shroud, Kenneth E. Stevenson and Gary R. Habermas (Hale, 1982).
The End of Atlantis, J.V. Luce (Thames and Hudson, 1969).
Atlantis: The Truth behind the Legend, A.G. Galanopoulos and Edward Bacon (Nelson, 1969).

MYSTERIES OF THE SEA

The World's Greatest Sea Mysteries, Michael and Mollie Hardwick (Odhams, 1967).
Famous Mysteries of the Sea, Brian Breed (Arthur Barker, 1965).
Invisible Horizons, Vincent Gaddis (Chiltern Books, 1965).
The Bermuda Triangle, Adi-Kent Thomas Jeffrey (New Hope Publishing Co., 1973).
The Bermuda Triangle, Charles Berlitz (Doubleday, 1974).
The Bermuda Triangle Mystery Solved, Lawrence David Kusche (New English Library, 1975).
Stories of Famous Ships, Richard Garrett (Arthur Barker, 1974).
Mary Celeste – the Odyssey of an Abandoned Ship, Charles Edey Fay (Peabody Museum, Salem, Mass., 1942).
Into Thin Air, Ralph Begg (David and Charles, 1979).
Mary Celeste, Macdonald Hastings (Michael Joseph, 1972).
The Joyita Mystery, Robin Maugham (Parrish, 1962).

MYSTERIES OF THE AIR

Great Mysteries of the Air, Ralph Barker (Chatto and Windus, 1966).
Space, Gravity and the Flying Saucer, Leonard G. Cramp (Werner Laurie, 1954).
Flying Saucers Have Landed, Desmond Leslie and George Adamski (Werner Laurie, 1953).
Flying Saucer Report, Roger Stanway and Anthony Pace (Newchapel Observatory, 1968).
Unidentified Flying Objects, Robert Chapman (Arthur Barker, 1969).
In Search of my Father, Ronald Howard (William Kimber, 1981).
The Search for Amelia Earhart, Fred Goerner (Bodley Head, 1966).
Who Destroyed the Hindenburg?, A.A. Hoehling (Robert Hale, 1962).
Airshipwreck, Len Deighton and Arnold Schwartzman (Jonathan Cape, 1978).

GHOSTS AND THE OCCULT

The Most Haunted House in England, Harry Price (London, 1940).
The End of Borley Rectory, Harry Price (London, 1948).
Report for Society for Psychical Research, 1954.
An Adventure, Jourdain and Moberley (various publishers and editions).
Pocket Guide to the West Indies, Sir A. Aspinall (London, 1954).
History of Barbados, Sir R.H. Schomburgh (London, 1844).
Madame Blavatsky, the Woman Behind the Myth, Marion Meade (Putnam, 1980).
Old Diary Leaves (Retitled: *Inside the Occult*), Henry Steel Olcott (Running Press, Philadelphia, 1975).
Reincarnation, compiled and edited by Joseph Head and S.L. Cranston (Causeway Books, 1967).
The ESP Reader (Castle Books, 1969).
Twenty Cases Suggestive of Reincarnation, Ian Stevenson (American Society for Psychical Research, 1966).
Encounters with the Past, Peter Moss with Joe Keeton (Sidgwick and Jackson, 1979).
Mind Out of Time, Ian Wilson (Gollancz, 1981).
More Lives than One?, Jeffrey Iverson (Souvenir Press, 1976).

MONSTERS
Ancient Mysteries, Peter Haining (Sidgwick and Jackson, 1977).
The Leviathans, Tim Dinsdale (Futura Books, 1976).
In Search of Lake Monsters, Peter Costello (Panther Books, 1975).
The Yeti, Odette Tchernine (Spearman, 1970).
Big Foot, John Napier (Dutton, 1973).
There are Giants in the Earth, Michael Grumley (Sidgwick and Jackson, 1974).
On the Track of Unknown Animals, Bernard Huevelmans (Hart-Davis, 1974).

PICTURE ACKNOWLEDGEMENTS

The photographs in this book are reproduced by permission of the following:

Aerofilms Ltd 81 above; *BBC Hulton Picture Library* ii, 51 above, 55, 61 above, 72, 163, 171 below; *BPCC/Aldus Archive* 123 below (© Press Association Ltd), 143 (© Associated Press), 203, 229 above; *British Museum* 93; *Bulloz Library* 67 below; *John H. Cutten Associates* 195 above; *Mary Evans Picture Library* 188 below (© Mary Evans/Harry Price, Coll., Univ. of London); *Fortean Picture Library* 225 below, 233 above (© René Dahinden); *Fotomas Index* 67 above; *Keystone Press Agency Ltd* 17, 23, 35, 159 below, 167, 170-1; *Mansell Collection* 51 below, 73 below, 86 above, 87, 132, 133, 135, 179 above and below right, 209; *Paris Match* 40 above; *Popperfoto* viii, 3, 7 above left and right, 27, 34, 41, 61 below, 73 above, 86 below, 152, 153 above, 176-7, 178-9, 188 above, 195 below, 225 above; *Ronald Sheridan* 81 below, 107 below, 111; *Syndication International* 19 below, 99; *Topham Picture Library* 7 below, 11, 13, 19 above, 40 below, 43, 44, 45, 75, 103, 107 above, 117 (© National Maritime Museum, London), 123 above, 149, 153 below, 159 above, 189, 197, 221, 229 below, 233 below, 236.

The map on page 127 is by Heather Sherratt.

INDEX

Abgar, King, 102
Adamnan, 222
Adamski, George, 150-2
Adventure, An (Jourdain and Moberley), 199
Aethelhere, King, 96
Akimaya, Josephine, 172
Alcock, John, 174
Alcock, Leslie, 79
Alexandra, Tsarina, 50
Allingham, Cedric, 155-6
Anastasia, 50, *51*, 52-4, *55*
Anderson, Anna, 52-6
Anderson, Augustus, 130
Angoulême, Duchess d', 88-9
Anna, King, 96
Annals of Waverley, 82-8
Antommarchi, Dr, 64-5, 68
Argonauts, the, 109
Arnold, Gordon, 47
Arnold, Kenneth, 124, 148-50
Arnott, Dr, 64-5
Arthur, King of England, 77-9, 82-3
Artois, Count d', 68
Ashe, Geoffrey, 105
Aspinall, Sir Algernon E., 202
Atlantis, 104-12
Axmann, Artur, 36

Banerjee, Professor Hemendra, 214
Barras, 88
Barry, Madame du, 193
Basselle, Colonel Norman, 164
Bauer, Dr Fritz, 33, 36
Beauharnais, Josephine, 88
Bede, 95
Bellstedt, Leutnant, 156-7
Bennett, the Reverend James, 83
Bentham, 142, 144
Beowulf, 94, 97

Berlitz, Charles, 125
Bermuda Triangle, the, 121-8
Bermuda Triangle, The (Berlitz), 125
Bernstein, Morey, 215
Besant, Annie, 159, 211
Bianca, Duchess of Savoy, 100
Bingham, Lord, 21
Black Horsemen, The (Wildman), 78
Blavatsky, Helena, 205-8, *209*, 210-11
Blavatsky, Nikifor, 205
Bloxham, Arnall, 164, 216
Bonaparte, Napoleon, 63-4, *67*, 68-9
Bonaparte, Prince Napoleon Louis Jérôme Victor, 66
Bordet, Abbé, 231
Borley, 184-7, *188*, *189*, 190-2, *236*
Bormann, Albert, 33
Bormann, Gerda, 30, 33
Bormann, Martin, 28-33, *34*, 35-7
Braden, Jim, *see* Brading
Brading, Eugene, 47
Bratfisch, 74
Braun, Eva, 31
Brewster, Samuel, 201
Briggs, Captain Benjamin Spooner, *135*, 136-8
Briggs, Mrs, 136-7
Briggs, Sophia, 136-7
Brown, Arthur Whitten, 174
Brown, Basil, 90-1
Brown, Beresford, 2
Brown, Charles, 4
Bruneau, Mathurin, 88
Buch, Gerda, *see* Bormann, Gerda
Buch, Major, 30
Buckingham, Duke of, *see* Stafford
Bulganin, N.A., 21-5
Bull, the Reverend Harry, 185
Bull, the Reverend Henry Dawson Ellis, 184-5
Burton, Maurice, 224

Camden, John, 79
Camelot, 77–83
Camelot and the Vision of Albion (Ashe), 105
Camps, Dr Francis, 2, 5
Cardington, Lord Thompson of, 175
Cathars and Reincarnation, The (Guirdham), 216
Caton, Rowland, 202
Cecilie, Crown Princess of Prussia, 54
Charny, Geoffrey de, 100
Charny, Margaret de, 100
Chase, Dorcas, 204
Chase, Thomas, 204
Chase family tomb, 200–2, *203*, 204–5
Chaubey, Kedar Nath, 213
Chenhalls, Alfred, 158–61
Christie, Ethel, 4–5, 8
Christie, John Reginald Halliday, 4–6, 7, 8–10
Churchill, 161
Clarke, Robert Bowcher, 202
Columba, St, 222
Combermere, Lord, 202
Commynes, Philippe de, 62
Conan Doyle, Sir Arthur, 131, 204
Connally, Governor John, 39, 46–7
Connally, Nellie, 39
Corliss, William, 128
Coulombs, the, 210–11
Crabb, Lionel ('Buster'), 22, *23*, 24–6, *27*, 28–9
Crantor, 104
Crawford, O.G.S., 92
Croyland, the Monk of, 58
Culverwell, Captain, 118

Dagobert I, King of the Goths, 96
Davies, Squadron Leader Lester, 231
Desault, Dr, 85
Deveau, Oliver, 129–30
Devi, Kumari Shanti, 161–2, 213–14
Died 1513, Born 1929 (Stewart), 165, 217

Dinsdale, Tim, 224, 226
Dönitz, Admiral, 31
Doveton, Sir William, 64

Eady, Muriel, 6
Earhart, Amelia, 165–6, *167*, 168–70, *171*, 172–3
Ecgric, King, 96
Eckener, Dr, 181
Eden, Sir Anthony, 25
Edmund Mortimer, Earl of March, 57
Edward I, King of England, 82
Edward IV, King of England, 58
Edward V, King of England, 57–63
Eichmann, Adolf, 33
Eisenhower, 162, 165
Elisabeth, Archduchess of Austria, 77
Elisabeth, Empress of Austria, 70–1, 74
Elliot, James, 200
Elwes, Dominic, 20
End of Borley Rectory, The (Price), 192
Erdmann, Colonel Fritz, 181–2
Ernst Ludwig of Hesse, Grand Duke, 54
Ethelred the Unready, King of England, 80
Evans, Beryl, 4, 6, 7, 8–9
Evans, Geraldine, 4, 8–10
Evans, Timothy, 4, 6, 7, 8–10

Fake Defector, The (Hutton), 29
Fedorovna, Dowager Empress Marie, 54
Ferrie, David, 47
Flood, Frederick Solly, 137
Flying Saucers Have Landed (Adamski), 151, 154
Forshufvud, Sten, 65–9
Fox, Kate and Margaret, 206
Foyster, the Reverend Lionel, 186–7, *188*
Foyster, Marianne, 186–7, *188*

Franz Josef, Emperor of Austria, 70–4, 77
Friedmann, Tadek, 33
Frogman Extraordinary (Hutton), 28
Frost, K.T., 79, 110, 112
Fuerst, Ruth, 5–6
Furneaux, Rupert, 9

Gaddis, Vincent, 122
Galanopoulos, Professor A.G., 106
Gehlen, Reinhard, 32
Gilliard, Pierre, 54
Glanville, Helen, 142–3, 190–1
Glass, Sandra, 96
Goebbels, 31
Goerner, Fred, 172–3
Golding, William, 234
Gondrecourt, Count, 70
Gooch, Stan, 234
Gould, Rupert, 223
Gregson, Captain W.E., 190
Grey, Lady Elizabeth, 58–9
Grierson, Philip, 95
Grünberg, Detective-Inspector, 54
Guirdham, Dr Arthur, 216–17

Hahn, Helena, 205
Hasler, H.G., 226
Hassenstein, Lieutenant-Colonel, 53
Hastings, Lord, 59
Hawkes, Gerald, 122, 124
Haynes, Lieutenant, 162, 164
Hébert, 88
Heenen, B.C., 106
Heiligenkreuz, Abbot of, 76
Henry IV, King of England, 58
Henry V, King of England, 58
Henry VI, King of England, 58
Henry, Don, 126
Herodotus, 109
Hervagault, Jean Marie, 88
Hess, Rudolf, 30

Hill, Clint, 39, 42
Hillary, Sir Edmund, *229*, 230
Hindenburg, 173–5, *176–7*, *178–9*, 180–2
Hitler, Adolf, 30–1, 175, 180, 182
Hodgkinson, 142
Hodgson, B.H., 228
Hodgson, Richard, 210, 213
Holmes, Father Arthur, 160–1
Home, Daniel Dunglas, 207
Howard, Leslie, 158–61, *159*
Howard, Ronald, 158
Howard-Bury, Colonel, 228
Howell, Mark, 80
Hoyos, Count, 74
Huevelmans, Bernard, 230
Hume, A.O., 210
Hume, Donald, 9–10
Humphreys, Christmas, 211
Hunt, Lord, 231
Hutton, J. Bernard, 28–9

Ilbery, Captain Josiah, 115
Inheritors, The (Golding), 234
In Search of My Father (Ronald Howard), 158
Invisible Horizons (Gaddis), 122
Invisible Residents (Sanderson), 125
Irene, Princess of Prussia, 54
Isis Unveiled (Blavatsky), 208
Iverson, Jeffrey, 216

James (disciple of Jesus), 102
Jat, Jasbir Lal, 214–15, 217
Jeffrey, Adi-Kent Thomas, 125
Jessup, Morris K., 125–6
Jesus Christ, 97–104
John, St 102
Johnson, John, 129
Johnson, Lady Bird, 39
Johnson, Lyndon, 37, 39, 46–7
Jones, Dr David, 69

Joseph of Arimathaea, 101
Josephine, Empress, 88
Jourdain, Eleanor, 193-4, *195*, 196-9
Joyita, 138-46
Joyita Mystery, The (Maugham), 146

Karapetyan, Lieutenant-Colonel Vargen, 231
Karolyi, Count Stephen, 76
Kaspar, Mitzi, 71
Keeton, Joe, 216
Kemptka, Erich, 31-2
Kendrick, Sir Thomas, 90
Kennedy, Jacqueline, 37, 39, 42
Kennedy, President John, 37-9, *40*, 41-8
Kennedy, Ludovic, 6, 9
Kennedy, Robert, 46
Kent, Dr J.P.C., 95
Khrushchev, N.S., 21-6, 37
Kleist, Baron von, 52-3
Koenigswald, Dr Ralph von, 230
Koot Hoomi, 210-11
Krumnow, Albert, 36

Lachouque, Commandant Henri, 66
Lafaurie, M., 95
Lairre, Marie, 190-1
Larisch, Countess Marie, 71, 76
Laurier, Dr John de, 128
Lebendorff, Tekla, 207
Ledger, P.C., 4
Lehmann, Captain Ernst, 180-2
Leland, John, 79
Leo XIII, Pope, 77
Lives to Remember (Underwood and Wilder), 216
Loch Ness Monster, 220-7
Lombard, Carole, 161
Louis XV, King of France, 192
Louis XVI, King of France, 83-4, *86*
Louis XVIII, King of France, 88

Louis Charles, 83-9
Lowe, Sir Hudson, 64-5
Lucan, Dowager Countess, 14-15, 18
Lucan, Frances, 14
Lucan, Lord, 10, *11*, 12-16, *17*, 18-21
Lucan, Veronica, 10-15, *17*, 21
Lucas, Nathan, 202, 204
Luce, Professor J.V., 106, 109
Ludwig, King of Bavaria, 71
Luke, St, 101
Lund, Charles, 130
Luomala, Dr Ellen Katharine, 139
Luther, Dr, 180

Maclennan, Hectorina, 8-9
Mal, Kanji, 213-14
Maloney, Kathleen, 8
Manahan, John, 56
Mantell, Captain Thomas, 148, 150
Marcello, Carlos, 47
Marchand, Louis, 65
Margaret of Anjou, 58
Marie Antoinette, 83-5, 194, 198-9
Marie Thérèse, 85
Marinatos, Profsssor Spyridon, 106-9
Mark, St, 98
Markham, Sir Clements, 60
Martin Bormann (McGovern), 36
Martinez, Juan, 33
Mary Celeste, 129-31, *132*, 133-8
Mary Magdalen, 102
Maugham, Robin, 146
Maxwell Scott, Ian and Susan, 10-12, *13*, 14-16
Maynard, Guy, 90
McCarthy, Henry, 141-2
McGovern, James, 36
Meade, Marion, 205
Miller, Glenn, 161-2, *163*, 164-5
Miller, Lieutenant-Commander Thomas Henry ('Dusty'), 139-142, *143*, 144-6
Mind Out of Time (Wilson), 217

Minos, King of Crete, 110
Minotaur, 110
Mitford, Bruce, 92
Moberley, Anne, 193-4, *195*, 196-9
Molinet, 62
Montholon, Count de, 64, 68
More, Sir Thomas, 59-62
Morehouse, Captain David Reed, 129-31, *133*, 136-7
More Lives than One? (Iverson), 216
More Than a Legend (Whyte), 224
Morgan, Flight Officer John, 125, 164
Morrison, Herb, 173-4
Morrison-Scott, Dr T.C.S., 228, 230
Most Haunted House in England, The (Price), 190
My Past (Larisch), 76

Napoleon, *see* Bonaparte
Naundorff, Karl Wilhelm, 88-9
Neanderthal Question, The (Gooch), 234
Nelson, Rita, 8
Nennius, 78
Neville, Richard, Earl of Warwick, 58
Nicholas II, Tsar, 50
Nicodemus, 102
Nimitz, Fleet Admiral Chester W., 172-3
Ninkovitch, Dr, 106
Nixon, Richard, 37
Noonan, Captain Fred, 166, 168, *171*, 172-3

ODESSA, 32
Olcott, Henry Steel, 207
Olga, Grand Duchess, 54
Orderson, the Reverend Thomas, 202
Oswald, Lee Harvey, 42, *43*, *44*, 45-8

Parsons, Dr, 142
Patterson, Roger, 232

Pearless, 141
Penda, King of Mercia, 96
Peter, Simon, 102
Peuthert, Clara, 52
Philipp, Prince of Coburg, 74
Phillips, C.W., 91-2, 96
Phythian-Adams, Dr John, 191
Plato, 104-6, 110-12
Plowman, Commander Peter, 140, 144
Plutarch, 109
Pocket Guide to the West Indies (Aspinall), 202
Pollock, Joanna and Jacqueline, 217-18
Pollock, John, 218
Pollock, Mrs, 217-18
Pompadour, Madame de, 193
Pontius Pilate, 98
Porshnev, Professor Boris, 231, 234-5
Pretty, Edith May, 90, 94
Price, Harry, 185-6, *188*, 189-92
Pronin, Dr Alexander, 231

Radford, Dr Ralegh, 79
Ranson, Detective Chief Superintendent Roy, 20
Redwald, 95-6
Reece, Arthur, 203
Reilly, Mr and Mrs, 4
Richard Duke of York (elder), 57-8
Richard Duke of York (younger), 57, 59-63
Richard III, King of England, 57-60, *61*, 62-3
Richardson, Albert G., 131
Rinaldi, Father Peter, 97
Rivett, Sandra, *13*, 14, 15, 21
Roff, Asa, 212
Roff, Mary, 212-13
Roff, Mrs, 212
Roff, Nervie, 212
Roosevelt, Eleanor, 169
Roosevelt, President Franklin D., 168-9

Rouse, George, 124-5
Ruby, Jack, 42-48, *45*
Rudolf, Crown Prince of Austria, 70-1, *72*, *73*, 74-7
Ryall, Edward, 216

Saga of Napoleon's Wallpaper, The (Jones), 69
Samona, Adela, 215
Samona, Alexandrina, 215
Sanderson, Ivan, 124-5
Sawyer, Claude G., 114-15, 118, 120
Schmeling, Max, 180
Schomburgh, Sir Robert H., 201-2
Scott, Sir Peter, 227
Scutt, Captain, 128
Search for Amelia Earhart, The (Goerner), 172
Search for Bridey Murphy, The (Bernstein), 215
Second Time Round (Ryall), 216
Secret Doctrine, The (Blavatsky), 211
Shackley, Dr Myra, 234-5
Shakespeare: *King Henry* IV, 58; *King Richard* III, 60
Shalikula, 235
Shand Kydd, Bill, 14-16
Shervington, Bill, 158-60
Shipton, Eric, 227-8
Sigebehrt, King, 96
Simon, Antoine, 84-5
Simon, Madame, 84-5, 89
Simon of Cyrene, 98
Simpson, Chuck, 141
Sinnett, Alfred, 210
Smith, Ethel, 186
Smith, the Reverend and Mrs Guy, 185-6
Smith, Dr Hamilton, 66
'Smith, Matthew', 24
Sokolov, Nicholas, 52, 56
Solon, 104-5
Speer, Albert, 30

Spehl, Eric, 182
Stafford, Henry, Duke of Buckingham, 60, 62
Steiner, Rudolf, 211
Stephanie, Princess of Belgium, 71
Stevens, Dr E.W., 212
Stevenson, Adlai, 39
Stevenson, Dr Ian, 214-15, 217
Stewart, A.J., 217
Stonehouse, Kenneth, 158, 160
Stoop, Michael, 16
Strange Planet (Corliss), 128
Strange Signes from Heaven, 150
Stukeley, William, 79
Stultz, Wilmer, 169
Stumpfegger, Dr Ludwig, 36
Sunex Amurex, 190-1
Sutton Hoo, 90-7
Svoboda, Franz, 56
Symonds, John, 211
Szeps, Moritz, 71
Szoegenyi-Marich, Ladislas von, 76

Taafe, Count, 77
Tanini, 141-2
Taylor, Charles, 122
Tchaikovski, Alexander, 53
Tchaikovski, Sergei, 53
Tchernine, Odette, 231, 234-5
Tekoka, 141
Ten Rillington Place (Ludovic Kennedy), 6, 9
Tensing, Sherpa, 230
Tepas, Quirinus, 160
Thaddeus, 102
Theseus, 110
Thompson, Captain, 166
Tighe, Virginia, 215-16
Tippit, Patrolman J.D., 42, 48
Todd, Thelma, 138-9
Tombazi, N.A., 228
Trafficante, Santos, 48
Troyes, Bishop of, 100-1

Turin, Shroud of, 97-8, *99*, 100-4
Turolla, Count Pino, 232
Twenty Cases Suggestive of Reincarnation (Ian Stevenson), 214
Two Stranglers of Rillington Place, The (Furneaux), 9
Tyrell, Sir James, 60

Underwood, Peter, 216
Unknown Earth (Corliss), 128

Valle, Eladio del, 48
Vaudreuil, Comte de, 199
Vennum, Mary Lurancy, 212-13, 217
Veronica, St, 100
Vespasian, 80
Vetsera, Baroness, 71, 74
Vetsera, Mary, 71-2, *73*, 74-7
Victoria, Queen of England, 77

Waddell, Major L.A., 228
Waddington, Ethel, *see* Christie, Ethel
Wakely, Chuck, 126
Waldegrave, Henry, 190

Waratah, 114-16, *117*, 118-20
Warren Commission, 46, 48
Warwick, Earl of, *see* Neville
West, Roland, 138-9
Wheeler, Sir Mortimer, 79
Whillans, Don, 231
Whitehouse, Sir George and Lady, 187
Whitehouse, Edwin, 187
Whyte, Constance, 224
Wilder, Leonard, 216
Wildman, S.G., 78
Wilson, Ian, 217-18
Woodville, Anthony, 59
Woodville, Elizabeth, *see* Grey

Xenia, Princess of Russia, 56

Yeats, W.B., 210
Yeti, The (Tchernine), 231
Yurovsky, Jacob, 50

Zana, 235
Zapruder, Abraham, 47